The Melville
Hawthorne Connection

Also by Erik Hage

Cormac McCarthy: A Literary Companion (McFarland, 2010)

The Melville–Hawthorne Connection

A Study of the Literary Friendship

ERIK HAGE

McFarland & Company, Inc., Publishers
Jefferson, North Carolina, and London

ISBN 978-0-7864-7076-1
softcover : acid free paper ∞

LIBRARY OF CONGRESS CATALOGUING DATA ARE AVAILABLE

BRITISH LIBRARY CATALOGUING DATA ARE AVAILABLE

On the cover: Nathaniel Hawthorne (left) and
Herman Melville (both Library of Congress);
sperm whale © 2014 Dorling Kindersley

Manufactured in the United States of America

*McFarland & Company, Inc., Publishers
Box 611, Jefferson, North Carolina 28640
www.mcfarlandpub.com*

To the memory of David P. Brown

This fabulous shadow only the sea keeps.
— Hart Crane, "At Melville's Tomb"

Table of Contents

Preface and Acknowledgments

This book ends with an idea presented by the American literary critic Leslie Fiedler, that to "be an American ... is precisely to *imagine* a destiny rather than to inherit one; since we have always been, insofar as we are Americans at all, inhabitants of myth rather than history." This is an idea at once held aloft and questioned in this book, as it is a collective fascination with myth that drives many toward the friendship between Herman Melville and Nathaniel Hawthorne. Yet it is also this fascination that sometimes drives one farthest from the essence of the friendship. And once the mythologizing and speculating end, the real understanding of the friendship begins. Too much has been written about the possibility of romantic involvement between the writers, based on little to no evidence whatsoever. Too many apocryphal accounts of the writers' initial meeting during a hike up Monument Mountain have likewise found their way onto the Internet and into our discussions. The point here is that there is much about the relationship that invites conjecture, but guesswork should never be confused with fact. There is no evidence that any drama presaged the rift between the two writers; rather it was a slow drift, driven by the circumstances of life: geography, literary pursuits relegated to the back burner, Hawthorne's stigmatic political affiliations, and Melville's (ultimately failed) pursuit of a government post in the Lincoln administration. Moreover, the two couldn't recapture the magic of those Berkshires conversations any more than, for example, reuniting college friends today could reignite the craziness of younger years. Time and circumstances have changed, and the past is relegated to memory.

Nevertheless, the friendship between Herman Melville and

1

Nathaniel Hawthorne will continue to fascinate because of the book that emerged during the heat of that friendship, *Moby-Dick,* and its subsequent high place in popular consciousness—and because of the mythologies that developed around both writers. That having been noted, the relationship is no less fascinating for the daily, human concerns and struggles that one encounters away from the glow of mythology (writing, financial cares, running a household with growing families, the sometimes bedeviled pursuit of book sales, and so forth). Of course, what sustains our attention is the work of the authors, and a large part of this book is concerned with the impulses that drove their writing and the possibility of counter-influence. This was, I argue, a friendship whose true basis—beyond an almost instantaneous mutual affinity and admiration for each other — was intellectual ideas and literary craft, and the conversations between the two hewed mostly to philosophical and spiritual rumination as well as to those matters that concern writers most: craft and publishing.

For a friendship that fully transpired during the 1850s, the relationship still draws a great deal of interest, and this book clearly has benefited from, and owes a debt to, the wealth of scholarship both writers have inspired, particularly throughout the whole of the twentieth-century and into the new millennium. And while the work you are reading has leaned heavily upon the rigorous work of generations of biographers and critics of both writers, my hope is that it also moves into new territory and helps sustain a long-term interest in the writers at an individual level, as well as in those spaces where they come together, both in life and in their literary affinities. Melville's personal letters to Hawthorne remain the most fertile terrain for study, even bereft as they are of the other half of the conversation. (Hawthorne's letters to Melville were presumably destroyed.) The richest details we can glean about Melville's personality during the time of *Moby-Dick*'s creation come to light there — and in the letters of Hawthorne's wife, Sophia, whose descriptions give us the fullest glimpse of the former mariner and represent wonderful writing in their own right.

It has also been a rewarding and wistful experience to reach back through the years and visit the places closely associated with Hawthorne and Melville. This book has involved many mini-journeys to, for example, Pittsfield, Concord and Salem in Massachusetts and Lansingburgh and Albany in New York — both to the writers' homes and to places of lore (the House of the Seven Gables, for example). And while it may be difficult in our contemporary times to get a sense of place in the nineteenth century, it is nonetheless a rich experience to be in these buildings and towns and to consider the lives that were lived there. Like many before me, I climbed Monument Mountain (in more than one season), stood in Melville's study at Arrowhead looking northward at Greylock; explored the Stockbridge Bowl, where Hawthorne lived; stood on the bank of the Hudson in Lansingburgh where Melville swam and boated; visited the Old Manse, where Hawthorne wrote some of his greatest stories; walked the streets of Albany around Melville's old haunts; spent many a day in the streets and buildings of Salem; sat in the New Bedford Seaman's Bethel that Melville visited before his whaling voyages; visited the Hawthornes' Raymond, Maine, home—the list goes on, of course. Biographers describe a sense of closely following their subjects but never catching them, but in my experience it's more about getting a certain essence. One must spend numerous days and nights during all seasons in Pittsfield and Lenox to partially understand living there—to get a feel for the roll of the seasons, the changing appearance of the trees and mountains, the bounty and then deprivation of sunlight, the crisp smell of pines and woodsmoke, the heavy buffeting of late-night winter wind against a wooden house. These things—the landscape, the seasons, the weather, the mountain views, the environment particular to the Berkshires—were certainly acutely felt by Melville and Hawthorne and left their psychological and emotional impressions.

Hawthorne's own notebooks contain close natural descriptions of his wanderings near his house: strolling the frozen lake wearing India rubber boots, taking close note of a cluster of ice-clasped berries and the path of snow-choked streams. Fall brought heaps of apples next to cider mills and the sight of the sphinx-like Monument Mountain, which seemed to him to be draped in an exotic shawl of bright colors. The writers' public lives were limited during the most intense period of the friendship, and one must get a sense of their sequestered existences, whether spent at the study desk or simply in their heads, using their keen sensitivity to take in all around them. What did Melville see when he looked out his study window at Greylock? He saw great hump of a cresting whale (as the story goes). Perhaps he did at times, but he also saw his crop field and the work that needed to be done there. May 1851 meant that the whale book was imminent, but that was put aside so that Melville could work harvesting the field in order to have enough food for his livestock for the winter following *Moby-Dick*'s creation. As a writer of this kind of biographical criticism you chase meaning and you chase essences; you strive toward several layers of accuracy, or as close as you can get to it.

But enough on that—for all of this is the terrain of the following chapters, which detail the quotidian struggles, unpack the myths, and probe layers in the author's works. This is a heady combination to consider over the course of a few years, and I am grateful to those who have read and commented on the product of my own travel, study, and sequestered hours before I saw fit to stick an enormous rubber band around the manuscript, lug it to the Voorheesville, NY, post office, and mail it to my publisher, satisfied that I had served Herman Melville and Nathaniel Hawthorne as well as I could. Thanks are due to many who helped along the way, including Melissa McFarland Pennell, professor of English at UMass Lowell; Randall A. Clack, professor of English at Wesley University in Delaware; Sharon Talley, professor of English at Texas A&M–Corpus Christi. As readers of the manuscript, they devoted their time and expertise to its improvement. Their thorough review and thoughtful insights were invaluable — and I deeply appreciate their generosity.

On a more personal note, I am indebted to my family, particularly the support and tolerance of my wife, Elizabeth. In addition, my father-in-law, who passed away shortly before I met my wife, serendipitously left behind a treasure trove of antiquarian Melville books and criticism that was perfectly suited to my already burning interest. As to that burning interest, I must thank my literature professors over the years, while I was both an undergraduate and graduate student, for inspiring me to read closer and in new ways— and for inspiring me to devote a good portion of my life to reading and thinking about literature.

Books beget books, and this project emerged as I finished a volume about the work of Cormac McCarthy, a contemporary author whose debt to *Moby-Dick* is unmistakable. McCarthy, an admirer of Melville, once said that he believed the novel could encompass all of the interests and disciplines of humanity. It is this that drew me back to *Moby-Dick*, which more than any other work seems to take up this challenge. But the story of *Moby-Dick* is also the story of the Melville-Hawthorne friendship — and the unmistakable debt that Melville and that book owe to the Salem native. The stories of literary friendships have always fascinated me, for a number of reasons. Thus, the course of a new endeavor was drawn. (In turn, an ore I struck during this journey has led me to embark anew, on a book about wilderness and the American writer.)

I thank Herman Melville and Nathaniel Hawthorne for hosting me this long while — and moreover, for the immeasurable education.

ONE

Friendship; or,
The Ambiguities

I feel that there can be no perfect peace in individualness.
—*Melville*, Pierre; Or, The Ambiguities, *1852*

I shall leave the world, I feel, with more satisfaction for having come to know you. Knowing you persuades me more than the Bible of our immortality.
— *Melville, letter to Hawthorne, November 1851*

He has a very high and noble nature, and is better worth immortality than the most of us.
—*Hawthorne on Melville,* English Notebooks, *November 1856*

But truth is ever incoherent, and when the big hearts strike together, the concussion is a little stunning.
—*Melville, letter to Hawthorne, November 1851*

Will he linger where I have lived, to remind the neglectful world of one who staked much to win a name, but will not then care whether he lost or won?
—*Melville marked this passage of Hawthorne's "Monsieur
Du Miroir" and wrote above it, "What a revelation"*
(*Melville's copy of* Mosses from an Old Manse, *Volume 1*)

    In certain ways the friendship between the American literary giants Herman Melville and Nathaniel Hawthorne will always remain partly shrouded, with a comprehensive understanding destined to remain just out of view. It often fully breaches like the white whale itself, revealed in all of its striking dimensions, as when Melville intoned to his friend, "I shall leave the world, I feel, with more satisfaction for having come to know you. Knowing you persuades me more than the Bible of our immortality."[1] But then it often plunges again, so that much like Ahab raptly peering into the depths we can see no more than a "white living spot."[2] Nevertheless, it is a relationship worth pondering, and pondering at length, for it would become, in retrospect, a whirlpool around which a transformation in American literature was turning. The relationship is also remarkable for the frankness of affection between the authors — Melville's is overt, even through the wit-burnished Shakespearean formality, arcane and ranging allusions, and intellectual probing of his letters. Hawthorne's is reticent and partially hooded, yet unmistakable and seen in glimpses from letters to others and in his notebooks. Saul Bellow, an American writer of a much later generation, once wrote in reflecting upon his departed fellow writer John Cheever that it was "extraordinarily moving to find the inmost track of a man's life and to decipher the signs he has left us."[3] It is equally (perhaps more) moving to consider the traces of a friendship and creative kinship between writers whose times are long past. And for those wanting to see as much as possible of Melville, who will always remain somewhat of a cipher, the richest and deepest remnants of his character are in his letters to Hawthorne. Between these and his books, we seem to behold an entire individual.

The creative and personal lives of Herman Melville and Nathaniel Hawthorne intersected during a literary apogee for both, even though commercial — and, to an extent, critical — fortune never fully smiled on them during their own lifetimes (though Hawthorne clearly received the greater nineteenth-century recognition). They were essentially, in varying degrees and depending upon the work in question, writers who often found themselves out of synch with the readership of their age. In their work and in their lives, the two men were defined by paradoxes, ambiguities, and contradictions. As Malcolm Bradbury and Richard Ruland have surmised, Hawthorne, "[l]ike many *modern* writers [emphasis mine] ... was an author who would not claim authority" in his works, a narrative tendency that ran counter to the literature of the age and that resulted in, at times, an underestimation of his achievements. Similarly, Melville dwelled in "symbolic *ambiguity*" and in many ways explored "the difficulty of reading signs, [and] the duplicitous nature of most moral assertions and deductions," an inclination that would induce critical derision and that would make him essentially a literary pariah during his own time — but, of course, a pioneer of a future age.[4] Although the two remain clearly different writers from each other, these essentially twentieth-century tendencies cast them out of contemporaneous place but posthumously established them as ahead of their own time. That they found each other and became friends for a time was remarkable, and perhaps inevitable, for their work (and often their personalities) separated them from other contemporary writers in the burgeoning landscape of American literature. Perhaps most importantly, the two were highly attuned and sensitive to each other's work, so much so that Melville and Hawthorne likely had no better and more intuitive reader of their work in their own lifetimes than each other.

The timing of the meeting was also significant. Only a few months prior to meeting Melville, Hawthorne, already a well-known spinner of murky, taut tales, published his first and greatest novel, *The Scarlet Letter* (1850). (It was his "first," discounting the anonymous youthful work *Fanshawe*.) And during the time that the two lived a mere six miles apart in the Berkshire Mountains of western Massachusetts he composed *The House of the Seven Gables* (1851) and began *The Blithedale Romance* (1852). Hawthorne would never be so prolific again. For his part, the younger Melville, already the author of five sea-adventure books written in rapid succession, was toiling away at the thorny, multifarious depths of *Moby-Dick* (1851), which of course would come to be regarded as one of the greatest works in the English language after his death. In due course, it would also come to be seen as a universal and cautionary allegory for colossal enterprises: American expansionism, the pursuit of capitalism, the search for the divine. Melville not only blew wide open the constraints and parameters of narrative and novel structure but shaped his own set of archetypes, one that prominently endures today. Everyone from Adolph Hitler to George W. Bush has been allegorized in popular print as Ahab, who has become the quintessential avatar of destructive obsession. Hawthorne, 15 years Melville's senior, would have a profound enough impact on that book to end up the sole honoree on the dedication page, where Melville inscribes, "In Token of My Admiration For His Genius, This Book Is Inscribed to NATHANIEL HAWTHORNE"; this, despite the fact that the book came out only fourteen months after they had met — such was the ardor of Melville's fraternal feelings.

Around this friendship revolved writings that have become centerpieces of American literature, though a full appreciation of *Moby-Dick*, which was largely underappreciated — even scorned — in Melville's lifetime, wouldn't come until the second decade of the twentieth century, when the modern world displayed a heightened sensitivity for his ambitious, multiperspectival, untidy, pessimistic, and essentially proto-modernist vision. Melville was writing during an age in which social, political, and military events and movements (Abolitionism, post–Mexican War, westward expansion, the Missouri Compromise, Fugitive Slave Laws) were sending the young republic into a long spiral that would lead headlong into the Civil War, an event that, as Pulitzer Prize–winning historian Louis Menand posits, "swept away almost the whole intellectual culture of the North along with it." The timing of the 1920s Melville revival is significant in this light, for as Menand points out, after the war transpired, "It took nearly half a century for the United States to develop a culture to replace it."[5] *Moby-Dick* was, as biographer Andrew Delbanco pointed out, the outpouring of a "twentieth-century imagination,"[6] and it took a twentieth-century modernist consciousness to apprehend its achievement.

The most intense period of Melville and Hawthorne's friendship came during a time when both writers were forging developments in a young country with a scant literary identity, one that was, as Hawthorne termed it, in its "tottering infancy."[7] Society, however, was not prepared to embrace their work in all of its ambiguities, complexities, and uncertainties. (Hawthorne's late novel *The Marble Faun*, while deemed problematical by many critics, is arguably his most striking example of these attributes.) Melville and Hawthorne did deeply comprehend each other's work, though, and understood its significance. In fact, Hawthorne was the most prominent and credible defender of *Moby-Dick* upon its publication. And when their common friend, the editor Evert Duyckinck, wrote a backhanded review of Melville's whale book in New York City's *Literary World*, Hawthorne penned a swift and firm rejoinder: "What a book Melville has written!" he protested. "It hardly seemed to me that the review of it ... did justice to its best points."[8] For his part, late into life and decades after Hawthorne's death, Melville still pored over his editions of his late friend's work at his home on Twenty-Sixth Street in New York City, contemplating, underlining, and making marginal notes, while the framed steel engraving of Hawthorne gazed down upon him from the study wall. (This was the very portrait that Hawthorne's wife, Sophia, had given him as a present in March 1851, all those years and a world away in the Berkshires.)

Currently, however, the only widely available full volume on the friendship is a collection of essays. The goal here is to revisit the literary kinship in a thorough manner while also shedding light on the compelling personalities of both writers. For example, Hawthorne's restraint, poise, and generally inward nature masked a profound *cafard* that could boil over into caustic hostility. Perhaps most alarming was his streak of misogyny and the violent prose he used to express it in his correspondence and notebooks. For the indignity of outselling his works—Harriet Beecher Stowe's readership, for example dwarfed his own—Hawthorne condemned a whole generation of emerging American women writers as "d——d scribbling women" who should be "forbidden to write on pain of having their faces deeply scarified with an oyster-shell."[9] In another outburst during his time as a United States consul in Liverpool, England, he lashed out at what he deemed the "common," overweight, and unattractive English women he encountered on the streets of that city. In this particular journal tirade, he went so far as to suggest that "surely, a man would be justified in murdering them—in taking a sharp knife and cutting away their mountainous flesh, until he had brought them into reasonable shape."[10] Yet, conversely, here was the man who also grew up worshipping his older sister Elizabeth ("Ebe"); and, furthermore, here was the writer who, in the form of *The Scarlet Letter*, sensitively deliberated on, as 2003 biographer Brenda Wineapple put it, the "complex predicament women faced as wives, mothers, daughters, and sexual beings."[11] Such was the extent of his particular empathy that in Hester Prynne he established one of the strongest and most interesting woman protagonists in nineteenth-century literature. Wineapple declares that Hester "still stands, statuesque, the heroine par excellence."[12] All of which is to say that Hawthorne was like the chiaroscuro paintings he so admired, his boldly contrasting lights and darks continually battling for purchase in both his life and his work. To Melville, however, he displayed, for a time at least, a kindness and openness that he reserved for only those in his inner circle.

Nevertheless, the friendship necessarily retains a tinge of mystery for both practical and abstruse reasons. On a basic level, one must deal with the fact that all Hawthorne's letters to Melville have been lost to time (presumably destroyed by Melville, most likely at Nathaniel's request), leaving a yawning gap in the record—though Hawthorne's wife, Sophia's, letters and Nathaniel's own journal entries give us revealing epistolary glimpses of the elusive and mysterious Melville at times. At another level, one will always approach this task without a three-dimensional understanding of the social and personal parameters of male friendship in the United States during the mid–1800s, particularly the insular nature of a friendship among well-known, well-heeled, yet in many ways struggling and often extremely isolated writers. As writer and political theorist Leonard Woolf (husband of Virginia) once surmised regarding his own autobiography, "The moment one begins to investigate the truth of the simplest facts which one has accepted as true it is as though one had stepped off a firm narrow path into a bog or a quicksand — every step one takes one steps deeper into the bog of uncertainty."[13] But even though this conundrum is exacerbated by the temporal distance between the writers' lives and the contemporary writer, there remains a compelling story to be told and a bounty of compelling signs and traces to perceive and piece together.

It is clear, too, that these men often necessarily dwelled in an atmosphere of savage autonomy, wrestling with their respective visions and surrounded by family who could only vaguely understand the full nature of their vocation and the inward-plumbing depths of those sequestered, inviolate hours. In each other, the writers found an empathetic soul, and in the work of Hawthorne, Melville found another author probing the darker recesses of human nature and psychology, regions into which he was embarking himself as he burrowed deeper into *Moby-Dick,* a book destined to find soundings far below its more apparent elements of adventure, proselytizing, and allegory. Perhaps even more importantly, each writer recognized the other as a visionary, more so than any of their contemporary critics could fathom. In a sense, Hawthorne also became a mirror that reflected Melville's own ambition and desire to plunge his muse headlong into a dark, variegated, "howling infinite."[14] (Thus, Melville's warning to family friend Sarah Morewood of *Moby-Dick*—"dont you read it.... A Polar wind blows through it, & birds of prey hover over it. Warn all gentle fastidious people from so much as peeping into the book"[15]—mirrors Hawthorne's own fretting that though, try as he might to write a "more genial book ... the Devil himself always seems to get into my inkstand, and I can only exorcise him by pensful at a time.")[16] Hawthorne biographer Brenda Wineapple justly posits Melville as an acolyte who not only yearned for literary companionship but who, now deep into the struggle of writing *Moby-Dick,* eagerly projected his own burgeoning literary fixations and aspirations onto Nathaniel.[17] And ultimately it was what Melville termed Hawthorne's "darkness" that fanned the muse already burning in him, as well as Hawthorne's propensity to blur the lines between the actual and imaginary, between the waking and dream worlds. Taking license from the vision of Hawthorne, and inspired by meeting the writer himself, Melville felt even more compelled to follow and fully realize his own emerging instincts, becoming a bracing explorer of the human unconscious long before Freud and Jung gave us language and form to articulate such explorations. During the next century, Jung would deem *Moby-Dick* "the greatest American novel" and would see in it "the richest opportunities for psychological elucidation."[18] John Updike described these tendencies in Melville's work as a condition in which "outer becomes inner [and] images take on a heated life of their own, freed from reality."[19] Or, as Melville wrote in *Mardi*, his first work to presage this shift, he had turned from straight ocean adventures to "the world of the mind; wherein the wanderer may gaze round, with more of wonder than Balboa's band roving through the golden Aztec glades."[20] Melville, ever the ribald adventurer, had found fresh, uncharted territory. For Hawthorne, the unconscious was often represented, as he ruminated in *The Scarlet Letter*, by "the wild, heathen nature of the forest, never subjugated by human law"[21] and therefore a place where (as he wrote in "The Birthmark") "Truth often finds its way to the mind close-muffled in robes of sleep, and then speaks with uncompromising directness," unfettered by the "self-deception [of] our waking moments."[22] In *The Scarlet Letter*, outer and inner sometimes seems delineated by the contrast between the forest and the market-place. As Hester Prynne warns her daughter, "Hold thy peace, dear little Pearl.... We must not always talk in the market-place of what happens to us in the forest."[23] Hawthorne, as early as the 1830s, was driven toward what F.O. Matthiessen labeled "hypnagogic" imagery; consider Hawthorne's description in "The Haunted Mind" (1834) of the experience of waking up in the middle of the night "when the mind has a passive sensibility, but no active strength: when imagination is a mirror, imparting vividness to all ideas, without the power of selecting them or controlling them."[24] Here, then, is the hinterlands that both writers would explore.

Beyond Hawthorne's profound influence on Melville, however, there is also clear evidence of *mutual* admiration and even influence. Since the revival of interest in Melville in the early twentieth century, a narrative strain has cropped up that suggests a significant imbalance in the friendship. In the telling, the young, ardent-hearted Melville desperately courts the more aloof and coldly Puritanical spirit of Hawthorne. This orientation has its roots in Lewis Mumford's seminal 1929 Melville biography, in which he represents the writer passionately trying to penetrate, to no avail, the "arctic ice" that housed Hawthorne's deeper intimacies.[25] Many writers have taken the position that the relationship cooled because of Melville's too-passionate pursuit of his literary soulmate or Hawthorne's chagrin at not being able to secure a governmental post for the younger author through his close friendship with antebellum president Franklin Pierce, an old Bowdoin College classmate. (Hawthorne's influence *was* sufficient to secure a consul post for himself in Liverpool, but ultimately, as he confessed in his journal, he simply lacked enough leverage to assist Melville.)[26] These assumptions are fueled by the absence of Hawthorne's letters to Melville, a *tabula rasa* onto which one can be inclined to impose his or her own interests. Even Andrew Delbanco, who has written one of the best critical biographies of Melville (*Melville: His World and Work*, 2005), suggests that the *Moby-Dick* author "may have gotten too close to some explosive secret"[27] in the private life of Hawthorne, inducing the older writer to push him away (an idea that has roots in the hardly credible Julian Hawthorne's book about his father). An earlier biographer, Edwin Haviland Miller (*Melville*, 1975), proposes—based on Melville's documented ardor and Hawthorne's missing responses—that the younger writer made a sexual advance, causing Hawthorne to flee his affections, another assertion that is not shored up with any evidence in the record.

Nevertheless, there seem to be more evident reasons for the eventual cooling of the relationship. Most obviously there was the matter of geography: For an eighteen-month tenure during 1850 and 1851, the Hawthornes rented a cottage on the Lenox/Stockbridge border in Massachusetts, only six miles away from the Melville's eventual Pittsfield home, Arrowhead. But the relative seclusion of the Berkshires (the Salem-reared Hawthorne preferred to be near the coast), the harsh winters, and an acrimonious and seemingly silly dispute with the landowner family, the Tappans, over the right to the fruit orchards on the rented property led to a hasty departure in November 1851, the month of *Moby-Dick's* publication. Melville did continue to stay in contact with both Nathaniel and Sophia Hawthorne, however, even when they relocated to England in 1853. And from one perspective the reason for the eventual drift was most likely one of those things that often occurs in human relationships, with no precise antecedent or cause. As Melville wrote later in life, in the poem "Monody," which many biographers and critics take to be an elegy to his friend after his passing (Hawthorne died in 1864, when he was nearly 60), "To have known him, to have loved him.... /And then to be estranged in life,/And neither in the wrong."[28] It remains commonplace, even in this age of digital communication, for the circumstances of life, geography, and familial and professional obligations to sometimes reduce the heat of friendship or to turn one's focus more intently elsewhere. In fact, in his post–Berkshires years, Hawthorne not only turned from Melville but largely from writing itself, as his governmental post and travel absorbed his attention.

All of which is to say that, at times, one must approach this friendship, particularly its eventual drift, with a healthy dose of poet John Keats's "negative capability"—that is, the capacity to be among "uncertainties, Mysteries, doubts, without any irritable reaching after fact & reason."[29]

Nevertheless, while it is

Herman Melville, 1861 (courtesy Berkshire Athenaeum, Pittsfield, Massachusetts).

important to keep pragmatic realities in mind, there was also likely another factor propelling the drift between the two writers during Hawthorne's final years: Melville's continual striving for a government post and Hawthorne's stigmatic political orientation during this time. In 1860, a few years after his final encounter with Hawthorne, Melville—after arriving home from a voyage around Cape Horn with his youngest brother, Thomas, a clipper ship commander—found himself again searching for a governmental job to halt his continual financial slide. He had first (unsuccessfully) sought a post when Franklin Pierce entered office in 1853, hoping that Hawthorne's influence would yield a result. Now, with Abraham Lincoln coming into office, Herman's family lobbied heavily for him, particularly John C. Hoadley, a brother-in-law who had served in the Massachusetts legislature. Though the Melvilles were Democrats, they weren't as stubbornly mired in traditional Democratic ideals as Hawthorne, and Herman did garner a meeting with Charles

Sumner, the Republican abolitionist senator from Massachusetts. And though the post never came to fruition, the pursuit of it would have been possibly dragged down by close association with Hawthorne, who was dead against the idea of war, was openly skeptical of Lincoln, and didn't even necessarily support the idea of a Union. For all his protests in the late 1840s, around the time of his Custom House dismissal, about being apolitical, Hawthorne was undeniably a political figure by this time. He had served as consul and was known as a dogged friend and celebratory biographer of the polarizing Franklin Pierce. To be associated during this volatile time with Hawthorne, who became ever more staunchly anti–Union as the United States headed toward war, would have been a distinct disadvantage. In the wake of *Moby-Dick*, and in light of his failure to earn a living as an author, Melville periodically and continually sought the stability of government work — that is, until actually landing a government position in 1866 as a New York customs inspector. This reality regarding the friendship doesn't hold the attraction of explosive secrets or secretive interpersonal conflict, and perhaps this is why it is rarely addressed. But the fact of the matter was that it was an urgent time, and Hawthorne had become a problematically political figure. For Herman, authorship and creative affinity was one side of the coin; earning a living and feeding one's family was the other. To be closely associated with Hawthorne in 1860 and 1861 was simply a liability to Melville's pursuit of a post under this administration.

But to return to the question of lopsidedness in the friendship: Despite the missing, presumably destroyed letters from Hawthorne, an absence that amplifies the impression of unrequited adoration, there is clear evidence of the older writer's deep and abiding admiration and affection for Melville. Additionally, Hawthorne was likely Melville's only important literary contemporary to recognize him for the literary innovator that he truly was. In 1856, well after the relationship's most intense years, Melville spent three days in Liverpool, England, visiting the Hawthornes en route to a solo exploration of Europe and the Holy Lands. (Melville's passport application, inscribed in the author's own hand, denotes such particulars as "Stature: 5 feet 8¾ inches," "Eyes: Blue," "Nose: Straight," "Mouth: Medium," "Hair: Dark Brown," "Complexion: Fair.")[30] Hawthorne wrote vividly and warmly of their time together in his notebooks, concluding, in the loftiest possible praise, that Melville "has a very high and noble nature, and [is] better worth immortality than the most of us."[31] In England, the con-

versation between the two had delved, as it had in the Berkshires, into
deep metaphysical and ontological waters. And Hawthorne marveled
at how the ruminative and intensely analytical Melville still seemed
to be struggling to find a belief system that could sustain him over
the long haul. "It is strange how he persists—and has persisted ever
since I knew him, and probably long before — in wandering to and
fro over these deserts.... He can neither believe, nor be comfortable
in his unbelief," wrote Hawthorne, whose consternation was tinged
with admiration: "[A]nd he is too honest and courageous not to try
to do one or the other."[32] The nature of the visit as well as Hawthorne's sentiments undermines the idea of a prior rift caused by
the discovery of an "explosive secret." The continual, loosely supported,
suggestion in the biographical record that Hawthorne eventually spurned
the author of *Moby-Dick* points to this ongoing problem created by
Hawthorne's absent correspondence, one best expressed by Jana L.
Argersinger and Leland S. Person — that is, that the "missing letters
create a space where scholarly desire can preempt the possibility of
reciprocal feeling."[33] Hawthorne undoubtedly reciprocated Melville's
affection, but the two were different spirits with different means of
expression. Hawthorne was frequently inward and inscrutable in
his social interactions; Melville swung between the poles of extreme
sociability — he was a renowned social raconteur — and utter withdrawal.
But in his exchanges with Hawthorne, Sophia, and their children, he
was at his most zealous and gregarious, and he was the rare welcome
visitor into that insular circle (though he occasionally exhausted
Hawthorne). Nathaniel even delightedly noted in his journals that little
Julian had told him "he loved Mr. Melville as well as me, and as mamma,
and as Una."[34] In fact, a couple of months after the Hawthornes had
fled the Berkshires the parents prompted six-year-old Julian to write an
affectionate letter to the *Moby-Dick* author, an act that seems to dispute
any suggestion of an uncomfortable schism.

Nathaniel's wife, Sophia Hawthorne, also expressed great admiration and affection for Melville, and she has left us with the most vivid
portraits of the sea-faring writer. She gushed in a letter to her mother
that she felt Melville was "a very great man" and wrote of his "keen
perceptive power." Most bracing and descriptive, however, are her
sketches of his physical presence and manner: "He is tall & erect
with an air free, brave & manly. When conversing he is full of gesture &
force, & loses himself in his subject." She was also enchanted by "a sin-

gularly quiet expression" in Melville's eyes (one later captured in the well-known 1861 Pittsfield, Massachusetts, daguerreotype of a seated Melville). "It is a strange, lazy glance, but with a power in it quite unique — It does not seem to penetrate through you, but to take you into himself."[35] Sophia's impressions were recorded during the earliest meetings between Melville and the Hawthornes, in September of 1850, at a time when Melville still possessed a certain celebrity status as the virile, robust author of early books such as *Typee* (1846) and *Omoo* (1847), both of which had a basis, albeit embellished, in the writer's own South Pacific adventures— and both of which staked out Melville as a travel writer and not an important literary figure. Her observations were certainly informed by those glimmerings, which, as Hershel Parker established in the 1990s, made him as much of a literary "sex symbol" as one could be in the United States in 1850.[36] In fact, in a comment with only slightly muffled tones of salaciousness, the typically prim Sophia wrote to her sister, "Mr. Typee

The Old Manse, Concord, Massachusetts (Library of Congress, c. 1900).

is interesting in his aspect — quite. I see Fayaway in his face."[37] This was, of course, an allusion to the erotic Polynesian woman in *Typee* and therefore a nudge and a wink regarding not only Melville's thinly veiled descriptions of sexual conquest in that novel, but his own suggestive virility. Sophia, an astute aesthete and a fine writer herself, as her letters demonstrate, also admired Melville's craft. Even after the Hawthornes had moved from the Berkshires, she wrote a letter to Herman detailing her admiration of *Moby-Dick*, which had just recently been published.

Most scholarship, however, focuses on Melville's sentiments toward Nathaniel Hawthorne, not only those expressed in his letters to the other writer but those in his August 1850 review of Hawthorne's collection of tales *Mosses from an Old Manse* (published in 1846). Compellingly, Melville wrote the review under the purposely misleading pseudonym of "A Virginian Spending July in Vermont," and it appeared in the New York City–based *Literary World* in two parts in mid- and late August of 1850. Therefore, there are layers of duplicity at work here: Melville not only shields his identity behind that of a genteel Southerner far from home, but also writes the review as if he had never met the author. But the fact of the matter is that Melville wrote the review in the immediate days after — and in the full flush of — his first encounters with Hawthorne. The meeting occurred during a hike up Monument Mountain with other local Berkshires celebrities, including Dr. Oliver Wendell Holmes, and a full day spent discoursing and engaging in other adventures, including a group romp through a rocky and shadowy ice glen. Melville, therefore, clearly possessed an idea of the character of the man behind the tales while writing the review, though he presents his revelations as someone enchanted by the works but estranged from the actual writer behind them; the truth, however, is that the real reviewer behind "Hawthorne and His Mosses" had become immediately and deeply enchanted by both the work and the flesh-and-blood presence of the man. It was also, to a degree, a reciprocal gesture: Hawthorne had favorably reviewed *Typee* for the *Salem Advertiser* in 1846, a few years before meeting Melville.

The review also traces the beginnings of Hawthorne's influence on Melville's craft, most tellingly when Melville discusses the "blackness" of Hawthorne's muse — that is, those turgid, plumbing, psychological tendencies that Melville was undertaking himself as he wrestled with the unwieldy book about the whale. And through this "darkness," Melville traced a lineage to Shakespeare, essentially pulling the circle tightly around the three of them, despite the fierce American nationalism he also displayed in the piece. While Melville wrote that "it is that blackness in Hawthorne ... that so fixes and fascinates me," he also found that very quality to be a canvas "against which Shakespeare [also] plays his grandest conceits":

> [I]t is those deep far-away things in him; those occasional flashings-forth of the intuitive Truth in him; those short, quick probings at the very axis of reality: — these are the things that make Shakespeare, Shakespeare. Through the mouths of the dark characters of Hamlet, Timon, Lear, and Iago, he craftily says, or sometimes insinuates the things, which we feel to be so terrifically true, that it were all but madness for any good man, in his own proper character, to utter, or even hint of them. Tormented into desperation, Lear the frantic King tears off the mask, and speaks the sane madness of vital truth.[38]

Most striking here is the degree of projection: He seems to be deliberating on his own burgeoning whale epic; for what better insight do we have to soaring, dark rhetoric and tragic complexity of Ahab and the flashing, lifting insights that close out many of the chapters of *Moby-Dick*? And Ahab — who undoubtedly bears the influence of Lear and MacBeth — is arguably one of the most Shakespearean of characters outside of Shakespeare's own canon. Consider Ahab's many Shakespearean ruminations and ravings, such as the speech addressed to the "pallid" flames leaping from the ends of the yard-arms and masts after lightning has struck them:

> Oh! thou clear spirit of clear fire, whom on these seas I as Persian once did worship, till in the sacramental act so burned by thee, that to this hour I bear the scar; I now know thee, thou clear spirit, and I now know that thy right worship is defiance. To neither love nor reverence wilt thou be kind; and e'en for hate thou canst but kill; and all are killed. No fearless fool now fronts thee.[39]

Melville, who had only become deeply acquainted with Shakespeare's works a few years before *Moby-Dick* (after procuring a large-print collection that suited his troublesome eyes), was ingrained by those readings while composing the novel; therefore, to suggest Hawthorne's Shakespearean lineage is to pull the cloak tightly over the three of them. In addition, *Moby-Dick*'s omniscient narrative flashings of insight — when the prose takes flight, seemingly breaking free from Ishmael's first-person —certainly finds kinship in the work of Hawthorne, particularly such murky tales as "Young Goodman Brown," "The Minister's Black Veil," and "The Birthmark," even though Hawthorne remains a tightly controlled writer next to the brazen, gusting prose of *Moby-Dick*. Hawthorne, the man and the writer, spurred on Melville's black impulses and made him fall in love with his own intentions anew. The South African writer J.M. Coetzee was writing autobiographically in 2002 when he penned the following lines, but they could have been describing Melville's own impulses in 1850 and 1851: "What he would write if he could ... would be something darker, something that, once it began to flow from his pen, would spread across the page out of control, like spilt ink ... like shadows racing across the face of still water, like lightning crackling across the sky."[40] It also must be underscored, if it is not clear already, that Melville was like blotting paper at this point in his writing life; he made up for his lack of formal education by becoming a voracious autodidact who rapidly absorbed influences, processing them through the prism of his own creative tendencies. In fact, in the years leading up to the composition of *Moby*-Dick, he seemed to be swallowing books whole.

Furthermore, in yoking himself to Hawthorne, through the *Mosses* review and in the soaring *Moby-Dick* dedication, Melville was forging a fiercely nationalistic alliance, suggesting that the destiny of future American writers was to eclipse their canonized English predecessors and to forge more modern frontiers befitting a new and expansive country. "Believe me, my friends, that Shakespeares are this day being born on the banks of the Ohio," he sermonizes behind the veil of the Virginian. "And the day will come, when you shall say who reads a book by an Englishman that is a modern?" Melville perceived his own work and Hawthorne's as a fresh generational groundswell of a distinctly American literature, one whose "ontological heroics" sought more profound depths than predecessors such as James Fenimore Cooper — whom Melville's mother, Maria, knew in his youth — or Washington Irving, who exerted an early influence on Melville. Both of those forbears, however, were arguably an extension and continuation of the literature of England. Therefore, the "Hawthorne and His Mosses" review, the very treatise that essentially announced his allegiance with Hawthorne (despite its pseudonymous nature), became not only one of the first reviews to fully engage the layers of Hawthorne's vision but, as Lewis Mumford would declare in 1929, "one of the keenest expositions of the situation of the creative writer in America" in the middle of the nineteenth century.[41] The September 1851 death of James Fenimore Cooper, whom Melville had admired in the past, must have only cemented his notions that he and Hawthorne represented a new visionary frontier in American letters during this literary blooming of the 1850s. Melville was separating himself and Hawthorne from the rest of the American pack, positing the two of them as resolute and unflinching truth-seekers. "For in this world of lies, Truth is forced to fly like a scared white doe in the woodlands," Melville writes in the review. "[And] only by cunning glimpses will she reveal herself."[42] Melville, desperate for literary fellowship, had essentially been groping around in uncharted literary "darkness"—far removed, for example, from the voguish Transcendentalism of Emerson — and suddenly he encountered another prominent American writer there as well, one who, as if by providence, abandoned his native coastal Massachusetts and moved into a small red cottage six miles down the road. The chance encounter recalls the "A Squeeze of the Hand" chapter in *Moby-Dick*, when Ishmael, hands blindly groping and squeezing in a large tub of spermaceti, "unwittingly" finds his "co-labourers' hands," the act transmuting them into "dear fellow beings."[43]

Obviously, this passage is most often cited for its bold masturbatory intonations, and the *Mosses* review and Melville's letters also contain enough potentially sexual imagery to titillate critics who would suggest more than Platonic intentions at work here. In "Hawthorne and His Mosses" Melville, as the Virginian, gushes, "But already I feel that this Hawthorne has dropped germinous seeds into my soul. He expands and deepens down, the more I contemplate him; and further, and further, shoots his strong New-England roots into the hot soil of my Southern soul."[44] (Melville did eventually "unveil" himself to the Hawthornes as the writer of the review, basking in the glowing response to the revelation.) Even in his letters to Hawthorne, out from behind the pseudonymous persona, Melville is, by any standard, profuse and suggestive. Responding to a letter in which the older writer complimented *Moby-Dick* in the most unequivocal and frank terms (a compelling reference is made to Hawthorne's "plain, bluff" letter), Melville becomes effusive: "I felt pantheistic then — your heart beat in my ribs and mine in yours ... I would sit down and dine with you and all the gods in old Rome's Pantheon." Then the imagery moves to even more explicit demonstration, as Melville attempts to fully convey "this infinite fraternity of feeling": "Whence come you, Hawthorne? By what right do you drink from my flagon of life? And when I put it to my lips—lo, they are yours and not mine." This is clearly the language of one who feels he has found a literary soulmate, and he finishes with a post-script flourish that cements the pairing: "The divine magnet is on you, and my magnet responds. Which is the biggest? A foolish question — they are *One*."[45]

This is the primary source material that, estranged from

Hawthorne's long lost letters, leads biographers toward provocative readings of the relationship, particularly Melville's passion for the older writer. There is no doubt that Herman Melville sees his and Hawthorne's relationship as a marriage of like minds, but there is little compelling evidence beyond the figurative. Furthermore, social history weighs in from all sides regarding the question of homosexual strains in the relationship. It could be misleading to contextualize the question with notions of sexuality in our own time. For example, how does one deal with the fact that in both "privileged society [and] working-class culture, letters between same-sex friends in the nineteenth century" often contained "emotional intensity and passionate references"?[46] Melville was also known to refer to the editor Evert Duyckinck, a friend with whom he had less of an affinity, as "my beloved."[47] One must also consider historian D. Michael Quinn's assertions that

> in nineteenth-century America, same-sex friends of all ages held hands while walking down the streets of cities or towns. Few people regarded it as remarkable when same-sex friends kissed each other "full on the lips" in public or in private. Fewer still saw anything unusual in the common American practice of same-sex friends sleeping in the same bed, sometimes for years at a time.[48]

This places Melville's passionate outpourings in a different light. Yet, of course, in a society where sexual relations among men were regarded so taboo and driven so far underground as to be referred to as "the sin that cannot be named" (the term "homosexuality" itself didn't yet exist in their time), we encounter a whole other set of problems and unanswerable questions. Melville also does compellingly write of "love-friendship missives" between boys in *Pierre*, a novel written after becoming well acquainted with Hawthorne. He expressed how such a boyhood friendship "sometimes transcends the bounds of mere boyishness and revels for a while in ... a love which only comes short, by one degree, of the sweetest sentiment entertained between the sexes." But Melville also qualifies it and extinguishes it: "as the advancing fruit itself extrudes the beautiful blossom, so in many cases, does the eventual love for the other sex forever dismiss the preliminary love-friendship of boys."[49] Late psychiatrist and Oxford professor Anthony Storr likely casts the most insightful light upon the matter in detailing Tennyson's close friendship with Arthur Hallam in his 1988 book *Solitude: A Return to Self*: "Their friendship was intimate and passionate, but neither overtly nor covertly homosexual. Pre-Freudian generations were more fortunate than our own in being able to freely admit 'love' for a member of the same sex, or of the opposite sex, without the implication that all love is necessarily sexual in origin."[50]

Beyond these relationship complexities, however, Hawthorne did show a keen interest in — even a fixation with — Melville's work. Sophia notes in a letter that upon meeting Melville, Hawthorne was fascinated enough by the new literary acquaintance to spend hours laying in the hay, poring through all of his books, including a re-reading of *Typee*, which he had positively reviewed in 1846. Through this exercise he gained what he termed in a letter to Evert Duyckinck "a progressive appreciation of the author." Furthermore, he deemed *Mardi* (1849) "so good that one scarcely pardons the writer for not having brooded long over it, so as to make it a great deal better."[51] Hawthorne, a writer who moved at a more deliberate and much less-prolific pace, divined Melville's reckless, head-long process. But his admiration was also unequivocal and cut against the grain of *Mardi*'s critical reception. He implicitly understood Melville's vision as few had, and he proclaimed that "no writer ever put the reality before his reader more unflinchingly than he does in 'Redburn' and 'White-Jacket.'"[52] These comments and Melville's writings to and about Hawthorne suggest that this was primarily a relationship of like minds, ideas, mutual affinity, and literary practice, and any attempt to pseudo-sexualize it moves one far afield — into complete speculation — and away from the most compelling and concrete aspects of this story. In fact, Melville, who was known in his work to be a great appreciator and describer of masculine beauty, nonetheless solely hurls his admiring prose against Hawthorne's intellectual gifts and craft (this despite the fact that Hawthorne was renowned for his Byronic handsomeness). Clearly the language is often what Newton Arvin characterizes as "aston-ishingly sexual," but, as Arvin also points out, for Melville this is the only adequate means of expressing "impregnation by another mind."[53] In her 1996 Melville biography, Laurie Robertson-Lorant outright con-demns the homosexual tack in an afterword fully dedicated to the ques-tion of Melville's sexuality, particularly the relationship with Hawthorne. Denouncing what she terms the "hopelessly politicized" landscape of sex and gender politics in academia, she finds it "restrictive to reduce Melville's writings to coy sexual disclosures, or his life to an elaborate lie."[54] Furthermore, Lorant supports the notion that Melville's letters to Hawthorne, which are often deemed homoerotic, are more about "self-discovery, psychological identification, intellectual excitement, and spiritual hunger."[55] She also highlights the essentially self-involved, self-gratifying bent in Melville's effervescing to and about Hawthorne: "These passionate letters express Melville's infatuation with the new self-image and artistic self-confidence Hawthorne aroused in him."[56]

And while there is *some* evidence to suggest that, if put on the scales, Melville's ardor outweighed Hawthorne's, it is likely not to the degree that apocryphal tellings propose. "Melville's demands might be greater than Hawthorne would have time or inclination to meet," wrote Sophia Hawthorne in the spring of 1851, after having lived near Melville for several months, a statement that suggested that Melville's passion-driven overtures and intellectual excitement had worn the older Hawthornes out at times.[57] (Additionally, the Hawthornes, both in their forties, were raising two young children and a baby — born later, in May 1851 — in the tiny red cottage, an exhausting prospect in and of itself.) Moreover, Hawthorne may not have had the capacity for displays of intimate friendship at that time; many who encountered him noted the writer's repressed nature, one that seemed an extension of a nearly debilitating shyness. Evert Duyckinck described Hawthorne as "a fine ghost in a case of iron" and also commented on his noticeably "nervous way."[58] Evert's brother George commented admiringly on Hawthorne's handsomeness but also noted his "sort of hesitating manner and a peculiar half timid smile."[59] Hawthorne was extremely secretive and contained; in fact, his own sister, Ebe, would tell his daughter Una in later years that her father "kept his very existence a secret."[60] Therefore, all things considered — Hawthorne's nature, family obligations, and so on — the openness and generosity that Nathaniel *did* demonstrate toward Melville was significant, in particular his invitation to have Herman stay overnight in the red cottage with him, Sophia, and their children, Una and Julian, who were six and four years old at the time that Melville met them. But Hawthorne, 15 years Melville's senior, was also at a different and less excitable stage in life and not prone to Melville's ebulliences and enthusiasm, much as Melville himself would finally surrender to a certain spiritual weariness in his 40s. This was a man, after all, who only five years after meeting Melville would write in his journal, "Really, I have no pleasure in anything.... Life seems so purposeless as to not be worth the trouble of carrying it on any further."[61] Years later, Ralph Waldo Emerson, reflecting on Hawthorne's funeral, wrote of "the painful solitude of the man, which, I suppose, could no longer be endured, & he died of it."[62] It is also important to note that Hawthorne would pass away in his sleep in Plymouth, New Hampshire (while on a vacation tour with longtime friend and former U.S. president Franklin Pierce), a mere 12 years after first meeting Melville; therefore, he was already at an advanced stage in his own life while in the Berkshires. One should consider as well that the very kind of intellectual companionship that Melville hungered for was of a variety that Hawthorne had already tasted. During the previous decade in Concord, Massachusetts, he had become well acquainted with Henry David Thoreau, whom he liked, and Ralph Waldo Emerson, for whom he did not care as much. During his college years at Bowdoin, Hawthorne met another budding literary icon, Henry Wadsworth Longfellow, who would describe the collegiate Hawthorne as a withdrawn and mysterious individual. It was a relationship that, nurtured by correspondence, would grow close in later decades. As to the dynamic between Melville and Hawthorne, Sophia details their conversational synergy in a letter to her sister, Elizabeth Peabody: "Nothing pleases me better than to sit & hear this growing man dash his tumultuous waves of thought up against Mr Hawthorne's great, genial, comprehending silences," she wrote. "[I]t is astonishing how people make him their innermost Father Confessor, is it not?"[63] This is the traditional portrait of Melville and Hawthorne: The younger writer passionately expostulating while the older writer remains genial and reserved, a portrait enhanced by the imposed silence of Hawthorne's missing correspondence.

Nevertheless, there are more complicated depths to the dynamic between the two that buck conventional portraits of the friendship. Why, for example, would Hawthorne write the following passage in his journal in 1856 (in Liverpool), describing Melville in terms that are traditionally ascribed to himself? "A week ago last Monday, Herman Melville came to see me at the Consulate, looking much as he used to (a little paler, and perhaps a little sadder), in a rough outside coat, and with his characteristic gravity and reserve of manner."[64] And what was it that Melville found so palpable in Hawthorne — and here we address mostly the person, not the writer — to have what Newton Arvin described as an overwhelming "sense that he had come upon another man to whom he could address himself with a fullness and a straightness that had no precedent in his experience"?[65] Of himself, Melville had confessed to Sophia that "he was naturally so silent a man that he was complained of a great deal on this account." But there was something about Hawthorne's presence and his "great but hospitable silence [that] drew him out," Melville noted, telling Sophia "that it was astonishing how *sociable* his silence was."[66] Hawthorne's silence, though, belied the fact that he had relocated to the Berkshires in the wake of what Hawthorne biographer Brenda Wineapple properly termed the "most trying year of his life."[67] During the previous year he had lost his mother and been unceremoniously fired from his post as surveyor and inspector at the Custom House in his hometown of Salem for political reasons, after a presidential administration shift. He arrived in western Massachusetts in May (months before Melville purchased Arrowhead) depressed and sickly, and he soon lapsed into a nervous fever. By the time he met Melville in August he was somewhat on the mend, revived by the tonic of the Berkshires mountain air and the boldly verdant surroundings. Nevertheless, there were simmering reservoirs of anger in Hawthorne. "I think it essential to my success as an author, to have some bitter enemies," he cryptically wrote to the publisher J.T. Fields on January 27, 1851, while residing at the red cottage.[68] Earlier, in 1849, soon after his Custom House dismissal, he had fantasized about wielding his greatest weapon to wound those who had wronged him. As he venomously asserted to Longfellow, "I cannot help smiling in anticipation of the astonishment of some of these local magnates here who suppose themselves quite out of the reach of any retribution on my part."[69] And, indeed, his opening "Custom-House" incantation in *The Scarlet Letter*—a highly unflattering portrayal of his former workplace, colleagues, and Salem itself—was aimed to fulfill that vendetta, cloaked behind the transparent conceit of setting the stage for the story to follow.

And while Hawthorne had fled Salem to be out of reach of all that unpleasantness, that port city had conditioned him to appreciate a proximity to the ocean. By contrast, in the Berkshires the William Tappan family had rented him a small red handyman's cottage on the perimeter of their estate. The house, which had uneven floors and drafty crevices, sat on the north edge of the cozy, bucolic, and picturesque "Stockbridge Bowl," which cradled Lake Mahkeenac. Melville, by contrast, was staying in Pittsfield at the large family estate soon to be dubbed "Broadhall" when he first met Hawthorne. The home had been in the Melville family for years and then had been converted into a boarding house in order to offset financial troubles. At the time of the Hawthorne-Melville meeting in August 1850, it was about to be purchased by family friends, the Morewoods. Shortly after meeting Hawthorne, Melville and his wife, Lizzie, would purchase the farmhouse, barn, and land roughly adjacent to the Broadhall property that Herman would dub "Arrowhead," based on the number of those artifacts unearthed on the grounds. (Herman and Lizzie, witnessed by Melville's cousin Robert, signed the house and land deeds on different dates in September 1850.)[70] An open, arable field where the Melvilles would grow various crops stretched away to the north side of the house toward the impressive hump of Mount Greylock, the highest point in Massachusetts, at around 3500 feet, which loomed like a cresting whale. (Much as *Moby-Dick* was dedicated to Hawthorne, the follow-up novel, *Pierre*, was dedicated to "Greylock's Most Excellent Majesty," a flourish that both displayed his love of his Berkshires surroundings and served as a humorous jab toward English writers of a previous age, who offered their dedications up to royalty.)

But the different abodes of the men did not directly parallel their literary fortunes. Melville was in a commercial and critical slump, having ground out five books in as many years with diminishing returns. The exotic adventures *Typee* (1846) and *Omoo* (1847) brought him recognition but unfortunately would come to represent the high point of his fame and commercial viability during his own lifetime. The more complex and digressive *Mardi* (1849), which first hinted at the idiosyncratic and fulsome depths of Melville's muse, was critically punished; therefore, he attempted to return to more marketable ocean-bound forms with *Redburn* (1849) and *White-Jacket* (1850), novels written in a flurry of haste even remarkable for the prolific Melville, who would later dismiss the works in the most disparaging terms. By contrast, Hawthorne had established himself as a great craftsman of short fiction during the 1830s and 1840s, and his first proper novel, *The Scarlet Letter* (1850), had arrived only two months prior to the relocation to the red cottage. The book was met with acclaim and sold out its first printing of 2500 copies within the span of two weeks, an impressive showing for an American author of that era.[71] His spirit may have been withering — and he and Sophia may have once endured poverty and near starvation in Concord during a long, slow ascent — but for this time his literary life was vibrant, and he was heralded by many as a man of genius. Here, then, were their respective literary destinies: Hawthorne's work was bound to be somewhat appreciated in his own lifetime, and then highly lauded soon after his death, while Melville, popular early on, would languish in obscurity for the remaining decades of his life, while bearing witness to Hawthorne's post-mortem fame, and then quite posthumously evolving into one of the most influential and celebrated novelists ever, based on his book about the whale. During their last meeting in 1856, Hawthorne had suggested in his journal that the noble, spiritually restless Melville was more deserving of immortality than most — but he had no idea that the forgotten *Moby-Dick* would become the source of that immortality.

In its time *Moby-Dick* clearly delineated the contemporary destinies of the two writers, having been greeted with some outright nasty critical reception and weak sales upon its release in November 1851. And though the book's dedication celebrated the influence of Hawthorne, *Moby-Dick* was also a testament to the differences between the two authors. Hawthorne diligently composed taut narratives with all of the fat boiled off of them and poised in a liminal space between sleep and waking and reality and fantasy. If these were romances he was toiling at, they were romances of an altogether different hue — a "rich duskiness of color" that called to mind the dramatic dark tones of a chiaroscuro painting.[72] Melville swung through dreamworlds too and led the reader into the figurative crevices and glens of human psychology, but *Moby-Dick* was a book of heaving ambition, bursting at the seams in a patchwork of brilliance and niggling imperfections. Melville's writing was as intense as the man, punctuated by flashes of philosophical and religious insight, heat lightning, and reaching prose; Hawthorne offered shorter books — finely woven webs of human intricacies that were intended to induce "new moral shapes to spring up to the reader's mind."[73]

The differences were evident in the writers' Berkshires work patterns as well. Hawthorne maintained deliberate and inviolate work hours early in the day. Melville was known to have kept regular hours for periods, but often the prose spilled out in lurches and brash flurries that came between significant periods of stalling. At Arrowhead, there were animals to feed, crops to be yielded, social appointments to be met, and family members to be carted hither and thither by Melville and his diligent horse, Charlie. In his spacious upstairs study on the north end of the house, he sequestered himself, writing in bursts, contemplating the landscape, and pacing the wide pine floor planks like Ahab on the *Pequod*. Beyond the north windows were the fields where crops had to be managed. Clangings from the kitchen fireplace and the cries of his toddler son Malcolm (affectionately dubbed "Barney" by his father) wafted upward into his imaginative space, as did, for a time, the hammerings and sawings of workmen building a porch ("piazza") below his window. Over in the cramped red cottage in Stockbridge, Hawthorne wrote in a small upstairs nook with a slanting ceiling, while Sophia maintained order, silence, and privacy until he descended from his morning sessions to re-enter the fold.

The adult experience of the two men obviously differed much as well. Melville, particularly in the years leading up to the meeting of the two writers, was known for his brazen, often perverse, and adventure-some spirit, qualities that, much like Hawthorne's restraint, translated to his own pages. Now in his mid–40s, Hawthorne had rarely travelled outside of his native New England (his longest trip had been to Niagara Falls); Melville had spent years at sea and had mutinied in the South Pacific, essentially island- and ship-hopping his way back home. As a young man, he had caused his family great anxiety with his desultory, explorative path through early life. In January of 1841, his eldest brother, Gansevoort, who had assumed the role of patriarch after their father's death (and who was soon to prematurely die himself), wrote their younger brother, Allan, that he was suffering from "ill health" and "exces-sive anxiety on account of Herman," who was 21 at the time.[74] Gan-sevoort, three-and-half years older than Herman, had spent the previous days scuttling around and helping the younger Melville ready himself for the whaling voyage he was bound and determined to undertake as a common seaman, making sure Herman was well fed and outfitted with the appropriate accoutrements. "Now that he has gone — not to return for three or four years," wrote Gansevoort in his elegantly looping hand (a far cry from Herman's sometimes indecipherable scrawl), he was finally able to relax. "It is a great consolation to me that I have done my duty towards him, thoroughly & conscientiously in this his last cruise upon land," he wrote to Allan with more than a hint of palpable relief.[75] But it was this very adventurous and hearty spirit that Hawthorne admired, as well as Melville's Spartan needs. In 1856, in England, during the two writers' last visit together, the older writer appreciatively wrote in his journal of Melville's ability to travel the world with few personal effects. "I do not know a more independent personage," Hawthorne muses. "He learned his travelling habits by drifting about, all over the South Sea, with no other clothes or equipage than a red flannel shirt and a pair of duck trowsers. Yet we seldom see men of less criticizable man-ners than he." And when Hawthorne reflects upon Melville's "wild and adventurous youth," there is a palpable strain of wonder at a person who is, in many ways, similar yet ultimately so different from himself.[76] (Melville, despite his incomplete formal schooling, clearly put something of his own aspect in a description of Ahab, who had "been in colleges, as well as 'mong the cannibals; been used to deeper wonder than the waves.")[77]

This paradox of Melville — the well-bred, patrician-born but raw adventurer and sea salt — was one of the many qualities of the man that stimulated Hawthorne and inspired him to let the author into his insular world. This is one reason why Hawthorne tolerated Melville's tendency for pop-in visits and why he went against the grain of own character by offering the newcomer lodgings at his own small house. Of course, Sophia's approval of Melville was a factor too, as was Melville's playful and affectionate orientation toward the Hawthorne children. (The Hawthornes also appreciated both Melville's pedigree and his marriage to the daughter of the esteemed Bostonian Judge Lemuel Shaw.) Decades later, as an adult, Julian would write, "There were few honester or more lovable men than Herman Melville."[78] But if Melville's robust embrace of existence impressed Hawthorne, that very quality sometimes caused Melville frustration over Hawthorne's reserve and his inclination toward comfort zones. Writing to Evert Duyckinck, Melville praised Hawthorne's work to the rafters, calling him a "wonderfully subtle" writer of stories with "deeper meanings ... worthy of a Brahmin" and claiming that he possessed a "genius immensely loftier, and more profound, too, than any other American has shown hitherto in the printed form." But Melville's consternation regarding Hawthorne's personality also surfaced. "Still there is something lacking — a good deal lacking — to the plump sphericity of the man. What is that? He doesn't patronise the butcher — he needs roast beef, done rare."[79] Many critics and biographers read Melville's comments as a scrutiny of Hawthorne's work, but Melville is clearly talking "of the man" (these are his very his words) that he encounters in their personal exchanges. In fact, in the next sentence he qualifies himself — "Nevertheless, for one, I regard Hawthorne (in his books) as evincing a quality of genius" — clearly showing that he is moving back and forth between the man and the works, trying to reconcile one with the other.[80] Hawthorne's personality doesn't match up to that compelling blackness that Melville encountered in Hawthorne's tales; but even Hawthorne's son Julian would proclaim of his father that "the man and the writer were ... as different as a mountain from a cloud" and marveled that he was "unable to comprehend how a man such as I knew my father to be could have written such books."[81] Nevertheless, it is easy to miss Melville's meaning in the letter to Duyckinck. In the 1850s, American celebrity culture was in its infancy, and his revelations are akin to someone who has adored the performances of a contemporary movie actor but then comes away disappointed when the off-screen actor lacks the vibrancy of the onscreen character. Melville had blurred the line between fiction and non-fiction in his early novels, basing them on his own often exaggerated and even distorted exploits. He regaled the Hawthornes and others with vivid tales of his South Pacific adventures and even acted as if he were standing on deck hauling away at ropes on a mountain ledge atop Monument Mountain during his first meeting with Hawthorne and other such "celebrities" as Dr. Oliver Wendell Holmes. Melville very much played and lived the part of "Melville the writer" at times and had indeed had experiences very much akin to those that he put to the page. And there was undeniably something performative in his engagement with Hawthorne, as evidenced by both his over-pouring and densely figurative letters to the older writer as well as his meetings with Hawthorne and family, during which he would play out his Polynesian adventures as he narrated them.

This performative bent was certainly evident on the occasion of Melville's 32nd birthday (August 1, 1851)—three months before the publication of *Moby-Dick*—when he treated himself to a surprise visit with his friend. On horseback, he encountered Hawthorne and Julian along the road to the red cottage and shouted out a theatrical greeting in Spanish, very much playing the part of the dashing *caballero*. For his part, Hawthorne didn't at first recognize the horseman as Melville, but was mildly and pleasantly surprised when he did. Hawthorne simply did not bring the same flair, energy, and verve to their interactions, and it was this perceived shortcoming that caused Melville to question the "plump sphericity" of the man's presence and bearing. In person, Melville expected Hawthorne to exude the layers and depths evident in his work, and the disparity between the man and the page was frustrating to Melville, a writer who had so often blurred the lines between non-fiction and literary invention and who had become accustomed to adopting the persona of both sea-adventures writer and sea adventurer. Melville's image of a "roast beef, done rare" in his letter to Duyckinck is carefully chosen, because to Melville his dear friend Hawthorne lacked a certain *sanguinity*, the very sanguinity that Melville so passionately offered up to Hawthorne. (An interesting dialectic between these contrasting personality types crops up in Melville's great short work, "Bartleby, the Scrivener," in which he presents the sanguine and reckless scribe Turkey—who, like Melville, had a preference for baggy pants—

and his sallow, sad, and nervous colleague Nippers. The two must dwell in close quarters at writing desks, yin to the other's yang.) Even in this circumstance of mutual admiration, Hawthorne projects a degree of coldness, an element of his temperament indelibly marked on him in formative years. Not long before meeting Melville, Nathaniel, the only son in a family of women, wrote in his journals as his mother lay dying, brooding over the "coldness of intercourse" between the two of them, a frostiness that stretched back to his own boyhood.[82] Indeed, Hawthorne had written something of himself into Hester Prynne, who kept all of her passions imprisoned within "a tomb-like heart."[83]

Melville's initial interactions with Hawthorne led him to the revelation that appeared in his review of *Mosses*: "On a personal interview, no great author has ever come up to the idea of his reader" (though he was yet again playing a part as he wrote those words, that of a Virginian who had never met Hawthorne).[84] Both in writing and in person, Melville had a greater range than Hawthorne, whose literary genius was distinguished by hermetic scope and painstakingly hewn deliberation, what the *Literary World* termed his "marvelous self-control."[85] Melville, on the other hand offered an "intellectual chowder" of a broader scale and variety.[86] In *Moby-Dick*, Melville could be grandiose one moment, ribald and comical the next. He could lure us into a densely figurative dream state aboard the *Pequod* in one chapter, systematically deconstruct the anatomy of the sperm whale in another, and then conjure up Shakespearean conventions in yet other parts of his narrative. He could also drop the rudiments of plot altogether and ponder the metaphysical and ontological. And he did all of this while keeping alive the concrete, everyday, life-threatening realities of life aboard a whaling vessel. Of course, though, Melville was far from a seamless writer, and he could be excessive where Hawthorne was fastidious. Consider the central symbols of the two writer's greatest novels: the tangible, elaborately embroidered detail of Hester Prynne's omnipresent, red "A" versus Melville's colorless whale, who remains absent and elusive, more phantasm than creature throughout much of the work. Melville's writing was also marked by liberation, not just liberation from traditional narrative structure but from social and religious orthodoxy, sexual repression, and bigotry.

The men's educational backgrounds vastly differed as well. Dire financial circumstances and the death of his father, Allan Melvill (the "e" was added during Herman's generation) in January 1832 in Albany, New York, prompted the family to withdraw Herman from Albany Acad-

emy when he was twelve. From then on, his formal education was spotty —
he did a short stint at the Albany Classical School in 1835 and briefly reen-
tered the academy in the fall of 1836. He also studied surveying for a time
at a vocational academy in Lansingburgh, New York, with the eventually
unfulfilled hopes of landing a position on the Erie Canal. Mostly, though,
Melville was self-educated. (In fact, he remained a sometimes shaky
speller well into his career as a writer.) In so many ways, in fact, he was a
self-fashioned individual, despite his pedigree. (Both of his grandfathers
were celebrated Revolutionary War heroes.) By contrast, Hawthorne —
despite emerging from similarly fallen gentility — experienced a complete
formal education, spending his college years among the Georgian-style
halls and tall pines of Bowdoin College, where he rubbed shoulders with
fellow students such as future poet Henry Wadsworth Longfellow and
future president Franklin Pierce. Both men, particularly Pierce, would
become dear friends. For his part, Melville was simultaneously self-conscious and prideful of his own path. His self-consciousness manifested
itself in the extensive canonical references and elaborate, reaching prose
of *Moby-Dick* (and the same in his letters to Hawthorne), as if he were
exhaustively showcasing the fruits of his self-studies. But Melville also
wielded his self-education as a mark of distinction that was part and
parcel of his ruggedly individualistic and adventuresome persona. Ishmael's assertion in *Moby-Dick* that "a whale-ship was my Yale College
and my Harvard" was clearly the author's personal credo as well.[87]

Yet there were strong affinities between the two writers' lives as well.
Most obvious was the fact that both had lost their fathers at a young age.
Hawthorne's father had been a sea captain who died of yellow fever in
Suriname when Nathaniel was not quite four years old. In fact,
Hawthorne's earliest, youthful writings were sea tales about "bronzed
pirates and hardy privateers, perhaps modeled on [George Gordon, Lord]
Byron's [*The*] *Corsair*."[88] Melville, like Hawthorne's father, had *lived* such
a life, though, and this certainly enhanced the attraction toward the
younger writer and likely figured into Hawthorne's favorable review of
Melville's debut South Pacific tale *Typee* years before meeting the author.
(Incidentally, during the time of their Berkshires association Melville
was right around the same age as Hawthorne's father when he died in
Suriname.) Melville's father, Allan, an importer of French dry goods,
died just short of his fiftieth birthday. Owing to the relatively primitive
medical diagnoses of the time, the exact circumstances of his death will
never be known. What is clear, however, is that — bedeviled by profound

illness, sleeplessness, and crushing anxieties about debt — Allan Melvill descended into a feverish state described in family letters as "deranged" and "maniacal" before passing away in the family home in Albany, New York, in late January 1832.[89] Twelve-year-old Herman was a close witness to the terrible, unfolding spectacle.

But this particular book is about more than the mere similarities and differences between the two writers and the sufferings and exultations they experienced: It is also about what happened when they came together. In that way, this is very much a story about *Moby-Dick*, a work in which Melville picked up upon Hawthorne's literary tones and inclinations, but then extended and bent them towards his own purpose, anticipating the modern novel and influencing countless 20th-century writers. That Hawthorne was one of the few of the time to see through Melville's idiosyncratic style and into the heart of his visionary practice was testament to his own acute sensitivity and idiosyncratic tastes. As Edward Wagenknecht pointed out in a 1961 "psychography" of Hawthorne, despite his reserve and restraint the writer was not in the habit of confining "his appreciation to conventional things"[90]; in fact, as biographer Frank Preston Stearns indicated in 1906, his taste was often "much in advance of its time."[91] Many reviewers were lukewarm, some savage, regarding *Moby-Dick*. By the time of the follow-up novel, the densely psychological and idiosyncratic *Pierre* (1852), most reviewers asserted that Melville had squandered his literary gifts; some pronounced him outright crazy. His own mother, convinced that the writing vocation was threatening his mental and physical health, desperately employed what social contacts she could during the 1850s in an attempt to get him away from the writing desk and into a government job (to no avail).

Andrew Delbanco describes it best when he suggests that *Moby-Dick* "was Melville's vampire book — it sapped him."[92] Of course, it also was the deflating response to this, his greatest effort and one into which he had poured so much of himself, as well as the redoubled exertion of *Moby-Dick* and *Pierre* back-to-back, that drained his creative resources and energy. (The latter book summoned him to similarly dark regions, though *Pierre* was land-bound, less successfully executed and immersed in esoteric familial, romantic, and social dynamics: "Leviathan is not the biggest fish; — I have heard of Krakens," he ominously boasted to Hawthorne while in the fresh thrall of it.)[93] But Melville did not surrender his novelistic muse before inventing a new form of literary expression. The very extravagant, unrestrained, and untidy elements that critics in his time disparaged would become the hallmarks of his legacy in the twentieth century. "Melville was the first American to write with such outrageous freedom," Delbanco attests, and "the first to understand that if a literary work is to register the improvisational nature of experience, it must be as spontaneous and self-surprising as the human mind itself."[94] *Moby-Dick* was a result of a high-wire recursive process, with Melville first writing the tale using the raw materials of his experience and imagination and then ingesting outside sources whole and padding and piecing out the novel with all sorts of arcane and digressive information about whales, whaling, and philosophy (among other topics — for example, there is a chapter about the color white). Of course he also took inspiration from his literary north stars: Shakespeare, of course, and Virgil's first-century Roman epic *Aeneid*, the latter of which, like *Moby-Dick*, was written during — and reflected upon — a period of great political and social transformation. Melville was writing his tale just after the Mexican War, a time of rapid and turbulent westward expansion for the United States (though, in the book, Ishmael is purposely unspecific about the time of the narrative). And, of course, innate in the politics of expansion was the question of slavery, a debate made even more explosive in the north by the enactment of Fugitive Slave Laws as part of the Compromise of 1850, which was designed to accommodate such expansion. This law mandated northerners to prosecute slaves who had escaped to their region and to return them to their southern "owners." (Melville's own father-in-law, esteemed judge Lemuel Shaw, was forced to uphold these laws in landmark cases — in Boston of all places, that city known as "the cradle of liberty.") *Moby-Dick* was "in the broadest sense a political novel,"[95] despite the relatively inert political life of its creator. The novel is fraught with shades of Melville's anxiety about both expansionism and slavery. The writer had condemned the South Pacific oppression of French Colonialism and American Protestant missionaries in his earlier writings, and throughout his life he showed himself to be an egalitarian humanitarian. Hawthorne's take on slavery was more thorny and complicated; for one, he stood steadfastly by his longtime friend President Franklin Pierce throughout his own life. (Pierce was travelling with Hawthorne when the writer died.) The New Hampshire-born Pierce had become an unpopular president among many northerners during his presidency, one accused of consistently kowtowing to and rolling over for pro-slavery interests. As Pierce's personal biographer, Hawthorne glorified his friend, turning a blind eye to what history would come to judge as weaknesses of conviction and ethics. (The administration's one oft-cited success was the Gadsden Purchase, the final puzzle piece in the contiguous, transcontinental United States.) Hawthorne didn't condone slavery, but he supported the letter of the law when it came to the Missouri Compromise. He also saw the dissolution of slavery as a threat to the Constitution itself and therefore the Union. He represented Pierce (and, by proxy, himself) as stalwart realists who, while understanding the abhorrent nature of the enterprise, nonetheless, apprehended that the institution could not be rapidly abolished "except by tearing to pieces the Constitution ... and severing into distracted fragments that common country, which Providence brought into one nation through a continued miracle of almost two hundred years."[96] In addition, he suggested that a forced and immediate abolition would harm the very people it sought to emancipate. (Hawthorne, like many, had some amorphous ideal of an organic and "gradual" abolition in mind.) In retrospect — and despite their different views — both Hawthorne and Melville seemed awkward and ill-fitted to the political exigencies of their time. During the period when his fame was dwindling and the tides leading to the Civil War were rising, Melville tried to capitalize on the last vestiges of his notoriety by becoming a traveling lecturer. And despite an environment of heated rhetoric and deeper and deeper divisions in the Union, the author stuck to such relatively quaint and non-germane themes as "Travel: Its Pleasures, Pains, and Profits" and "Statues in Rome." (Had Melville lived to see the very literary modernism he anticipated and influenced fully rear its head, he might have empathized a bit with William Butler Yeats' sentiment, "The best lack all conviction, while the worst / Are full of passionate intensity.")[97]

Melville did throw smatterings of sociopolitical commentary into his works, but despite his family's clear Democratic roots he himself remained a political cipher throughout this life. And one could argue that the most resonant moments in *Moby-Dick* are neither social nor political; they come when Melville was inspired to explore matters both metaphysical and psychological within the framework of the whale hunt, often placing the reader in a place seemingly poised between unconscious and conscious, what Freud would term in later years "preconscious." ("Everything unconscious ... that can easily exchange the unconscious condition for the conscious one, is therefore better described as 'capable of entering unconsciousness,' or as preconscious," wrote Freud.)[98] In Hawthorne, Delbanco argues, Melville had "found a writer in touch with

the dreamworld that he himself had begun to explore."[99] Consider the
"Mat-Maker" chapter in *Moby-Dick,* wherein Melville gradually transmutes a routine, mundane afternoon on deck into a figurative dream
state, or rather a "hypnagogic" state, hinged between dreaming and
wakefulness. He introduces this idea by noting the "still and subdued"
atmosphere. Queequeg and Ishmael are industriously immersed in weaving a mat, but this dream-tinged scene also invests the slow, regular
movement of the activity with metaphysical poignancy. First, though,
Melville establishes the atmosphere that his language has lapsed us into,
noting that "such strange a dreaminess did there then reign all over the
ship and all over the sea."[100] The industrious mat weaving seems "as if
this were the Loom of time," notes Ishmael, "and I myself were a shuttle
mechanically weaving and weaving away at the Fates":

> There lay the fixed threads of the warp subject to but one single, ever
> returning, unchanging vibration, and that vibration merely enough to
> admit of the crosswise interblending of other threads with its own. This
> warp seemed necessity; and here, thought I, with my own hand I ply my
> own shuttle and weave my own destiny into these unalterable threads.[101]

Melville uses these psychological borderlands as a wedge into the metaphysical, as if it was the state that allowed one to glimpse through the
keyhole and toward the larger questions of the temporal, metaphysical,
and ontological. In Hawthorne, Melville found a fellow writer deeply
attuned to these psychological and metaphysical states, not only in his
work, but in their talks together. Hawthorne encapsulated one of their
Berkshires conversations, which stretched deep into the night, as being
"about time and eternity, things of this world and of the next, and books,
and publishers, and all possible and impossible matters."[102] It was the
deepest and most intimate intellectual engagement either would ever
experience. And in Melville, Hawthorne ultimately recognized a writer
who would put these matters to a deeper (and more risk-taking) test on
the page than he ever had, even if for Melville it meant estranging himself
from all that was commercial and palatable to his public. Herman envisioned his destiny as he was finishing up the whale book, lamenting to
Hawthorne in June 1851, toward the end of his *Moby-Dick* labors, "Dollars damn me.... What I feel most moved to write, that is banned, — it
will not pay. Yet, altogether, write the *other* way I cannot. So the product
is a final hash, and all my books are botches."[103] By this he meant they
were commercial botches, for Melville more than suspected his own
artistic greatness, even if his work was not suited for the buying public.

"Though I wrote the gospels in this century, I should die in the gutter," he bemoaned in the same missive.[104]

But let us not forget that *Moby-Dick* is dedicated to the "genius" of Hawthorne, and without Hawthorne — namely, the inspiration of both the man and his work — Melville would not have possessed the full vision to compose his essentially twentieth-century work. In fact, the possibility of an existence on any metaphysical plane without Hawthorne was something Melville found unsettling. In May of 1865, at the age of 45, a year after Hawthorne had died, and well after most of Melville's readership had abandoned him, the *Moby-Dick* author pulled Hawthorne's *Mosses from an Old Manse* from the shelf. This was the collection of tales that had once inspired him to sound his deepest literary depths and to pen a review that would cement their allegiance. Melville seemed to be seeking traces of his old friend, who had departed the world at the age of 59. While reading and contemplating the Hawthorne sketch "Monsieur du Miroir," Melville underlined the latter half of the following statement: "Will he linger where I have lived, to remind the neglectful world of one who staked so much to win a name?" Melville then wrote on the page, "What a revelation." Melville knew full well the sacrifices of his immersion in his novels, and Hawthorne too had sputtered out as a productive writer after their Berkshires glory (before garnering posthumous fame). It is even more important to note that he also marked another nearby sentence: "He will pass to the dark realm of Nothingness, but will not find me there."[105] In his time, Melville had borne witness to the premature death of his father and brother and had endured years at sea and desertion on a remote island. He had seen his literary reputation climb and then fall and had braved the fall of his family's fortunes as well as his own descent into debt. He had brought himself to the brink of mental and physical collapse with his literary pursuits and had just witnessed his own country in the throes of the Civil War. Yet, at this moment, the idea that he wouldn't encounter his late friend again, in any realm whatsoever, was unbearable. "This," Melville scrawled upon the page in response to Hawthorne's ominous lines, "trenches upon the uncertain and the terrible."[106]

It was not only the specter of their old friendship that Melville endured in his later years; as a failed and forgotten writer plying away at a workaday job as a customs inspector on the New York City piers and writing reams of poetry that few would read or respect (he had abandoned prose altogether), he also bore witness to Hawthorne's posthumous fame. Through the late 1860s and into the 1870s, Melville became a satellite in the Hawthorne universe; his scant reputation was now as a lesser-known writer who had once been friends with Hawthorne. Throughout this period, he would also witness release of Hawthorne's notebooks from America, England, and his travels in Europe. The first two contained mentions of Melville, and one wonders how the younger writer received them, both his brief mention in the American journals and the generous deliberations in the English writings. By the 1870s, in his fifth decade of life, Melville became reduced to, as Hershel Parker declares, a minor role in Hawthorne's life and posthumous fame.[107] As Hawthorne's posthumous comet soared, Melville had to live with the fact that his own work had countenanced some of the harshest and cruelest criticism that had ever been penned by the critics of the age. The Boston *Post* had once declared that *Pierre* must have been written "in a lunatic hospital." London's *New Monthly* proclaimed the style of Melville's whale book to be "maniacal — mad as a March hare — mowing, gibbering, screaming." The *Daily Times* (Boston) insisted in 1852, "No man has more foolishly abused great original powers."[108] These went beyond reviews of his works; they were attacks on his character. (He had experienced this to a lesser degree in certain ecclesiastical reviews of his early novels, in which his critiques of Protestant missionary work in the South Pacific were met with astringent assaults on his very morality.) In later life, it seemed to Melville that the only vestiges of his fame came early in his writing life, when he was known — in an appel-

Herman Melville, 1868 (courtesy Berkshire Athenaeum, Pittsfield, Massachusetts).

lation that would come to make him wince — as "the man who lived among the cannibals."[109] By the 1870s, Melville was both awash in the posthumous fame of Hawthorne and in his own sense of literary failure, as an artist and as a provider for his family. As Parker describes it, "The dead Hawthorne was having a great vogue ... and the living Melville might as well have been dead, since his fame was already posthumous."[110] In other words, Melville's literary reputation was a curiosity from a bygone age, never to be recovered (in the minds of critics who still bothered to mention him at all). Additionally, his domestic life was unraveling; by the mid–1870s, his wife was describing him to others as having deteriorated into "a frightfully nervous state," and, in a theme that came up again and again in Melville's later years, she raised desperate questions regarding his mental health.[111]

One effort that had exacerbated his already tenuous state of mind was *Clarel*, his epic poem based on his Holy Lands travels and sculpted out in diligent and rhymed meter. Here, he seemed to want to rival John Milton, and he did, at least in terms of length: When it finally appeared in 1876, in two volumes, the poem stretched to 18,000 lines, much longer than *Paradise Lost*, or, for that matter, *The Aeneid, The Odyssey,* or *The Iliad.* This was the work in which he bundled together all of his impressions of the Holy Land, his own spiritual conundrum, and the spiritual turbulence of the times around him. The onset of that trip had also proven to be his last audience with Hawthorne (in Liverpool). Fittingly, the poem also dealt with his evolving views on Hawthorne, amid all of the posthumous attention. Presenting himself as "Rolfe" and Hawthorne as "Vine," Melville contemplated both the chasm between them and their affinities. The poem, begun sometime in the years following his son Malcom's death at age 18 (from a gunshot wound while in his bed — arguably either accidental or suicide) would occupy his life for nearly a decade. After working the piers all day as an outdoors customs inspector, he would retire to his study to craft a few lines, limiting himself to rhymed, octosyllabic meter. (How compelling that he would self-impose such stylistic confinement in his writing late in life. This was a world away from the liberation he allowed himself in *Moby-Dick*.) Melville would later say, in a self-effacing, dismissive statement cultivated by years of literary disappointment, that it was "a pilgrimage or what not, of several thousand lines, eminently adapted for unpopularity."[112] What Walter E. Bezanson concluded in the 1930s, though, was that within the pilgrimage and all of the musing over spirituality was another dead serious motif: a "tournament of merits" between Rolfe and Vine, through which Melville measured himself against the now quite fashionable (and quite dead) Hawthorne.[113]

But what of Hawthorne? Had he extracted any influence from the younger writer? This is a region that remains largely unexplored — and a region into which this volume will embark. Nevertheless, with Hawthorne being one of the first readers and genuine appreciators of *Moby-Dick*—and with Hawthorne's innate receptivity to art of the unconventional sort — it is impossible to think that the eventually groundbreaking novel didn't leave its mark on him. Hawthorne had been impressed by Melville's early work during his marathon reading sessions of the younger author's pre–*Moby-Dick* works in the barn in Stockbridge. And since his letters to Melville are lost to time, one can only imagine what layers Melville's crowning achievement stirred in him at the time. But consider the advancement of Hawthorne's own prose in his last novel, the admittedly flawed and Italy-based *Marble Faun*, particularly in this one prolonged, constantly unspooling sentence:

> When we have once known Rome, and left her where she lies, like a long decaying corpse, retaining a trace of the noble shape it was, but with accumulated dust and a fungous growth overspreading all its more admirable features; — left her in utter weariness, no doubt, of her narrow, crooked, intricate streets, so uncomfortably paved with little squares of lava that to tread over them is a penitential pilgrimage, so indescribably ugly, moreover, so cold, so alley-like, into which the sun never falls, and where a chill wind forces its breath into our lungs; — left her, tired of the sight of those immense, seven-storied, yellow-washed hovels, or call them palaces, where all that is dreary in domestic life seems magnified and multiplied, and weary of climbing those staircases, which ascend from a ground-floor of cookshops, coblers' [*sic*] stalls, stables, and regiments of cavalry, to a middle region of artists, just beneath the unattainable sky; — left her, worn out with shivering at the cheerless and smoky fireside, by day, and feasting with our own substance the ravenous little populace of a Roman bed, at night; — left her, sick at heart of Italian trickery, which has uprooted whatever faith in man's integrity had endured till now, and sick at stomach of sour bread, sour wine, rancid butter, and bad cookery, needlessly bestowed on evil meats; — left her, disgusted with the pretence of Holiness and the reality of Nastiness, each equally omnipresent; — left her, half-lifeless from the languid atmosphere, the vital principle of which has been used up, long ago, or corrupted by myriads of slaughters; — left her, crushed down in spirit with the desolation of her ruin, and the hopelessness of her future; — left her, in short, hating her with all our might, and adding our individual curse to the Infinite Anathema which her old crimes have unmistakably brought down; — when we have left Rome in such a mood as this, we are

astonished by the discovery, by-and-by, that our heart strings have mysteriously attached themselves to the Eternal City, and are drawing us thitherward again, as if it were more familiar, more intimately our own home, than even the spot where we were born![114]

This — the only capable language of handling the twisting emotional gyres of repulsion and attraction — is not the tightly controlled prose of an earlier Hawthorne (or of any Hawthorne heretofore recognizable). And the contemporary reader will recognize in the tumbling strands the language of later writers — the dense outpourings of William Faulkner, the bursting-at-the-seams conception of more recent writers like Cormac McCarthy and Toni Morrison. This is their language, but it is a daring and singular voice inherited from Herman Melville (the Melville of *Moby-Dick*, not the much later *Billy Budd*). *The Marble Faun* was essentially Hawthorne's most modern novel, not only based on such prose but also in the unresolved nature of the story line, something that frustrated contemporary readers. The influence of Melville on Hawthorne is a largely unexplored question, but this volume takes the tack that Hawthorne, one of the few significant individuals to truly recognize and appreciate Melville's gifts in his own time, was ultimately influenced by the book about the whale, the very book that, paradoxically, was dedicated to his own genius. He was also egged on by Melville's praise of his craft in "Hawthorne and His Mosses." At a literary level, they fed off of each other. Who was influenced more by the other? Perhaps it is best to contemplate Melville's own lines to Hawthorne: "The divine magnet is on you, and my magnet responds. Which is the biggest? A foolish question — they are *One*."[115]

Historically, these lines and Melville's dedication of *Moby-Dick* to Hawthorne perhaps sealed their alliance, despite the shifting tides of their individual glory. (Melville, with the enduring force of one book, has now arguably eclipsed Hawthorne.) Indeed, seen from one perspective, the two writers were bound to share the same fate — that is, to be underappreciated in life, then to be reevaluated, rescued from oblivion, and to become influential long after death. This book will dwell in those spaces where the writers intersected and overlapped, in their lives and in their work, serving as both a biography of a friendship and a context through which to view their unique literary achievements and ongoing legacies.

Two

The Freshness of
Primeval Nature:
Monument Mountain
and the *Mosses*

Thou who wouldst see the lovely and the wild
Mingled in harmony on Nature's face,
Ascend our rocky mountains.
> —*William Cullen Bryant, "Monument Mountain"*

And the day will come, when you shall say who reads a book by an
Englishman that is a modern?
> — Melville, *"Hawthorne and His Mosses"*

In a countryman, this sudden flame of friendship would have seemed
far too premature, a thing to be much distrusted; but in this simple
savage those old rules would not apply.
> — Moby-Dick

It is a pity that Mr Melville so often in conversation uses irreverent
language — he will not be popular in society here on that very count —
but this will not trouble him.
> —*Sarah Morewood, letter to Evert Duyckinck*

It was August 1850, and the United States was convulsing. To the
west, California, soon to become a free state, was in the throes of the
Gold Rush, with gold seekers crawling all over its northern reaches like
an ant colony, having come by ocean — enduring the long sweep around
Cape Horn — or overland along the arduous California Trail. These ships
and prairie schooners carried what still remains the largest mass migra-
tion in the nation's history; in fact, from 1848 to 1850 San Francisco
swelled from a population of 800 to 20,000.[1]

But the vast western territories acquired in the Mexican War only heightened the friction over the slavery issue back east, and amid an environment of utter sectionalism, the Republic was coming apart at the seams. By September, the Compromise of 1850 would temporarily stall the move toward secession and civil war, but a key component of the Compromise, the Fugitive Slave Act of 1850 — a measure aimed at mollifying pro-slavery factions so that California could be admitted as a free state — would stir up enmity even more, paving the way to deepening division and, of course, a decade later, eventual war. (Despite his anti-slavery position, Herman Melville's father-in-law, esteemed Boston Judge Lemuel Shaw was constitutionally compelled to make a controversial ruling supporting the Fugitive Slave Laws, one that led to violent unrest.) Northerners were against these laws for various reasons, not just because it made them agents of slavery but also because it was perceived as an encroachment on their own rights and the authority of state and local law. There were, of course, also rifts within the North and many complicated crosscurrents in perspective; in fact, some northern businessmen primarily feared secession because of the potential economic impact. Pulitzer-Prize-winning historian Louis Menand goes so far as to conjecture, that they "feared secession far more than they disliked slavery."[2] The mill towns in Massachusetts, for example, depended heavily on the cotton that came from the South. The northern Unionists (that is, those who wanted to preserve the Union) were of course disparaged by the northern Abolitionists, who put principle above everything else, including the existence of the Union.

Against this turbulent backdrop, America's literary power was beginning to crest, breaking away from European ideas and influence and working its way into a shape of its own — though it takes the power of retrospection to fully realize the dimensions, especially where Melville and Hawthorne are concerned. 1850 to 1855 was a period that legendary critic F.O. Mathiesson has somewhat inaccurately called the "American Renaissance." (His other term "first maturity," or Malcolm Bradbury and Richard Ruland's suggestion, "American Naissance," swing much closer to the mark.) But one gets the idea; for during this period Ralph Waldo Emerson's *Representative Men*, Henry David Thoreau's *Walden*, Harriet Beecher Stowe's *Uncle Tom's Cabin*, and the first version of Whitman's *Leaves of Grass* all appeared. Most importantly, the years saw three novels from Hawthorne — *The Scarlet Letter*, *The House of the Seven Gables*, *The Blithedale Romance* — and four (with diminishing commercial returns) from Melville: *White-Jacket, Moby-Dick, Pierre,* and *Israel Potter.* And this is not to mention the remarkable shorter work, "Bartleby, the Scrivener."

Amid this cultural maelstrom — the Gold Rush, the slavery debate, Naissance, and all — and out in the sylvan insularity of the Berkshires, two of the greatest creative forces in the history of American Literature came together in the glow of friendship for a time and then eventually made a slow drift apart as the years wore on. In retrospect, we understand that without this meeting, *Moby-Dick* would never have assumed its known shape, and that this novel and Hawthorne's *The Scarlet Letter* would come to influence the lineaments of the American novel well into the twentieth century. At the time, however, it was difficult for a novelist to get a strong foothold in a country that still fawned over writers such as Dickens. Therefore, when Hawthorne and Melville first met, it was not a collision of self-conscious literary giants but a meeting of, in many ways, like-minded writers that would evolve into great personal and artistic affinity as well as mutual commiseration. Their success at the time could be described as moderate — that is, until the mostly negative reception of *Moby-Dick* began a definitive spiral in Melville's writing life that the follow-up, *Pierre,* would only hasten downward (though a handful of reviewers on both shores did appreciate the deep wonders of *Moby-Dick*). Both men also very much wrestled with what it meant to be an American writer, all the while forging works that would posthumously make them quintessential national authors and forbears of the rich and variegated landscape that has become American letters. The credit cannot go to predecessors such as James Fenimore Cooper, Washington Irving, or, even earlier, Charles Brockden Brown; these writers' talents still oscillated in the margins of the British literary universe. There was Edgar Allan Poe, of course, who died in 1849, but his histrionics, more explicit macabre bent, and pioneering efforts in the detective motif represent a different, less complex and penetrating brand of influence than the groundbreaking works of Melville and Hawthorne.

At the time when Nathaniel Hawthorne first met Herman Melville, the younger author was still a man poised between worlds, having not fully shaken off the residue of his sea travels and economic hardship, despite the fact that he had married well and seemed to be settling into agreeable domesticity. Melville's roots were undoubtedly refined and patrician; having descended from privileged lineages and two Revolutionary War hero grandfathers, he had been raised in an atmosphere of elegantly lapsed wealth and self-conscious social engineering. Yet he had also tasted the life of a common sailor for months and years at a stretch, becoming accustomed to humility and toil, his breeding and accent earning him little rank in those watery reaches of the world. The boy who was raised among sitting rooms, furniture heirlooms, and lofty family connections had also, before thirteen years of age, witnessed the death of his father and his immediate family's descent into bankruptcy. The straitened financial circumstances stalled his formal learning, and he would never complete his secondary education, let alone legitimately stroll the bucolic grounds of a New England college.

Melville's most crucial formative years were spent on various ocean vessels, including a whaling ship, during an era when whale men still brought small craft treacherously close to 40-ton leviathans and hurled roped harpoons at them. He had dwelled long months among the lower-caste egalitarianism of the cramped forecastle, a place where issues of race, nationality, and background often faded, as if the idea of native soil and birthright had been left behind with the land itself. It was a place of bawdy banter, crowded bodies, and, for some, frustrated hours spent carving images (sometimes pornographic depictions) into whale-bones. At a strikingly young age, he left everything behind for years of a perilous existence in far reaches, a time punctuated by defection, hazardous travails on South Pacific Islands, incarceration for mutiny, and toil as a farmhand in the fields of Tahiti — not to mention a stint as a bowling-pin setter in Hawaii. Now, just turned 31, he had long abandoned his seafaring ways for the life of a family man and writer. But he had been able to translate his previous existence into relatively successful books that walked a hazy line between fiction and nonfiction. His first two novels, *Typee* (1846) and *Omoo* (1847), had made a name for him and successfully carved out his reputation as an exotic adventurer whose exploits were not only audacious but sexually suggestive.

The handsome young man who encountered Nathaniel Hawthorne on August 5, 1850, still smelled of brine and faraway places, his skin tawny and his thick brown hair, which he wore swept back from his forehead, highlighted from weeks engaged in outdoor pursuits in the Berkshire Mountains: long days spent fishing Pontoosuc Lake, hiking the surrounding hills and mountains, and dare-devilishly ramming around the rough dirt roads in a pine-box carriage. He could still summon up the persona of the itinerant seaman from the pages of his books, and, when he was in one of his gregarious (as opposed to his pensive) moods, he regaled visitors or hosts with vibrantly orated tales of his life among ship crews and South Pacific natives. With his background and breeding, he was clearly comfortable among the Berkshires elite with whom his family associated, but he sometimes talked a little louder than the others, was impulsive and abrupt in his ways and less fastidious in dress, as if such things only mattered to him to a degree. Of course there was also that remarkably hirsute face, his luxuriant nut-brown beard extending down his shirtfront. (In *Pierre; Or, the Ambiguities* Melville would deem a "flowing beard" to be "the most noble corporeal badge of the man."[3])

Hawthorne, in his mid–40s, did not possess Melville's innate hunger for risk and adventure. He mostly clung to New England until his later years, when he worked in the consulate in Liverpool, England, and took to exploring Europe. Even his frail wife, Sophia, had voyaged to Cuba before their marriage, but Hawthorne was, in so many ways, a creature of restraint and safety. He had moved from Salem to the Berkshires months before, in May, in a state of nervous exhaustion brought on by the death of his mother and the travesty of a politically charged dismissal from his post at the Custom House. Hawthorne, a Democrat who insisted he had only passing involvement in politics, had been unceremoniously let go by the Salem Whig party when Whig candidate Zachary Taylor won the presidency. He was relatively slender yet physically impressive — a handsome, dark-haired man with a sizeable, dome-like forehead, heavy eyebrows and large, deep-set, grayish-colored eyes that pooled the light and often glowed with silent but penetrating comprehension. He was relatively tall, just under five-feet-eleven, and walked strong and erect but sometimes had the tendency to carry his head slightly to one side, as if in consideration of all that he passed. He still looked a little sickly around the edges from his recent struggles, but the mountain environs of spring and summer had done much for his constitution. Interestingly, many noted throughout his life that that there was a certain feminine aspect intertwined in all of his "manly" gravity and nobility, and often a nervous tinge to his relations with acquaintances and strangers. Henry Wadsworth Longfellow's wife, Frances, described Hawthorne as the "most shy and diffident of men,"[4] and during Hawthorne's Concord, Massachusetts, period, Transcendentalist figurehead (and father of author writer Louisa May Alcott) Bronson Alcott recalls Nathaniel being so "ill at ease" during two rare visits that he soon sought "excuse for leaving politely forthwith," citing a too-hot stove or too-loudly ticking clock, and bolted homeward.[5]

Hawthorne was also a riddle and paradox to those who knew him; he could be parsimonious with words, making conversations either strangely one-sided or downright awkward. Much like the plots of his works, he also seemed to be waging an inner war between the light and dark sides of his nature. Having descended from authoritarian Salem Puritan stock and having been exposed to a fine formal education, he could also show great compassion and affinity for those less fortunate than he. At the Custom House, he displayed sensitivity for the plight of the wharf laborers and did his best to accommodate them so that they could get in as many hours of wages as possible. When he lived among the Transcendentalists at Brook Farm, he may have held great skepticism for the utopian experiment, but he also displayed kindhearted attention to Frank Farley, a farmworker struggling with what we would today recognize as mental illness. Melville, in fact, saw an "omnipresent love" pulsing through Hawthorne's fiction, and another dear friend, Longfellow, traced a similar strain in his old Bowdoin College pal. Yet there were clearly capricious reservoirs of anger in Hawthorne as well; here, after all, was a man who declared it necessary to his literary success to have "bitter enemies,"[6] and here was the same writer who had used the prefatory "Custom-House" section of *The Scarlet Letter* to lampoon his old co-workers, his quill dripping with venom at the remembrance of his abrupt dismissal. (This is not to mention his notoriously brutal misogynistic screeds against woman writers in his notebooks.) In later years, he railed against "those jackasses in Washington" when they tried to lower his salary at the Liverpool consulate, and, when, during his consulate service, he finally traveled through Europe, he claimed to "detest Rome."[7] This was not unusual; so often Hawthorne, the perennial malcontent, came to loathe wherever he was residing at the time. But if Hawthorne was characteristically depressive, prone to isolation, and ill at ease in company beyond his inner circle ("I had always a natural tendency ... toward seclusion," he once proclaimed),[8] he was uncharacteristically aglow around Melville, sparked by what his wife termed the "freshness of primeval nature" and "true Promethean fire"[9] in the thirty-one-year-old author. In fact, Hawthorne's publisher and friend James T. Fields would claim, "I never saw Hawthorne in better spirits"[10] on the occasion of that first day of their meeting (Monday, August 5, 1850), which began with a steep hike up the area's celebrated Monument Mountain in Great Barrington, Massachusetts, on an overcast and gray day.

The multi-person jaunt was actually a calculated trip meant to showcase the local celebrity elite for some visiting literati from New York City (in hopes, of course, that they would duly record it for posterity and public consumption in a metropolitan journal). The locally based Dr. Oliver Wendell Holmes, Sr. — the celebrated lecturer, physician and writer — was on hand, looking prim and diminutive and nearing his 41st year. The New York City interlopers consisted of Melville's guests, publisher Evert Duyckinck and writer Cornelius Matthews, both of whom had been part of the core of literary elites who gravitated toward the fashionable politics of the Young America Movement in New York City during the previous decade. They were the kind of insider hipsters to whom Melville simultaneously felt drawn toward and repelled by while living in New York City. Herman had been an associate and friend with Duyckinck since 1847, and Duyckinck, like many, relished having a genuine literary article like the "retired Sea-Dog" Melville in his orbit.[11] (Duyckinck also possessed one of the most impressive library collections in the country, a fact that was not lost on Melville, who consistently tapped into that reservoir.) The well-known legal scholar and reformer David Dudley Field, Jr., a local who was close to Hawthorne's age, had organized the trip as a way to bring together the worlds of New York City and New England literary life, yet two more worlds that Melville straddled. The overdressed, dandyish essayist and publisher James T. Fields, who had published *The Scarlet Letter*, was also on hand, as were his young wife, David Field's daughter Jenny, and a prominent local, Henry ("Harry") Sedgwick, in his mid–20s at the time and a member of a celebrated Stockbridge, Massachusetts, family. Melville was acutely aware that he was surrounded by estimable reputations, fortunes, and, of course, formal educations: Holmes' from Harvard, Fields' from Williams, and Hawthorne's from Bowdoin. He was also fully cognizant that Hawthorne and Holmes were estimated among the small, self-conscious troupe for their genius — and that, though a respected writer, he was not. His role in the assemblage was that of the adventurer and writer of sea tales; that is, the ruddy mariner of his earliest books, *Typee* and *Omoo*, with a whiff of the exotic about him. And he played the role to the hilt. But Melville also possessed a desire to be appreciated for more profound, less literal depths in his prose, depths he had hinted at in his third book, *Mardi*, and fathoms that he was beginning to plumb in deeper fashion in his new work about the whale fishery, which he had begun earlier in the year. The Melville who first made Nathaniel Hawthorne's acquaintance on the Monument Mountain hike was a writer striving to break the critical constraints of being perceived as an American Daniel Defoe — that is, a spinner of light sea romances. Melville was preparing to pack his new book with layers of metaphysics, psychology, sermonizing, and the kind of cavernous darkness that he would come to admire in Hawthorne's works. The meeting, then, would become, as Ruland and Bradbury assessed, "one of those seminal literary relationships based on a primal shock of recognition." Furthermore, it would come to nourish "the essential spirit, the lightness and also the darkness, the symbolic inclination and the philosophical scope of *Moby-Dick*."[12] The meeting with Hawthorne, simply put, was one of the most important personal encounters in his writing life.

The hike up Monument Mountain consisted of a 720-foot, steep and winding ascent through the kind of glades that could have sprung from a Hawthorne tale, and the type of environment that had been a tonic to the author ever since his teenage rambles through the untamed Maine wilderness of his family's property in the 1820s. The pitched trek up Monument was a challenge to the more delicately genteel among the group; nevertheless, everyone, flushed with the nature of the company and the prospect of the day, eagerly clambered toward the summit, grouping or pairing off in conversations and picking their way along a small brook that trickled with mountain run-off. Duyckinck monopolized Hawthorne early on, the small, slender Knickerbocker taking full advantage of the opportunity to talk about *The Scarlet Letter* with one of his favorite authors. Melville was content to bide his time and, in the meantime, show off his agility and athleticism while scaling the steep mountainside. A good portion of the way up a thunderstorm began rolling across the sky. Duckinck remembered that it came from the south, seeped across the horizon, and "dragged its ragged skirts" directly toward them. The group sought shelter in a shallow overhang worn into the underside of a gigantic mossy boulder (not so much an actual "cave," as many have asserted).[13] Those who could not fit into the shelter — where some of the party were pressed against the rock wall, sitting on the damp, desiccated earth — benefited from the ingenuity of Dr. Holmes, who fashioned an umbrella out of evergreen boughs. Holmes also raised morale by producing a bottle of champagne and a silver mug from an India rubber bag he had been carrying on the way up the mountain. They huddled together, talked about all things literary and shared from the mug until the flash storm passed.

The final ascent left everyone winded, as they carefully stepped up a sheer and winding natural staircase of rocks and quartz outcroppings. The summit, at around 1,650 feet above sea level, was a tumbling effusion of gigantic pale boulders and rocks, with nary a flat piece of ground on which to stand. Hawks drifted below, swooping in slow arcs, as the captivated crew picked their way among the boulders and pointed out distant checkpoints. Below, the Housatonic River, in its richly verdant valley, snaked its way across the floor of the world. (In clearer weather, the group would have spied Washington Irving's Catskills to the west, rising like gray, distant ghost mountains.) As to Melville, he was in full "Mr. Omoo" mode, and spying a wedge-like and jutting rock at the dizzying, absolute rim of the precipice, he swung himself upon it like a horseman, sitting astride the peaked formation with all of the world falling away below him. The top-mast duties of ship life had clearly inured him against any paralyzing fear of heights, and it was as much statement as performance, as if to show the chasm of bravery and physical experience between him and the others. From his precarious perch, Melville entertained the others by pretending to be on a ship's bowsprit, tugging and hauling at invisible ropes. The writer was in high spirits; he was away from his New York City home and back in his beloved Berkshires, the landscape that had enchanted him since he was young. He was also among esteemed literati friends and acquaintances, and had become a writer of some note — one who was known and read and had a reputation, albeit one lacking marks of genius and greatness already bestowed upon Hawthorne. Here was a day he could only have imagined during his impoverished, toilsome years at sea. He had also just celebrated his third anniversary to Elizabeth (Lizzie, nee Shaw), on August 3 and his 31st birthday on August 1. Moreover, he was plying away at a budding manuscript in which he was beginning to truly stretch his literary powers — and he more than suspected its emerging greatness. Add to that the prospect of a friendship with another brilliant writer, the potential of which Melville may or may not have been aware of atop the rocky summit of Monument Mountain, and he was on the cusp of an *annus mirabilis*, one that would culminate with the publication of *Moby-Dick*.

On this day, Melville was certainly at his entertaining and social best, but there was an unfortunate undertow to his current Berkshires stay. While he would play magnanimous host to Duyckinck and Mathews during this visit to the Berkshires, the ancestral, stately "Melvill" family home in which they were all staying in Pittsfield, formerly owned by his debt-prone uncle and now under the charge of his cousin Robert, was being put up for sale after having been converted to a boarding house for visitors (good enough, in fact, for the likes of Henry Wadsworth Longfellow and his wife). "The family has gone down & this is their last season," Duyckinck knowingly wrote home to his wife from his trip.[14] Melville seemed to want to compensate for this reality with both his physical and literary prowess, and he was perhaps all too attuned to Duyckinck's and Mathews' awareness of the situation. As to Hawthorne, who was already acquainted with Melville's work after having positively reviewed *Typee* in Salem a few years before, he observed everything in his characteristically detached manner while becoming increasingly interested in this Melville character. Also hanging back, but for other reasons, was Oliver Wendell Holmes. The little doctor, who was from deep Berkshires roots and was renowned for his superior intellect and wit, found himself wildly out of sorts in this lofty, rugged place. He warily stayed far back from the precipice, clutching his India rubber bag, and anxiously peering toward the view below, noting that the whole thing made him nauseous, inducing a sensation, he said, that was like ingesting ipecac.[15]

Duyckinck's sidekick, the writer Cornelius Mathews, who has gone down in American literature lore (whether rightly so or not) as a notoriously long-winded attention sucker, decided at this point to read aloud from local poet William Cullen Bryant's "Monument Mountain," a work that espouses the natural beauty of the landscape and conjures the folklore of a heartbroken Native American woman who leaped from the mountain's peak. The situation at least provided an opportunity for more drinking — toasts to Bryant and then to other poets of the Republic, including Hawthorne's old college mate and friend, Henry Wadsworth Longfellow, followed as the bottle was once again presented from Holmes' bag. After all of the literary rites were performed and the bottles of champagne were emptied, the troupe headed back down the mountain, this time relying upon inertia, gravity, and the headiness of drink to whisk them along. Legend would have it that Melville and Hawthorne were pressed together in intense discourse during the rainstorm and all of the revels, but it is more likely that, due to the group dynamic, they primarily enjoyed smatterings of dialogue when the opportunity presented itself. But these exchanges, intermittent as they may have been, increasingly induced a magnetic pull between the two writers as more and more affinities began to surface between them. The climb, the revels, and Melville were drawing Hawthorne out of his diffident, protective encasement, and with the rest he headed over to the Field cottage in nearby Stockbridge for a hearty afternoon dinner of freshly slaughtered turkey and beef,[16] which was of course washed down with more spirits and more heady conversation, the kind one would expect from a gathering of such literary lions. (Some of the guests borrowed dry articles of clothing from Field, including Duyckinck, whose diminutive feet were swimming around in Field's large slippers.) Holmes, ever the instigator and satirist, lit up the table by launching a debate surrounding the currently vogue-ish studies of ethnology. And to posit himself as conversational gadfly — while perhaps poking fun at his own frail, diminutive stature — he suggested that Englishmen were physically superior to Americans.

Holmes couldn't have known the strong literary nationalism that was beating in Melville's breast at the time, for during the seafaring writer's prolific burst of creativity, pumping out five novels from 1846 to 1850, he had been constantly struggling with what it meant to be an American writer with a nascent identity in a young republic. This was one of the attractions to Hawthorne, someone whose work Melville would estimate to be in league with Shakespeare, but also to be distinctly "American." Here, after all, was the man who only days later would, under a pseudonym, pen a review of Hawthorne's story collection *Mosses from an Old Manse* in which he would declare, "And the day will come, when you shall say who reads a book by an Englishman that is a modern?"[17] This was a rejoinder to English writer and Anglican clergyman Sydney Smith's rhetorical question from the *Edinburgh Review*, which had been hanging in the air since 1820 and continually galling many a would-be American writer: "In the four quarters of the globe, who reads an American book?" In penning the Hawthorne review for the *Literary World*, Melville was laying a shot across English literature's bow in the name of Hawthorne — and, secretly, "Melville." Not the "Melville" of his previous works, but the sense of his own expanding literary power as he embarked upon the whale epic. So suffice it to say that Melville, the omnivorous autodidact who had been an active member of debating societies during his youth in Albany, leaped at the opportunity to shoot down any idea of English superiority and to go head-to-head in a healthy debate with Holmes, the dean of Harvard Medical School and one of the most respected minds in New England. There was also an undercurrent to the conversation that the two were clearly aware of: In his early twenties, Holmes had penned a well-known poem, "The Last Leaf," that both paid tribute to and gently lampooned Herman's beloved paternal grandfather, Thomas Melvill, Sr., a Boston Tea Party participant who, in old age and a couple of decades into the nineteenth century, was still in the habit of wearing a three-cornered hat and breeches as he tottered on his cane along the streets of Boston. Holmes likely didn't see much merit in the pro–English position he was taking, but rather was trying to draw the table out into spirited debate. For his part, Melville went after the idea like a shark hitting a chum line. "Melville attacked him vigorously," Duyckinck wrote with some satisfaction to his wife the next day.[18]

During the flurry of toasts, dining, and debate Hawthorne was in more elevated social spirits than his old friend and publisher James T. Fields was accustomed to witnessing, and he remembered over two decades later that the writer "rayed out in a sparkling and unwonted manner" during the feast and merriment.[19] Nevertheless, Hawthorne, by nature, was reticent to jump in and scrap it out with Holmes, though he surely shared Melville's views. As Duyckinck related, Hawthorne only "looked on" during the verbal skirmish, increasingly showing interest in the vigorous ex–mariner with the keen intellect as the debate swung around the table.[20] (Duyckinck's account, written the next day, in the immediate afterglow, is surely more accurate than Fields' retrospection through the decades that Hawthorne "stoutly" took part "in favor of the American [side].")[21] Holmes, ever the ironic wit and provocateur, then deemed himself convinced of American superiority and switched sides, according to Cornelius Mathews' account. And in a Swiftian streak of satire, he deemed that, yes, Melville was not only right, but that he had come to the conclusion that "in less than twenty years it would be a common thing to grow in these United States men sixteen and seventeen feet high; and intellectual in proportion."[22] As humor began to outweigh intellectual debate, the conversation tilted toward sensationalism and salaciousness. Alleged sea-serpent sightings were common in the nineteenth century among sailors and landlubbers alike, and talk turned to a recent alleged sighting in New York Harbor.[23] Tongues also wagged about a giant set of cattle testes on display in nearby Great Barrington.

Fortunately, before the conversation could descend further, prolific historical writer J.T. Headley, who was living in nearby Stockbridge, and his brother-in-law popped in, prompting the party of literary men to head off to explore the nearby Ice Glen on Field's property. The Glen was in a deep, sunless ravine, with large glacial boulders littering its fissure. It was another blackly romantic, Hawthorne-like landscape: all large, strikingly verdant mossy rocks boulders and deep, dark crevices that held pockets of ice well into the summer. Ancient trees stood like tall sentinels on the peaks of either side of the ravine. Headley, Melville, and Hawthorne took the lead—clambering around, through, and over the boulders and murky hollows—with the less rugged among them (the slight Duyckinck and Holmes, the soft and plush Mathews, the dapper and overdressed publisher James T. Fields) pulling up the rear. Alcohol, enthusiasm, and boisterous company powered the literary collective along the treacherous course, and Hawthorne—enlivened by the company and booze and displaying an uncharacteristically playful side—ominously called out from a hidden, dark trough that the Ice Glen would bring inevitable and "certain destruction" upon all of them.[24] (Melville wrote some of the Ice Glen into *Moby-Dick*, remembering its verdant hues as he describes an idyllic island ravine in Chapter II, "A Bower in the Arsacides": "It was a wondrous sight. The wood was green as mosses of the Icy Glen; the trees stood high and haughty, feeling their living sap; the industrious earth beneath was as a weaver's loom, with a gorgeous carpet on it.")[25]

Having avoided certain destruction, the group trooped back to David Dudley Field's house, an elegantly simple colonial brick structure, skirting along the meadows and fields surrounding the Housatonic River. Back at the house, there was more chatter and tea, and the arrival of another prominent local visitor, the tall and stately Elizabeth Sedgwick, eager to weigh in with the literary elite. Elizabeth ran a well-heeled school for young women in nearby Lenox and was sister-in-law to writer Catharine Maria Sedgwick. As 10 P.M. rolled around, the Pittsfield contingent—Duyckinck, Mathews, and Melville—hopped on the train to head home. A kindly brakeman named Conklin stopped near the Melvill farm, rather than taking them all the way to the downtown Pittsfield depot, sparing the three a considerable foot-trek in the dark.[26] With Mathews and Duyckinck bedded down in their guest rooms and Melville having quietly slipped into the room he was sharing with Lizzie, all could collapse into slumber knowing that even though August 5, 1851, was slipping away, it had been a day that they had sucked the very marrow out of. It was a complete day in many ways, with no mental or physical stone left unturned. And for Melville, it was the beginning of a friendship with Hawthorne—and by proxy a whole new course for his current book. All involved took something away from August 5—a significant memory, many distinct impressions—but it would primarily be cemented in history as the day that Hawthorne and Melville met, with all of the other participants falling away into supporting roles in the annals. As to Hawthorne, the day left him uncharacteristically magnanimous, and he extended a couple of rare invitations as a way of bringing himself closer to Melville.

* * *

The Hawthornes' temporary home, offered to them rent-free by the wealthy Tappans (though Hawthorne insisted on giving them fifty dollars), was a small red cottage on the northeast rim of the Stockbridge Bowl and on the southern edge of the property known as Tanglewood. The meadows behind the home sloped gradually toward the basin of gently rippling Lake Mahkeenac, which was cozily encased all around by low mountains. Though it lacked Hawthorne's accustomed proximity to the ocean, it was an idyllic setting in which even he couldn't be completely miserable for long, at least during the early, warmer months. (The drafty, poorly constructed little workman's cottage was not so desirable during the formidable Berkshires winters.) Throughout the spring and summer, it was a world of birdsongs and natural beauty, with ducks leveling downward in flight and gracefully alighting on the lake surface as Hawthorne, Sophia, and the two small children — Julian and Una — picnicked by the shore, having made the short walk with a basket from their back door. Hawthorne's youngest, Rose, would be born in the cottage in May 1851, a year after the family's first arrival.

This was where Melville, Duyckinck, and Mathews called upon Hawthorne late in the morning on August 8, 1850. Accompanying them was Melville's just-arrived brother, Allan, four years Herman's junior and an attorney in New York City, which was currently sweltering like a kiln in the August heat. Hawthorne's wife, Sophia (née Peabody), was on hand, as were the two children and her mother, who was visiting from eastern Massachusetts. Duyckinck took notice of the tasteful manner in which Sophia had decorated and outfitted the small house, admiring the fine art pieces on the walls and the serene window views of the sparkling lake at the bottom of the sloping meadow. Mrs. Hawthorne had draped the windows and main table in deep red cloth. In the drawing room was to be found a bowl and pitcher that Hawthorne's long-deceased sailor father had brought back from the Far East. In the front room lay a purple and gold carpet that Sophia's longtime friend Caroline Sturgis, wife of successful New York Broker William Aspinall Tappan (they were the owners of the property), had given her when they moved in. "My house is an old red farmhouse," Hawthorne wrote to one of his friends from the Custom House in Salem. "I find it very agreeable to get rid of politics and the rest of the damnable turmoil that has disturbed me for three or four years past."[27] Indeed, despite the complaints that Hawthorne would later voice about landlocked mountain seclusion, the red cottage would become a prolific literary workplace and sanctuary for him.

Hawthorne gave the four visitors some champagne, pulling out a couple of bottles that an admirer had given him and, as Duyckinck noted, "popping the corks in his nervous way." Hawthorne's social unease did not take one bit of the bloom off of Evert's estimation of the man and writer, however. "Hawthorne is a fine ghost in a case of iron," wrote Duyckinck to his wife the next day. "[He is] a man of genius and he looks it and lives it."[28] Meanwhile, the distance between Melville and Hawthorne was constantly closing, and Herman and the rest were reluctant to leave Hawthorne's company, heading down to the lake with him and lingering as long as possible, before heading to Stockbridge for an arranged get-together with J.T. Headley at the hotel. Hawthorne may have appreciated the attention of all of the guests, but it was Melville that he was singling out for his attentions—and a rare invitation for the younger writer to stay with him and his family for a few days at the red cottage was imminent. It didn't hurt that Sophia, ever-protective guardian of Nathaniel's sphere, was a bit in awe of Melville as well. "Mr Typee is interesting in his aspect—quite," she wrote to her sister Elizabeth of the visit. "I see Fayaway in his face."[29] In a couple of lines, Sophia had fused the handsome young man she had met—a man in the full, rugged flush of his beloved Berkshires outdoors—with the exotic, suggestive myths he had woven about himself in his earliest South Pacific novels, *Typee* and *Omoo*. It also didn't hurt that Melville would come to deeply admire Hawthorne, for that was a fan club that Sophia presided over and in which she was chief worshipper. A few months into her association with Herman, she would become unbridled in her praise of the sea writer, deeming him a "man with a true warm heart & a soul & an intellect—with life to his fingertips—earnest, sincere & reverent, very tender & modest."[30] During the August 8 visit, Duyckinck didn't quite measure up as well as Melville for Sophia, but he was nonetheless seen as agreeable and a gentleman. Mathews simply came off unfavorably as a "very chatty gossiping body."[31] (Herman's brother Allan, a lawyer who resided in no literary universe, apparently wasn't noteworthy enough for Sophia's ink.)

The guests finally did tear themselves away from Hawthorne and met up with J.T. Headley at the large hotel in Stockbridge, where they were greeted with bottles of wine and more conversation, and then all whiled away the afternoon lounging on the piazza and reading newspapers before Melville whisked them away again in his pine chariot, taking yet another new route through the Berkshires backroads. But at one point during all of the sightseeing and visiting from August 6 to 8, Melville and Duyckinck had come to an agreement: Melville would pen something about Hawthorne for Duyckinck's New York City journal the *Literary World*. This was a double score for Evert; it established his association with Hawthorne, whom the Boston literary scene (including James T. Fields) had laid strict claim to for so long. The ambitious little New York editor had championed Hawthorne for some time and had published *Mosses from an Old Manse* in his culturally nationalist Library of American Books collection, through Wiley & Putnam, along with Melville's *Typee*. (Duyckinckck was also Edgar Allan Poe's editor at Wiley.) The review was also a success for Duyckinck in that he had finally gotten Melville to cave in and pen a review, something he had been reluctant to do since after the critical savaging of his more aspiring and psychological book *Mardi*. Moreover, Herman had been avoiding, as biographer Hershel Parker terms it, "the dangers of dissipating his forces on miscellaneous writing" while he carved out the ambitious conception of *Moby-Dick*.[32] The question for both Melville and Duyckinck was what, exactly, Melville would review. *The Scarlet Letter* would have been the timely option, but no one had a copy on hand — such was the downside of making editorial decisions on the fly. Additionally, there was no time to have a copy shipped to the Berkshires, as Evert and Mathews had plans to leave on Monday afternoon, the 12th, and would need to carry Melville's writing back to New York with him. (Melville began penning the piece on Friday, the 9th.) It was decided that Herman would write something about the collection of tales *Mosses from an Old Manse*, which had been published four years before, in 1846. Herman's aunt Mary had given it to him as a gift not long before, and he had just sat down with it for the first time on August 7, in the fresh flush of just having met the author of the collection and one day before calling upon him in the red cottage. (Melville's stay with the Hawthornes wouldn't be realized until September 3.)

* * *

"Hawthorne and His Mosses" stands as a fascinating document in the history of American literature for many reasons. In it, Melville not only expressed his deepest and most abiding admiration for Hawthorne's craft, but he also, in retrospect, allowed readers to see into the recesses of his emerging imaginative efforts regarding *Moby-Dick*. "Hawthorne and His Mosses" was more than simply a review, for in the piece Melville also came to engage that which concerned an emerging American literature at the time, including the anxiety of British and European influence. And he was thinking of his own burgeoning novel as he addressed one of the great dilemmas, as articulated by Hershel Parker in 1996: "how as an American, a democrat, to write a tragedy equal to Shakespeare's without setting it in some heroic past or presenting it in Shakespearean rhetoric."[33] Melville placed before the reader the central identity crisis of a writer carving out a national literature in a young republic. As to the Shakespearean problem of setting, there was no need for a heroic past when there was the American dominance of whaling and the ocean, as well as less literal terrain to explore — that is, psychological terrain poised between sleep and waking and between conscious and unconscious. This was the setting Melville had begun to embark upon with *Mardi* — and while Melville had backed off after that book, offering up the hasty adventures *Redburn* and *White-Jacket* to the commercial tastes of the time, Hawthorne now gave him new license to light out for those less-literal hinterlands anew. For another biographer, Laurie Robertson-Lorant (writing in 1996), "Hawthorne and His Mosses" became, despite some of the hyperbole and occasional messiness in thought, "a kind of literary Declaration of Independence for American writers" in which Melville not only articulated his vision for his own writing (via that of Hawthorne) but "his struggle to reconcile democratic values with high literary standards."[34] But the device — the entry point in the review — for all of this was Hawthorne's tales, and Melville posited himself as the older writer's one true audience, a penetrating reader who could not be thrown off the scent of Hawthorne's genius by that writer's subtleties and orderliness, by a literary mode in which truth only reveals itself through "cunning glimpses." As Hawthorne biographer Brenda Wineapple (writing in 2003) put it, "Hawthorne may have hoodwinked the multitude with his tidy tales, but he didn't outfox everyone; certainly not Herman Melville."[35]

But beyond this appreciation of Hawthorne, the undeniable backbone of the piece is Melville's aforementioned deliberation regarding the state of an emerging literature in the young republic. "Hawthorne and His Mosses" has been continually scoured, since the 1920s, for deeper hints about the nature of the Melville-Hawthorne relationship, and too often the one (and only) line that could be bent toward a titillating interpretation has been amplified and represented as a dominant theme in the piece: "I feel that this Hawthorne has dropped germinous seeds into my soul. He expands and deepens down, the more I contemplate him; and further, and further, shoots his strong New England roots into the hot soil of my Southern soul."[36] Nevertheless, beyond the heaping admiration of Hawthorne, "Mosses" offers acute insight into Melville's state of mind, anxieties, and passions as he began to move into the deepest stages of the composition of *Moby-Dick*. Most apparent is the exhausting level of mental energy that drove his autodidactic efforts. In the piece, Melville not only speaks confidently and insightfully of Shakespeare, whom he had truly only just recently discovered, but he also writes eighty percent of the review before having even finished reading *Mosses from an Old Manse*—and admits as much to his readers. Most of the way through the essay, Melville fesses up: "To be frank (though, perhaps, rather foolish), notwithstanding what I wrote yesterday of these Mosses, I had not then culled them all." But, he explains, "[I] had, nevertheless, been sufficiently sensible of the subtle essences in them to write as I did."[37] Here were the Melville intellect and creative powers at work—all that the writer felt he needed was a *taste* of the man and his work and he was off and running, spewing out words and insights and connections.

This is the energy that drives *Moby-Dick*, which more than any novel ever written, is full to bursting with disparate references, modes, and themes, all the product of the author's scattershot, voracious self-studies and hyperactive mind. That Melville emerged from the publication of that novel exhausted, feverish, and ultimately sapped is no wonder, for everything he was taking in—including the relationship with Hawthorne and his work—rushed through him and was processed through the Melville conduit and into the pages of the whale epic. And in the composition of the book, Melville doggedly followed his mind wherever it chose to roam, his hand only loosely on the rudder. How else can one explain so many digressive and plot-less passages, chapters, including one full chapter, VLII: "The Whiteness of the Whale," that speculates upon the color (or lack thereof) white? Here were the qualities of the book that incited critics to lambaste it and that prompted Evert Duyckinck to deem it "intellectual chowder." But Melville is already anticipating the risks inherent in his muse as he writes of Hawthorne in the

"Mosses" piece and, more ostensibly, of himself as he prepares to delve into the furthest reaches of his new book. "[I]t is better to fail in originality than to succeed in imitation," he preaches. "He who has never failed somewhere, that man can not be great. Failure is the true test of greatness."[38] These lines point not only to the raw nerve and innovative spirit of the *Moby-Dick* author, but to his idea of an "American" literature, one that must ultimately completely break away from the English mode. In Hawthorne, Melville — behind the mask of a southerner vacationing in New England, a device that seeks to cohere on the page, and through a national literature, a republic that is in reality fracturing — locates "the new and better generation" of American writer par excellence. (The "southern" identity is also injected in order to make this a call for *all* American writers, despite the fact that Hawthorne is quintessentially a New England writer and profoundly steeped in those environs.) Hawthorne is New America: The smell of the country's "beeches and hemlocks is upon him," America's "broad prairies are in his soul," and "if you travel inland into his deep and noble nature, you will hear the far roar of his Niagara."[39] Other prominent American writers—for example, James Fenimore Cooper and Washington Irving — have thus far, from Melville's perspective, simply "furnish[ed] an appendix" to the well-read English authors by wielding their overt influence. He is also obstinate in his insistence that American readers and critics turn their affections away from England and toward native writers, warning against lavishing "embraces upon the household of an alien. For believe it or not, England, after all, is, in many things, an alien to us. China has more bowels of real love for us than she."[40] And in conjuring up England's ultimate literary figure, Shakespeare, as a comparison to the grand example of Hawthorne, Melville also seeks to dethrone the bard in America, slinging criticism at the "absolute and unconditional adoration" of the Shakespearean canon. "But what sort of belief is that for an American ... who is bound to carry republican progressiveness into literature, as well as into Life?"[41]

What one can glean from all of this is that Hawthorne's works (and person) have not only enchanted Melville, but have incited him to speculate upon and turn around in his head his own literary intentions and aspirations as an American writer. But one cannot solely rely on what he makes explicit in "Hawthorne and Mosses" — that is, one cannot blindly buy into the message that Melville is so ardently trying to impress upon the reader; for taken together. the "Mosses" essay and the completed *Moby-Dick* show an author both burdened and fueled by oppositional tension and paradox. As much as he holds aloft an American ideal (most fully realized, in his mind, by Hawthorne) — a "progressive" literature emblematic of the American spirit and divorced from English culture — the whale book is as much the creation of a new form of American literature as it is beholden to influences from abroad, particularly Shakespeare, despite Melville's protestations in "Hawthorne and His Mosses." His subject matter, however, displayed clear leanings toward his home country. "To produce a mighty book, you must choose a mighty theme," Melville would declare in the very pages of *Moby-Dick*.[42] At an obvious level, the prospect of dispatching with such a leviathan in its own environs is in itself a gargantuan undertaking, but at a nationalistic level, whaling was also a mighty theme. The pervasiveness of products harvested from whales was undeniable during the time that Melville was writing (particularly whale oil in lamps); add to that the clear American dominance of the industry, which had come to far outpace the English, and one has a quintessentially American — and, of course, "mighty"— subject. Another implicit tension in the piece emerges from Melville's prescience regarding the reception of *Moby-Dick*, which was still a long way from completion. (The book's American publication would arrive over a year later, in November 1851.) Melville speaks inspirationally in his Hawthorne essay about originality and innovation, but, as previously pointed out, he weds such achievements to failure in the public eye. Because Melville is pondering his own ambitions and intentions as he discusses Hawthorne, the strange effect is of a self-directed pep talk littered with predictions of critical and commercial failure. He becomes like the coach in the locker room who incites his team to do their best while predicting they will lose, based on score, while playing a beautiful game. That Melville, in his lifetime, would live out this paradox shows the writer's hyper-acuity regarding the nature of his work. Melville's sentiments about and to Hawthorne are littered with such rhetoric — in the "Mosses" essay he deems *Mosses from an Old Manse* "too deserving of popularity to be popular,"[43] and in a letter to Hawthorne, while deep in the thrall of *Moby-Dick's* creation, he bemoans, "What's the use of elaborating what, in its very essence, is so short-lived as a modern book? Though I wrote the Gospels in this century, I should die in the gutter."[44] The fact of the matter was that Melville was pouring every ounce of himself into what he believed would not only be his grandest artistic achievement but in all likelihood a complete public failure bound to be understood an appreciated by precious few in his lifetime. Melville becomes, in the review, the type of reader he wants for himself — that rare, sensitive, highly attuned individual who can recognize and appreciate the tiered depths of his work. "Where Hawthorne is known, he seems to be deemed a pleasant writer, with a pleasant style — a sequestered, harmless man, from whom any deep and weighty thing would hardly be anticipated: a man who means no meanings."[45] But Hawthorne is so much more than the dominant public perception regarding him: He possesses a "great, deep intellect, which drops down into the universe like a plummet," and his tales are charged with a "mystical depth of meaning."[46] Melville is still stinging from the public reception to his own third book, *Mardi*, which sought out less literal and more figurative and psychological terrain ("the world of the mind," as the writer deemed it), yet he plans to probe even deeper in the whale book — is resolved to leave behind a reputation as the "man who lived among the cannibals" or as the "American Defoe" and signal a new direction for American literature — and all of his ambitions and anxieties regarding this herculean effort are roused by the "genius" of Hawthorne and exerted into the lines of "Hawthorne and His Mosses"; the essay is, in many ways, a forecast of *Moby-Dick*, which was, at the time, still very much a private endeavor.

In the piece, Melville singles out the Hawthorne tale "Young Goodman Brown" for particular praise. In truth, he doesn't probe too deeply into the axis of Hawthorne's craft, but in this tale he does see the hallmarks of what he somewhat vaguely terms that author's "blackness" or "darkness" — and it is these turgid depths of Hawthorne's works that most compel Melville. There is much in this story that would appeal to the younger writer's sensibilities, certainly the unveiling of pervasive hypocrisy for one — that is, the notion that the most pious, upstanding, and devout members of a society may also be drenched in sin (and more in servitude to "the devil" than to any degree of moral obligation). In Melville's own early works, he unveiled what he saw as the hypocrisy of the Protestant missionaries working in the South Pacific, who under the guise of Christianizing did more harm than good and scaled the heights of selfishness rather than selflessness. Hawthorne's darkness, then, becomes "Truth" for Melville. "For in this world of lies, Truth is forced to fly like a scared white doe in the woodlands; and only by cunning glimpses will she reveal herself."[47] This is the kinship, claims Melville, that Hawthorne shares with Shakespeare: "Tormented into desperation,

Lear the frantic king tears off the mask, and speaks the sane madness of vital truth."[48] Note again the kind of paradox and oppositional tension that Melville is drawn to: "sane madness"; in fact, when the *Literary World* misprinted it as "same madness" it gave Melville fits, so important was that contradiction to him. (He would explain this error to Hawthorne's wife, Sophia, after he was "discovered" to be the author of the glowing review.) It was a paradox that would play itself out in Ahab, who — though undeniably mad — has layers of clear-eyed insight that often emerge in his rhetoric, and who even displays keen awareness of his own paradox: "All my means are sane, my motive and my object mad."[49] For Melville, this blackness he ascribes to Hawthorne becomes the canvas upon which the worthy writer can ply the profoundest of ideas— and, of course, "Truth." That blackness, Melville tells us, is the very "background, against which Shakespeare plays his grandest conceits."[50]

It is this idea of "blackness" that Melville carries forth into *Moby-Dick*. Surely it was something he had already had in mind — and something his readings of Shakespeare, Dante, Milton, and others had already impressed upon him — but to see it in a fellow American who was not only writing at the same time but with whom he had a growing and warm personal acquaintance led to a "shock of recognition"[51] that prompted him to approach his growing whale book with renewed energy. In "Young Goodman Brown," Hawthorne whips up a black maelstrom to accompany the shattering of Goodman's "innocence" (sexual and otherwise) and the character's dark realization, or the revelation of "truth," that there "is no good on earth":

> And, maddened with despair, so that he laughed loud and long, did Goodman Brown grasp his staff and set forth again, at such a rate that he seemed to fly along the forest path rather than to walk or run. The road grew wilder and drearier and more faintly traced, and vanished at length, leaving him in the heart of the dark wilderness, still rushing onward with the instinct that guides mortal man to evil. The whole forest was peopled with frightful sounds— the creaking of the trees, the howling of wild beasts, and the yell of Indians; while sometimes the wind tolled like a distant church bell, and sometimes gave a broad roar around the traveller, as if all Nature were laughing him to scorn. But he was himself the chief horror of the scene, and shrank not from its other horrors.[52]

Similarly, in *Moby-Dick*, as the fateful inevitability, madness, and true "reality" of the Pequod's mission becomes more and more imminent, Melville paints this scene that reflects both an outer and inner world (within Ahab and Ishmael, that is) and transmutes the smoke- and fire-laden labor of converting blubber to oil into something more elevated and horrible:

> Their tawny features, now all begrimed with smoke and sweat, their matted beards, and the contrasting barbaric brilliancy of their teeth, all these were strangely revealed in the capricious emblazonings of the works. As they narrated to each other their unholy adventures, their tales of terror told in words of mirth; as their uncivilized laughter forked upwards out of them, like the flames from the furnace; as to and fro, in their front, the harpooneers wildly gesticulated with their huge pronged forks and dippers; as the wind howled on, and the sea leaped, and the ship groaned and dived, and yet steadfastly shot her red hell further and further into the blackness of the sea and the night, and scornfully champed the white bone in her mouth, and viciously spat round her on all sides; then the rushing Pequod, freighted with savages, and laden with fire, and burning a corpse, and plunging into that blackness of darkness, seemed the material counterpart of her monomaniac commander's soul.
>
> So seemed it to me, as I stood at her helm, and for long hours silently guided the way of this fire-ship on the sea. Wrapped, for that interval, in darkness myself, I but the better saw the redness, the madness, the ghastliness of others. The continual sight of the fiend shapes before me, capering half in smoke and half in fire, these at last begat kindred visions in my soul.[53]

And as the crew gets closer and closer to the chase, and therefore their own violent fate, Melville presents us with the ominous image of the ship's burning masts after a lightning strike:

> All the yard-arms were tipped with a pallid fire; and touched at each tri-pointed lightning-rod-end with three tapering white flames, each of the three tall masts was silently burning in that sulphurous air, like three gigantic wax tapers before an altar.[54]

Melville uses the turgid, flickering imagery in these two passages—the flames, the human figures, the candles—to conjure up those intentions he attributes to Shakespeare and Hawthorne in the "Mosses" review: "those occasional flashings-forth of the intuitive truth ... those short, quick probings at the very axis of reality."[55] And it is an utter "blackness" that provides the background and canvas for these flashings and probings, for these "grandest conceits," asserts Melville. In "Young Goodman Brown" one can see these intentions in Hawthorne's work; moreover, one can see what Melville (unspecifically, and at a loss for the *mot juste*, for once) terms this "blackness," a host of images he uses in his own work to accompany his own "flashings forth" right down to the evocations of candles. But for the lack of a ship, this passage from "Young Goodman Brown" could be Melville's own:

> At one extremity of an open space, hemmed in by the dark wall of the forest, arose a rock, bearing some rude, natural resemblance either to an altar or a pulpit, and surrounded by four blazing pines, their tops a flame, their stems untouched, like candles at an evening meeting. The mass of foliage, that had overgrown the summit of the rock, was all on fire, blazing high into the night, and fitfully illuminating the whole field. Each pendant twig and leafy festoon was in a blaze. As the red light arose and fell, a numerous congregation alternately shone forth, then disappeared in shadow, and again grew, as it were, out of the darkness, peopling the heart of the solitary woods at once.[56]

This is not to say that Hawthorne influenced the larger shape of *Moby-Dick* — and the novel clear boasts a tidal wave of influences beyond Hawthorne — but the mark of the older writer upon Melville was instantaneous and promethean, and *Moby-Dick* would have never bore out many of its shades and tones were it not for Melville's encounters with the works and the man.

* * *

On August 17, the very day that the first installment of "Hawthorne and His Mosses" was published in the *Literary World*, Melville paid a visit to the Hawthornes in the little red cottage near Lenox. The Hawthornes were still blissfully unaware of the complimentary piece on Hawthorne, let alone the true identity of "the Virginian" who wrote it. Melville brought along a package that Evert Duyckinck had sent along to Nathaniel from New York City, without knowing that it contained copies of his own five published books, including *Typee*, which Hawthorne had praised in a review in a Salem newspaper in 1846. Duyckinck knew that Hawthorne wasn't in possession of any of Melville's books at the time, including the copy of *Typee* that Duycknick himself had sent to Hawthorne to review years before — Evert was also aware that Hawthorne's not-too-easily aroused interest had been significantly stirred up by the younger author and that the books would satisfy that ever-increasing interest and curiosity. (Duyckinck, ever the witness to and sounding board for the friendship, also sought to nourish it in its early stages.) The main business of the visit to the red cottage was to shore up plans for Melville to be the couple's guest for an extended visit, based on the invitation that Hawthorne — well out of character — had impulsively put forth during the revels on August 5. A pact was made to host Herman early in the next month, September, a time of year, assured Melville, when the Berkshires—in the late throes of glowing, verdant summer—was one of the most pleasant places to be on earth.

Hawthorne had a seasonal habit of "loafing summers and setting to work at the first frost," as Hershel Parker put it[57]; therefore, there was time for reading before he would begin carving out the stirring book about a home and family in Salem that would come to be known as the *House of the Seven Gables* upon its publication in early 1851. Thus unburdened for the moment of literary toil, Hawthorne—in anticipation of Melville's visit in a few weeks—stretched himself out on the hay of the barn and plowed through the ex-mariner's literary output up to that point, gaining a growing admiration for the writer as August waned and the bird and insect songs thrummed around him. He re-read *Typee*, revisiting, in the fresh bloom of acquaintanceship, what he had found alluring about it when he had favorably reviewed it in 1846, and then he traced the writer-mariner's development through *Omoo, Mardi, Redburn,* and *White-Jacket*. That Hawthorne, in between the publication of the *Scarlet Letter* and on the verge of writing *Seven Gables*—and therefore in the fullest flush of his own literary powers—would commit such an intent and lengthy gaze upon Melville's work was a testament to his keen interest in the seafaring author. Hawthorne emerged from his Melville immersion more impressed than ever and even more convinced that this was a man that he wanted to spend time with and to come to know even better. On the 29th of August, Hawthorne wrote to Duyckinck, offering up what was from him rare and high praise. He had read all of Melville's works, he wrote, and he was quite impressed. In particular, he was struck by *Mardi*, the book that—in Melville's explorations of less literal and more psychological landscapes—clearly prefigured *Moby-Dick* and that also, in that very reaching and exploration, elicited much critical derision. It was, surmised Nathaniel, a "rich book, with depths here and there that compel a man to swim for his life." He was unremittingly frank in his praise: "It is so good that one scarcely pardons the writer for not having brooded long over it, so as to make it a great deal better."[58] It was still early in their friendship, but Hawthorne—divining both Melville's extraordinary talent and headlong, hasty writing process—had already proven himself to be Melville's most attuned and sensitive high-profile reader; no other figure of such literary merit would read Melville so deeply and so well in his lifetime. (And he hadn't even published *Moby-Dick* yet.) Of Herman's two most recent works, *Redburn* and *White-Jacket*—books that Melville himself, who had churned them out in a haste that was even remarkable for him, dismissed as mere salary fodder—Hawthorne wrote, "*No writer* [emphasis mine] ever put the reality before the reader more unflinchingly than he does."[59] Even if *Redburn* and *White-Jacket* weren't, as a whole, Melville at the height of his powers, Hawthorne recognized the flourishes of an unparalleled writer.

Consider what Hawthorne saw in *White-Jacket:* for example, the narrator's over one-hundred-foot fall from the topmast, which becomes a long frozen moment of metaphysical scrutiny, and the type of prolonged examination, inflation, and elevation of a passing moment or brief sensation that would figure much later in modernists such as Faulkner and Hemingway. Here, for the first time, was the kind of written examination of a moment that prefigured a later generation, what Hemingway would theorize as "the sequence of motion and the fact which made the emotion,"[60] or, as T.S. Eliot admiringly said of Hemingway's work, "[H]e seems to me to tell the truth about his own feelings at the moment when they exist."[61] F.O. Matthiessen made this connection between the Eliot quote and the *White-Jacket* fall (in *American Renaissance* [1941]), seeing the scene as illustrative of "the innermost nature of Melville's developing power."[62] Judging from Hawthorne's comment regarding his "progressive appreciation" of Melville, Hawthorne, ever systematic and meticulous, read Melville's books chronologically; therefore, this plunge from the yard arm in *White-Jacket* (one of the last moments in the most recently published work) would have been fresh in his senses when he wrote to Duyckinck that "no writer ever put the reality before the reader more unflinchingly"—and surely no character in fiction has (literally) fallen with more poetic force, as Melville deliberates in mid-air:

> I fell—down, down, with lungs collapsed as if in death. Ten thousand pounds of shot seemed tied to my head, as the irresistible law of gravitation dragged me, head foremost and straight as a die, toward the infallible centre of this terraqueous globe. All I had seen, and read, and heard, and all I had thought and felt in my life, seemed intensified in one fixed idea in my soul. But dense as this was, it was made up of atoms. Having fallen from the projecting yard-arm end, I was conscious of a collected satisfaction in feeling, that I should not be dashed on the deck, but would sink into the speechless profound of the sea ... there was a still stranger hum in my head, as if a hornet were there; and I thought to myself, Great God! this is Death! Yet these thoughts were unmixed with alarm. Like frost-work that flashes and shifts its scared hues in the sun, all my braided, blended

emotions were in themselves icy cold and calm.... Time seemed to stand still, and all the worlds seemed poised on their poles, as I fell, soul becalmed, through the eddying whirl and swirl of the maelstrom air.[63]

In Melville's rendering, all practicalities are mixed with deeper mysteries: The tangible weight of falling, the palpable direction of his plunge, and the realization that he will strike ocean and not ship are intermingled with the emotional and mental abstractions of a person poised between life and death. All of the narrator's cumulative life sensations become "one fixed idea" in his soul that is perceived as *dense* (that is, something tangible and palpable to his senses) but also "made up of atoms" (that is, beyond the realm of human sensation). When Hawthorne expressed his admiration at how Melville "put the reality before the reader," this is an example of what he meant: the intermingling of carefully hewn sensations—what is really like to fall; the practical thoughts and the movement of the body through the air—with the uncanny sensations that pass through the soul as one heads toward possible death (that is, an utter strangeness and abstraction that, paradoxically, only heightens the "reality" of the experience). Matthiessen identifies the *White-Jacket* scene as "the first extended instance when the two halves of [Melville's] experience, his outer and inner life, are fused in expression."[64] but it is even more than this—it is at once outer, inner, *and* metaphysical, a fusing still evident when White-Jacket hits the water, until his brush against a living thing confirms his own vitality, and he, in a sense, snaps out of it. Again, Melville's acute description of concrete realities—here, hitting the water and sinking—are bound up with metaphysical sensations, those sensations that transcend the natural world (what Melville places in the "soul"):

> As I gushed into the sea, a thunder-boom sounded in my ear; my soul seemed flying from my mouth. The feeling of death flooded over me with the billows.... I wondered whether I was yet dead, or still dying. But of a sudden some fashionless form brushed my side—some inert, coiled fish of the sea; the thrill of being alive again tingled in my nerves, and the strong shunning of death shocked me through ... and there I hung, vibrating in the mid-deep. What wild sounds then rang in my ear! One was a soft moaning, as of low waves upon the beach; the other wild and heartlessly jubilant, as of the sea in the height of a tempest. Oh soul! Thou then heardest life and death.... The life-and-death poise soon passed; and then I found myself slowly ascending and caught a dim glimmering of light.[65]

Taken together, Hawthorne's immersion in and sensitive reception to the younger author's books and Melville's essay "Hawthorne and His

Mosses" display a remarkable and immediate mutual affinity. If either writer had a more attuned reader in their lifetime, they have yet to come to light. That the two could also share a friendship bond only heightened this intellectual, creative, and spiritual affinity. In fact, Hawthorne's recording of their last conversation in *The English Notebooks* pointed to a common tenor in their conversations throughout their relationship, the search — particularly Melville's — for a spiritual belief system.

Hawthorne's old Bowdoin classmate Henry Wadsworth Longfellow, who had become a close correspondent in later years, sent the two issues of the *Literary World* containing "the Virginian's" review from his dwelling in the small seaside community of Nahant, Massachusetts, on August 24, 1850, the same day that the issue containing the second installment went public. "I have rarely seen a more appreciating and sympathising critic," wrote Longfellow to his fellow alum. "I do endorse all he says about you."[66] (The Hawthornes had likely obtained copies of the reviews prior to receiving the Longfellow package.) The two-part essay created quite a stir when it reached the Hawthorne cottage in the Berkshires. *The Literary World* was a high-profile and respected publication centered in New York City, and Melville's anonymous piece had heaped upon Hawthorne's work a new kind of appreciation, one that separated him from the pack of laboring American authors, singling him out for genius and greatness. Sophia was beside herself with awe and appreciation upon reading "Hawthorne and His Mosses," and turned, as she so often did, to writing to her sister Elizabeth Peabody of all matters Nathaniel. "At last someone speaks the right word of him," she effused. "I have not before heard it. I have been wearied & annoyed hitherto with hearing him *compared* to Washington Irving & other American writers.... At last someone dares to say what in my secret mind I have often thought — that he is only to be mentioned with the Swan of Avon — The Great Heart and the Grand Intellect combined."[67] Writing to Duyckinck she displayed a more restrained hand, but no less conviction, deeming the writer of the "Mosses" piece the "first person who has ever in *print* apprehended Mr Hawthorne ... the word has at last been said which I have so long hoped to hear, & said so well." Turning to the disposition of the critic, she offered up one of the most astute (and likely accurate) characterizations of Melville, while not even yet knowing the true identity of the writer: "The freshness of primeval nature is in that man, & the true Promethean fire is in him." Sophia also passively and politely prodded Duyckinck to reveal the identity of the reviewer. "Who can he be, so fearless, so rich in heart, of such fine tuition?" she pointedly wondered. Is his name altogether hidden?"[68] As to Nathaniel himself, he took it all in with appreciative humility, writing in his own letter to Duyckinck, who had become the sun around which this happy drama orbited and unfolded, that the writer of the essay was "no common man; and, next to deserving his praise, it is good to have beguiled or bewitched such a man into praising me more than I deserve."[69]

Sophia's discovery of the identity of the writer would coincide with Melville's prolonged visit with the Hawthorne's at the little red cottage, which stretched from September 3 to September 7. The association of the highly attuned writer of the essay with Melville, this genteel but exoticized author known for his far-flung travels and life among the "cannibals" (brought to life through exaggeration and distortion in *Typee* and *Omoo*), left Sophia febrile. Here was not only a man full of rare experience and personality, but a formidable ally to share in her belief system, which centered around worshipping Mr. Hawthorne above most everything else. And Melville proved to be the perfect guest as well, attentive to Sophia, Nathaniel, and the children, and hardly a bother or an intrusion, even in the tiny confines of the rented house on the rim of the Stockbridge Bowl, which was a far cry from the spacious, great-halled Melvill[e] family home across the way in Pittsfield. On the second day of the visit, September 4, Melville and Hawthorne headed by carriage over to Herman's familiar haunts in Pittsfield. Once there, Tappan took the train to Albany, while the two writers spent the day and dinner time with Herman's cousin Robert Melvill, who had taken over stewardship of the large home (soon to be dubbed Broadhall) in its last days as a family property. The Melvill curse of mismanagement and debt had finally wrested it from the clan. For now, it would serve as a boarding place for vacationing lodgers until the new owners, the Morewoods, moved in and took over.

During the time of his stay at the red cottage, Melville respected the sanctity of Hawthorne's industrious mornings upstairs in his cramped writing space, where now, in the early bloom of his writing season, he was tracing out the lineaments of *House of the Seven Gables*. Melville would tromp off for a lengthy walk through the idyllic Indian summer morning or would shut himself in the sitting room to pore over the Hawthornes' copies of Ralph Waldo Emerson's works, sitting beneath an engraving of Raphael's "The Transfiguration" that Emerson himself had given to the couple. Melville had been drawn into an intimate family sphere entered into and witnessed by few. The authors also spent time engaged in long walks and probing conversations. Hawthorne was in the midst of a prolific peak; Melville was poised before a tipping point when the whale book would transmute from simple adventure to something greater and more complex — the type of mounting work that, he told Hawthorne, he desired to write above anything else. Here, in retrospect, were the seeds of American literature: walking, talking, planning — meditating upon things of this life and beyond. The only close witness to the developing kinship was Sophia, who took in Melville's person deeply, showing a sensitivity of observation that matched Herman's own. Her words remain the most resonant, direct, and full characterizations of the author, with whom she spent much time in conversation; and from her perspective one gets a sense of Melville's heightened responsiveness, sensitivity, and intensity toward that which aroused him. It is certainly a quality that resonates in his writing (including his essay on Hawthorne), but we learn from Sophia's eloquent writings that it reverberated through his person as well. Having spent time conversing with him one evening on the veranda of an elegant nearby home inhabited by her friends the Tappans—"in the golden light of evening twilight, when the lake was like glass of a rose tint," as she described it[70]— she offered up this appraisal to her sister Elizabeth: "Mr Melville is a person of great ardor & simplicity. He is all on fire with the subject that interests him. It rings through his frame like a cathedral bell."[71]

Sophia Hawthorne was an artist, a painter, and literary history is richer for the sensitive perception she showed in absorbing and describing the many shades of Herman Melville. Even before she knew that he had written the tribute to her husband in the *Literary World*, she left biographers with a compelling word portrait of the author. In a letter to her mother fraught with adjective after adjective she attempts to convey all that she perceives in him, registering it all in one long swoon: He is "warm," "earnest," "tender," "reverent," and "modest," she tells her mother, and also keenly "perceptive." He is also "tall & erect" and "manly," she writes, with a "straight & rather handsome" nose, a mouth that is "rather expressive of sensibility & emotion," and a "strange, lazy" gaze that is nonetheless powerful, seeming to take "deepest note of what is before him." She also describes how he loses himself in passionate conversation, holding forth with "gesture & force." There is neither "grace nor polish," she notes with a tint of admiration.[72] In describing Herman in such a concrete and physical manner, Sophia is also keenly aware of the sexuality infused in Melville's literary persona by his early Polynesian tales *Typee* (in particular) and *Omoo*. Writing about the South Pacific, he had pushed the envelope in a culture where only the most oblique and indirect references to sexuality were acceptable, describing for example (in *Typee*) the blissful daily evening massage sessions during which several young native women attended to him, lathering "fragrant oil" on his limbs and kneading him with their palms. "I see Fayaway in his face," Sophia had written to her sister the first time she had met Melville, immediately dialing into Melville's semiautobiographical association with the naked Marquesan woman character from his book, whose very name suggested a world (and a world of eroticism) away from staid, mid-nineteenth-century New England. Having represented his two early books as his own adventures, Melville cut a romantic figure, and that reputation was colored with more than a little eroticism. Of course, Sophia had little idea about the lineaments of the tremendous book that Melville was currently crafting across the way in Pittsfield, and clearly no one alive at the time could predict the impact *Moby-Dick* would have on subsequent generations—yet she does conjure up a multidimensional portrait of the writer that is consonant with the nature of that work. From Sophia, one gets the sense that *Moby-Dick*, in all of its wondrous and lively literary shades, is also an expression of the very personality of Herman Melville. While certain people, including Melville himself and Hawthorne's own son Julian in later life, would marvel at how distant and remote Hawthorne's own personality seemed from the expression of his tales, Melville's very being would seem to breathe forth from *Moby-Dick*'s pages. Looking back on the written evidence, the Hawthornes and Herman Melville make a compelling triangle. Little mention is ever made of Herman's wife Lizzie in the record of this trio (for reasons unknown), and they seemed drawn tightly together into an insular world by the energies of admiration: Melville's for Hawthorne, Sophia's for Melville (in particular *for* his admiration of Hawthorne), Sophia's unyielding worship of Hawthorne, and Hawthorne's tempered but unquestionable admiration of and affinity toward Melville. Furthermore, Herman displayed an attentiveness and tenderness to all of the Hawthornes, including the children, that endeared him to the fold. And while it wasn't Nathaniel Hawthorne alone that inspired Melville to pull up stakes in New York City and to and settle in the Berkshires—it had been a beloved family locale since his youth—certainly Hawthorne was on his mind when, in late September, he finalized the purchase of the

Herman Melville's Arrowhead, Pittsfield, Massachusetts (Library of Congress, c. 1945).

large drafty farmhouse and parcel of land that would come to be known as Arrowhead, after a turning of the fields unearthed several of those artifacts, and moved his budding family to Pittsfield, a mere six miles from the red cottage. Here was where he engaged in the true heavy lifting of *Moby-Dick*, which he had started in the spring, and here was where the book began to take its dynamic and exploratory form and where Melville's imagination poured forth. In truth, he wrote the book under the gaze of Hawthorne; he needed to have Hawthorne down the road to accomplish it, and he wrote of his progress in heaving letters to the older writer (a partial explanation of the dedication of the book to Hawthorne). Nathaniel would, of course, also become the first true reader of the work — not just one of the first to read it, but the first great mind to perceive greatness in it, just as Melville had been the first in print to apprehend the dark depths of Hawthorne's stories, which heretofore had often been seen as no more than antiquarian and dusky, yet interesting tales. Under Hawthorne's gaze, Melville rose full up to his greatest heights of creativity and ambition. The mere presence of the man to whom the book would be dedicated seemed to unlock something in the younger writer and to give him permission to explore uncharted forms and themes. Surely, all of this was already contained in Melville, but Hawthorne, and Hawthorne's work, became key catalysts. Nearing the end of *Moby-Dick's* creation (in June 1851), he wrote to Hawthorne, "Shall I send you a fin of the *Whale* by way of a specimen mouthful? The tail is not yet cooked — though the hell-fire in which the whole book is broiled might not have unreasonable cooked it all ere this."[73] Hawthorne was the mirror to which he held up his work while writing it, and while it is not clear whether he took up Melville's offer to sample the unfinished tome, it was clear that in a world of thousands of potential readers, Melville wrote with the singular Hawthorne very much in mind.

It was the early fall of 1851; Melville and Hawthorne had met and become fast friends. For the next year-plus, the relationship would become one of mutual affinity and empathy — one of drinking and talking "ontological heroics" late into the night, of pouring out frank letters to each other over six miles of bumpy and wooded road. For the two, it was mutual comfort and inspiration while trying to eke out a living through writing in the remote, rural environs of the Berkshire Mountains in western Massachusetts, far from the bustle and fellowship of Boston and New York City intellectual circles. For us, though, staring backward into the marks and traces left behind, the friendship becomes the seeds of a literature, an American literature that finally attempts to stretch into new regions and expand within the growing national consciousness. "But already I feel that this Hawthorne has dropped germinous seeds into my soul," penned Melville behind the mask of a southern reviewer, but he was speaking for himself as he wrote of Hawthorne: "He expands and deepens down, the more I contemplate him."[74]

THREE

Loomings; or, Early Lives of the Authors

Talk not of the bitterness of middle-age and after life; a boy can feel all that, and much more.... And never again can such blights be made good; they strike in too deep, and leave such a scar that the air of Paradise might not erase it.

–Melville, *Redburn*

In our cities families rise and burst like bubbles in a vat.

–Melville, *Pierre*

"I have loved you like a father ... and at a time like this I should have something of a father's authority. I charge you to be gone that I may die in peace."

–Hawthorne, "Roger Malvin's Burial"

Full fathom five thy father lies;
Of his bones are coral made;
Those are pearls that were his eyes:
Nothing of him that doth fade
But doth suffer a sea-change
Into something rich and strange.

— William Shakespeare, *The Tempest*

Part of the allure regarding the friendship between Hawthorne and Melville arises from the contrasts between the two: the gap in both ages and personality and, of course, the different means of literary expression — Hawthorne's tightly wound tales of melancholy, beauty, devilishness, and anguish contrasting with Melville's probing, effusive, eloquent, and disorderly tomes. But there is also enough similarity in the circumstances of their early lives to suggest a mutual empathy that sustained the friendship.

Both, of course, lost fathers at early ages; Hawthorne's father, the sea captain Nathaniel Hathorne (the "w" was added to the family with the next generation), died at the age of 32, far from his Salem home and family in Surinam, in South America, having contracted yellow fever during his merchant travels. He left little behind for his family other than a yawning absence that would pervade many of his son's protagonists with "an air of unresolved paternity," as biographer James R. Mellow would phrase it.[1] Nathaniel Hathorne's sea pursuits were never lucrative, but he did leave behind raw material for his namesake child's imagination. He had visited places such as China, Calcutta, and Sumatra, and he had ably guided his ship around Cape Horn, earning him his captain status. This was a world beyond the two narrow, adjacent streets in Salem that contained and sheltered a good portion of Hawthorne's early life—the crowded homes on Union and, later, Herbert Streets. Around Salem, however, Captain Hathorne was known for his melancholy and private nature.[2] Clearly *this* was part of the son's inheritance as well.

Melville's father, Allan Melvill (also a letter short of his direct descendants, who acquired a final "e"), would also die intestate, having spectacularly failed as an importer of French goods in New York City before fleeing his creditors and taking his family to live in his wife's native Albany, where he died at 49 years of age after suffering from fever and dementia. Herman was only 12 years old, and the death would drastically shift the course of his life as he left behind childhood schooling for the world of the workforce and adult concerns. Allan Melvill had spent his final years in pleas for loan after loan, the new debts piling upon the old; false promises constantly being made regarding new ventures that would clear the sheets. All were failed enterprises, though the Melvill household managed to convey a degree of affluence, buffering Herman and his siblings from his father's fall. As the third oldest, Herman did come to awareness by degrees, however; in fact, the first significant boat voyage of his life was not an ocean journey—it was a steamboat flight up the Hudson River from New York City to Albany, with Herman and his father bearing the family's larger possessions (such as furniture) and Allan looking backward over his shoulder as he narrowly avoided debtor's prison. The rest of the family had gone ahead to Albany to set up house, with Herman's oldest brother, Gansevoort, playing the role of surrogate parent. Herman, eleven years old and the second oldest boy, was left to accompany his father on this ignominious river voyage.

As to Herman's place in the clan, Gansevoort was the family's star; the oldest brother took to well to schooling, was socially at ease, and was destined for political life. By contrast, the Melville parents sought "realistic" expectations for Herman. Allan had him sized him up as a young boy as "very backward in speech & somewhat slow in comprehension." Nevertheless, his father did relay to Herman's uncle, Peter Gansevoort, that the boy's understanding of "men & things" was "both solid & profound" and that he possessed a "docile & aimiable [*sic*] disposition."[3] From his parent's perspective, Herman wasn't book smart like Gansevoort, so there was only a need for the barest of education. A "practical activity" such as "Commerce" is where his future and limited talents lay, an industry that could mostly "dispense with ... book knowledge."[4] And while the prediction seems patently ridiculous in retrospect — his son would, after all, produce one of the quintessential books in all of literature — Herman would never have a chance to prove his father wrong in the latter's lifetime, something that undoubtedly clung to him throughout life.

Allan Melvill's final descent cast aside any buffer between the children and their circumstances. "I am destitute of resources and without a shilling," he wrote pathetically to his own father, Thomas, in December 1830, seeking monetary assistance. He added that he "may soon be prosecuted for my last quarters rent ... I know not what will become of me."[5] Allan, who had been born to a proud lineage — with a Revolutionary War hero father who reared him with fine education and travels abroad to France — had seen business opportunity after business opportunity appear and then dissipate. He felt the hounds on his tail: He was nearly fifty years old, with eight children and a wife that he couldn't care for on his own, and at the time he was scraping by as a clerk in a fur and hat business in Albany. On November 29, 1829, he took a business trip to New York City, hoping to summon up another round of appeasement for his creditors — and it was the return voyage that finally did him in. He had taken the steamer *Constellation* up the Hudson River from New York City, but when the vessel met an insurmountable ice obstruction in Poughkeepsie, New York, on December 8, the passengers had to dismount and continue by land. Allan had little choice but to proceed in an open one-horse wagon, with little buffer from the frigid temperatures. Having spent the night in Rhinebeck, he then hopped aboard an open two-horse wagon that took him to the town of Hudson and, finally, he was conveyed in a covered sleigh that pulled up on the east side of the

river, in Greenbush, New York, straight across the broad expanse of the
Hudson from Albany. It was 4:45 P.M., during a time of year when this
meant pending darkness, and the temperature, as he recorded in his
diary, was "2 below 0."[6] The last stage of his journey was on foot, crossing
the thick ice of the river with only the dusky, weak light from distant
Albany windows to mark his destination. The trip sapped him, and afterward he fell into a fever, through which he tried to work, lest he fall
even further into the financial abyss.

He stayed on his feet through December, but by early January the
shark's tooth was clearly upon him. Bedridden, he tremulously marked
two passages from Psalm LV in his Bible: "My heart is sore pained within
me: and the terrors of death are fallen upon me" / "Fearfulness and trem-
bling are come upon me and horror hath overwhelmed me."[7] It was Allan
Melvill's last statement to the world, as he soon fell into dementia. His
brother Thomas—summoned from Pittsfield, Massachusetts—arrived
to find Allan "under great mental excitement—at times fierce, even
maniacal."[8] Herman's father hung on for over two weeks more and then
died on January 28. The death was quite different from that of Hawthorne's father in distant Suriname, an unwitnessed expiration of life in
a faraway, exotic place, all relegated to a son's imagination. Herman was
a boy on the verge of adolescence, living in a house suffused with the
month-long, ghastly demise of its guiding figure. "Talk not of the bitterness of middle-age and after life; a boy can feel all that, and much
more," he would write in *Redburn* (1849), which used as raw material
his first ocean voyage, to England. "And never again can such blights be
made good; they strike in too deep, and leave such a scar that the air of
Paradise might not erase it."[9] The experience was also refracted into the
pages of *Pierre* (1852), which Melville wrote in his early 30s, immediately
after *Moby-Dick*. In the novel, one finds that the titular character's father
"has died of a fever; and, as is not uncommon in such maladies, toward
his end, he at intervals lowly wandered in his mind."[10]

Despite these tragic losses and sinking fortunes that befell their
families in their early lifetimes, both Hawthorne and Melville came from
lineages whose importance and influence in the early republic was
unmistakable. Nathaniel's great-great grandfather, William Hathorne,
was one of the earliest English settlers of the Massachusetts Bay Colony.
Born of a stout Puritan orthodoxy, he acquitted himself well in the New
World, rising through the ranks as a major in the Salem militia after
leaving Dorchester for that locale in 1636, and eventually assuming a

prominent role as a deputy in the House of Delegates and a magistrate. His descendant, the author Nathaniel, would remember him for his staunchness: as an officer of the court he brutally punished heretics and illegal fornicators (he rained down his Puritan cruelty on Quakers in particular), and he once even rose up and defied an order from King Charles II to return to England to explain the disorderliness of the bur- geoning colony. William's son John would become the ancestor that cap- tured Nathaniel's imagination the most, however: As a judge during the Salem witchcraft trials in 1692, he helped bring about the hanging of nineteen young women and the torture (and eventual death) of another. Hawthorne the writer would get much mileage out of a particular piece of family folklore, which held that one of the condemned hissed out a curse from the gallows, damning John Hathorne and all of his descen- dants. (A similar curse is central to *The House of the Seven Gables*.) When Arthur Miller composed the play *The Crucible* in the early 1950s, John Hathorne became the ultimate villain of the piece: a sadistic, ice-cold automaton bent on sending the innocent to the gallows. (Miller's ren- dering, however, did coalesce several historical figures into the one char- acter of Judge Hathorne.) It is fitting that Nathaniel Hawthorne would come to represent a quintessential American writer, for his heritage sprang from the country's nascent colonial roots. And Salem's rich, turgid tales of devilry, witchcraft, and anguish coursed through his household and veins. It was no wonder that the first collection of his work was a two-volume set called *Twice-Told Tales* (1837 and 1842), for he had inherited his material and themes as much as his genealogy. The unmistakable craftsmanship, however, he could call his own.

Of course there was also Salem itself coloring Hawthorne's early consciousness through its unusual prosperity and infusions from distant worlds. With its bustling commerce via the Far East, Salem *was* America's sense of multiculturalism for a time, As Salem historian Robert Booth describes it, "In its streets were the goods and aromas of far-off places; at the heart of its downtown was the museum of another world. Salem was not like the rest of America."[11] Here is the Salem less told in the annals of history for lack of luridness — the "golden empire" beyond the tantalizing twin mythologies of witchcraft and persecution.[12] Nathaniel Hawthorne was born in the comet tail of Salem's prosperity, when duties collected at its port were still an economic engine of the country — and in a time before the intense turn to industrialization, manufacturing, and westward expansion. Hawthorne came to life in a city that had the most wealth per capita in America, despite only having around 10,000 citizens and being far from the highest population center.[13] Salem also boasted the young country's first millionaire, merchant E. Hasket Derby, who died in 1799. Faraway items filled the city's port with aromas and sights: pepper, porcelain wares, and tea — even opium and Asian birds' nests (for that rare delicacy, bird's nest soup). Salem's commerce in the China Trade also influenced the look of homes; the Federalist houses of the wealthy merchants often boasted touches from afar — balustrades and lattices bore Eastern designs and within well-acquitted homes one could find Chinese fans and goods made from ivory and silk.

Like Hawthorne's Salem ancestors, Herman Melville's predecessors also figured prominently in the early history of the country and saw it through its bloody transition from English rule to sovereignty. "One basic fact linked the lives of Melville's grandfathers," wrote biographer Andrew Delbanco. "[B]oth had been born English and had become, by violence, American."[14] His paternal grandfather, Major Thomas Melvill (who was of Scottish heritage), had participated in the Boston Tea Party — and such was his adherence to the past that in later years he proudly showed visitors a vial of tea leaves from that event. He also adorned himself, even as an old man, in Revolutionary-era garb, strolling the streets of Boston in breeches and a three-cornered hat. The spectacle of his fading glory, idiosyncracies, and anachronisms were prominent enough for Oliver Wendell Holmes to pen a poem entitled "The Last Leaf" about the old man in 1831, nearly two decades before the physician, writer, and professor encountered Herman Melville and Nathaniel Hawthorne on Monument Mountain and hotly debated with Melville across a dinner table. Thomas Melvill, who married Priscilla Scollay, from another prominent Boston family with Scottish roots, profitably lived out his post–Revolutionary years as an inspector of customs and then naval officer in his native city. He provided his sons, Thomas Jr. and Allan, with fine schooling and then sent them to France for further refinement as young men. Both, unfortunately, would come to be known in adulthood primarily for their debts and failed enterprises, turning again and again to their father for temporary relief.

Herman Melville knew his paternal grandfather, but his maternal grandfather, Peter Gansevoort — an even greater hero than Thomas — died seven years before Herman's birth. Peter, a giant of a man for the time at six-foot-three, would go down in Revolutionary War lore as "The Hero of Fort Stanwix." The colonel openly defied a surrender ultimatum and held off a British siege of that fortress (in present-day Rome, New York), cementing his legend. (Herman Melville would name his second son Stanwix in tribute to this ancestral legend.) Peter Gansevoort had descended from the line of aristocratic Dutch that would establish Albany and its surrounding environs, and he lived out his days in a variety of prominent and lucrative roles. He milled lumber in Saratoga County in the town that would come to be stamped with his family name, Gansevoort; he was the sheriff of Albany; he was a commissioner charged with holding treaties with the Indians at the northern and western frontiers; and he was appointed a brigadier general in the army. His son, also Peter, inherited the management of all of his assets, and one of his foremost duties would eventually become taking care of his sister Maria and her large brood of children after Allan Melvill's death. These then were the bloodstreams of Herman Melville, Bostonian Scots–American and Dutch Patroon aristocracy — lines that had figured in the turbulent and bloody creation of America — and his enses were filled with the bustle of early nineteenth-century downtown New York City, where the harbor more than hinted at the ocean and the world beyond, and, later, landlocked Albany, which hugged the broad spine of the Hudson, a distant promise and reminder — with its teeming ports— of the oceans to which it led.

Both Hawthorne and Melville also found sweet relief and escape in more rural and forested environs while still in their youth. For Hawthorne, sanctuary came in the still raw and forested environs of Raymond, Maine (a part of Massachusetts at the time). His mother Betsy's family, the Mannings, didn't have a lineage of seafarers or esteemed judicial presences like the Hathornes— they were more grounded and practical folk — but Nathaniel's grandfather, Richard Manning, unlike the Hathornes, left his family comfortable after his death through a stagecoach business and the acquisition of land. Much of that property surrounded the frontier-like environs around Lake Sebago in Maine, where as a boy Nathaniel, who had been known to play the invalid and depend on crutches for long stretches in Salem, roamed the forests, fished the lakes, and hunted game. In Maine, he grew flushed, strong, and hearty. This was far from Salem, a city of judgment and categorization, and it was far from the Herbert Street house packed with the chatter and bustle of family members and only a short stroll from the hive-like business of the wharf. Nathaniel had been a cherubic, fatherless boy, with dark curls and peaches-and-cream skin, who had been doted upon by uncles and aunts—it had made him fragile. But an extended stay in the wilds of Maine had changed him. "[H]e became a good shot, and an excellent fisherman, and grew tall and strong," his older sister Ebe (Elizabeth) recalled in later years. "His imagination was stimulated, too, by the scenery and by the strangeness of the people; and by the absolute freedom he enjoyed."[15] Sent back to Salem for a proper course of education, he moped around the Herbert Street house. "He sighs for the woods of Raymond," noted his aunt Mary, living in close quarters with him.[16] "How often do I long for my gun and wish again that I could savigize [*sic*] with you," he wrote to his younger sister Louisa (Maria Louisa), who remained back in edenic Maine with his mother and older sister Ebe. Salem, the very city that would supply and nourish his literary energies, would also crop up again and again in Nathaniel's life as a place of suffocation and frustration.

For the young Melville, natural, forested freedom came in the Berkshires of western Massachusetts, the very environment that would provide the backdrop for both his friendship with Nathaniel Hawthorne and the creation of his greatest work, *Moby-Dick; or, The Whale*. Like Hawthorne, Melville knew spiritual suffocation at a young age as well, and in the wake of his father's death, Albany became such a geographical place for him, as he was thrown into the work force as an adolescent. But there was always the Melvill family farm in Pittsfield, which was just over the New York border in Massachusetts. The young Melvill savored the visits—the bracing air and mountain views, the agrarian rhythms and cycles. In the summer of 1837, on the cusp of eighteen, he was charged with the substantial responsibility of overseeing the farm as his uncle Thomas sought fortunes (that is, more debts and disgrace) in the frontier regions of Illinois. The privations, suffocation, and social strictures of Albany fell away as Herman worked in the open air. Rising like a sentinel in the distance was Mount Greylock, a constant companion that would later loom in his study window as he traced out the whale epic. His older brother, Gansevoort, and younger brother, Allan, were pointed in the direction of law careers while Herman, stamped by his parents early on as possessing humbler and less intellectual acumen, was sent to the fields. That was fine with him, and in the words of Hershel Parker, "Unconfined at last, he expanded physically and emotionally to match the landscape."[17] Besides the oceans themselves, the Berkshires became the most meaningful geographical relationship of his lifetime. When Evert Duyckinck visited the area during the memorable late summer of 1850 in which Melville met Hawthorne, he commented on Melville's remarkable affinity with the landscape surrounding the farm, noting that he knew "every stone & tree."[18] That very sense of wonderment that made Melville such an acutely sensitive writer began to emerge in the Berkshires as he surveyed the mountains, lakes, and striking verdancy of the region. As previously noted by Parker, the expansive environs stimulated a similar expansiveness in Herman, one that would eventually find an outlet when he discovered himself as a writer.

* * *

Beyond these affinities, however, Melville and Hawthorne's early paths through life and their individual developments as writers were strikingly different. Hawthorne, born 15 years before Melville, was certainly the more sheltered of the two in the wake of his father's death. Melville, just a boy, would find himself tossed into the work force and pulled from school after his father's death; Hawthorne was, frankly, a bit coddled, enjoying the close oversight of his mother's family, the Mannings. (The Hathorne side left him rich imaginative fuel for his literary imagination, but not much else; he was closely connected to his Manning side, but not to his paternal heritage.) In the wake of his grandfather Richard Manning's death, he fell under the watchful paternal gaze of not just his mother, Betsey (Elizabeth), but of his uncles, Richard and Robert Manning. There was a certain Shakespearean parity to these two father figures of Nathaniel; Richard, having injured his spine or leg in a carriage mishap around 1810 (when Nathaniel was 5 or 6 years old), was the more soulful and unconventional uncle — a likely result of his injury and longtime physical and spiritual suffering. Robert was more practical and intractable, yet visionary in his own way, becoming a master orchard keeper and horticulturalist over the course of his lifetime. Eventually evolving into one of America's top pomologists, he would publish a book cataloguing fruit varieties and have a significant hand in the creation of the Massachusetts Horticultural Society.

Richard would set off for the family's raw Maine property when Nathaniel was around 8 or 9, carving his own fiefdom out of a veritable frontier and leaving his pining nephew with a sense of abandonment back in Salem. In seeming reaction, Nathaniel — having injured his leg playing with a bat and ball at school — echoed the role of Richard, playing the part of the "cripple" for over a year, being schooled at home and undergoing what was clearly an overkill of medical treatment. It was, however, the beginning of Hawthorne's self-education, which for him meant a sharp turn inward and voracious reading habits. Introspection and absorption dominated his early life, as did his older sister Ebe, his closest confidante and perhaps sternest judge. Under his sister's watchful eye, he lounged around, using the benefit of his presumed infirmity to absorb writers such as John Milton, Alexander Pope, and Lord Byron. Ebe, his most perceptive observer early on, would later recall him as overly pampered, but she also heralded his self-development. "If he had been educated for a genius," she observed, "it would have injured him excessively. He developed himself."[19] But lying around on the carpet in Salem with his nose in a book was only part of his development. In 1816, he was bounced between the father figures, his uncles, being sent from Robert to Richard, from the districted and urbane streets of Salem to the wilds of Maine. The prospect of reuniting with Richard in Maine and getting away from Salem had been dangled in front of Nathaniel, and the delay of that offer had sent him back to the crutches and alleged affliction. Finally, nearing twelve years of age, he, his mother, and sisters packed off for what would become a land of enchantment for the Hawthornes. "Stay here one summer," swooned Ebe, and "you will not be reconciled to live in any other place."[20] It did her delicate brother good to be in such an outdoor paradise of forest and lake. "It was a new place, with few inhabitants, *far away* 'from churches and schools,'" she would surmise in later years. His "imagination was stimulated too," by scenery, landscapes, people, and unfettered freedom utterly unlike that of Salem.[21]

Hawthorne also bore the benefit, later, of a formalized education, rubbing elbows at Bowdoin College in Brunswick, Maine, with young men who would go on to make their mark on the country. And here is where Hawthorne's and Melville's development as writers and individuals take sharply divergent paths. As one of 38 students entering in the fall of 1822, Hawthorne would live out a collegiate existence typical of privileged young men in America, drilling in Latin and the classics, falling into trouble for drunken revelries, and becoming acquainted with classmates such as future U.S. president Franklin Pierce ("the worst, or ... the weakest, of all our Presidents," as Ralph Waldo Emerson concluded)[22]; Henry Wadsworth Longfellow; congressman Jonathan Cilley, who famously died in a duel while in office; and Horatio Bridge, a vaunted Navy commodore who would head up the branch's supply organization under several administrations. With Pierce and Bridge,

Hawthorne formed intense, lifelong friendships, while Longfellow, with whom he corresponded in the years well after Bowdoin, would become a close friend long after graduation, as well as the first notable champion of Hawthorne's stories. After university, Nathaniel, unsure about any direction in life and unwilling to assert himself upon the world, retired back to his third floor room in the family house on Herbert Street and very deliberately became a writer, plundering his genealogy and the history of his native region for raw material. He took influence from American predecessors Washington Irving and John Neal. Literary history may have reduced the latter author to obscurity, but Hawthorne had seen much in Neal while reading him in college, and he furthermore had been sparked by Neal's cry for an American literature that distinguished itself from and flew in the face of English writing. "It is American books that are wanted of America; not English books," spat Neal, anticipating Melville's much later cry in "Hawthorne and His Mosses," "[N]or books made in America, by Englishmen, or by writers, who are a sort of Bastard English."[23] James Fenimore Cooper, heeding a similar call, had already published the first of his Leatherstocking books, *The Pioneers* (1823), and was about to publish what would become his most famous novel, *The Last of the Mohicans* (1826), using distinctly American frontier experiences as raw material. Hawthorne's classmate, Longfellow, was also laying the groundwork for his own entry into American letters. A clearly better student than Hawthorne, Longfellow had given the commencement address for their graduating class, and then, before taking a teaching position at their alma mater, had traveled Europe, where in Madrid he had become acquainted with and fallen under the tutelage and influence of Washington Irving.

Hawthorne's was a less glorious path than his classmate's, and though he developed in a third-floor room long yards from the Salem Harbor rather than in the far reaches of the Pacific — and though he had the benefit of a formal and privileged education — he was, like Melville, essentially an untutored and rabid autodidact. "All really educated men," he would come to believe, "whether they have studied in the halls of a University, or in a cottage or a work-shop, are essentially self-educated."[24] Thus, having not necessarily made the most of his time at Bowdoin, he became a studious devourer of documents and books in his post-graduate life. He studied the histories of the Puritans and Quakers. He plumbed the depths of his Hathorne ancestors. (He was soon to adopt the "w.") And at the Salem courthouse he pawed through artifacts once owned by alleged witches. Driven by what his sister Ebe coined "the Puritan instinct that was in him,"[25] he absorbed the history of New England. But in his typical manner, he developed very much in private. (By contrast, Melville regaled family and friends with tales of his adventures— developing his narrative meter in very much public and oral fashion — before first putting pen to paper with *Typee*.) Thus, he would send Ebe to the local library, the Salem Athenaeum, for him, and thus *Fanshawe: A Tale*, his first and self-published attempt at a novel, was anonymous. Though reticent and reclusive, he was far from agoraphobic, however; he liked events and crowds into which he could blend as a quiet observer. And at the sound of the Salem fire alarm, he would be drawn toward whatever conflagration it announced. Fire strangely attracted him, claimed his sister. In fact, Nathaniel condemned to fire the remaining copies of the unpopular *Fanshawe*, the ceremony fusing two of his attractions, flames and anonymity. He would condemn all of his earliest work to the same fate, and his own wife, Sophia, would only learn of *Fanshawe* after Nathaniel's death. As to Hawthorne's reclusiveness, isolation was fine, as long as there was family chattering and moving around beneath the floorboards and as long as there was bustling and vibrant Salem paces from his door. Decades later, Lenox would provide a more genuine form of seclusion — one he would come to find unsettling.

Hawthorne received a slim inheritance upon the death of his grandmother, enough to sustain his lack of a marketable vocation, and by the late 1820s he was deeply mired in drafting the short tales for which he would become famous. The first significant publication of his stories was in *The Token*, an annual gift book timed in advance of Christmas and published by Samuel Griswold Goodrich, who also wrote under the alias Peter Parley. Thus, such masterpieces of the short form as "Roger Malvin's Burial" and "My Kinsman, Major Molineux" were given public life, though still without an author's name attached to them. The tales were undeniably American in subject matter, but they were strikingly unique and otherworldly as well, possessing the layers that Melville would come to recognize and draw inspiration from for *Moby-Dick*. ("Deep as Dante," he exclaimed.) This was, as Brenda Wineapple has come to describe it, "historical fiction within a psychological theater" intimating both "real time and internal time."[26] Despite a newfound readership, Hawthorne remained not only anonymous, but poorly compensated; between 1831 and 1832, Goodrich bought ten stories of his for a sum that was only somewhere between 50 and 70 dollars.

Further material for his literary pursuits came during those rare instances when "Hawthorne, the Herbert-Street recluse" became "Hawthorne, the traveler." He had become accustomed to summer jaunts with another of his uncles, Samuel, who traveled all over New England for reasons of business and health (a tubercular condition), and throughout his entire existence as a writer summer was a downtime for Nathaniel. His creative engine, noted biographer James R. Mellow, "needed a touch of frost before they revived."[27] Hawthorne relished filling his storehouse with images and anecdotes of local rural characters, many of them encountered in the pubs that the two frequented during these jaunts. (Hawthorne, throughout college and late into life, was known to like the drink.) In the summer of 1832, he planned to take his most extensive trip yet, through New Hampshire's White Mountains over to Burlington, Vermont, and Lake Champlain, and then all of the way across New York to Niagara Falls. Compared to the globe-spanning of Melville, it was travel of a smaller scope, but it was suitable to Nathaniel's needs and enough to stoke his creative furnace for a planned collection of tales, *The Story Teller*. (Sections of the planned piece saw print, but the collection was never published as a complete book.) Hawthorne traveled in what would become his typical manner — that is, perennially disappointed by what he saw (Niagara Falls wasn't spectacular enough; Lake Champlain didn't smell like his native coast) — and turning his nose up at much of the imperfect and lowly humanity along the way. But despite finding "a wretched sense of disappointment"[28] in the presence of wonders such as Niagara's thundering cataract, his acute, unique, and ever-probing writer's senses did find sublimity in the unexpected — for example: the sounds, through a drawn curtain in the crowded sleeping quarters of an Erie Canal boat, of a woman undressing, which he traced with salacious detail. "[T]he twang, like a broken harp-string, caused by loosening a tight belt; the rustling of a gown in its descent ... the unlacing of a pair of stays. My ear seemed to have the properties of an eye," he wrote.[29] Or the nighttime images of a drained forest swamp, glimpsed by Hawthorne as the canal boat glided along the desolate, flat expanse between Utica and Syracuse: "perhaps a hundred trunks, erect, half overthrown, extended along the ground, resting on their shattered limbs or tossing them desperately into darkness." Filtered through his sensibilities they became "ghostlike — the very land of unsubstantial things, whither dreams might betake themselves, when they quit the slumberer's brain."[30] This was the quality of his vision that enchanted

Melville and made Hawthorne's works endure long after the nineteenth century: the fusing of the natural and dream worlds, the very contemplative space that Melville, in the fresh thrall of Hawthorne, would explore in *Moby-Dick*. "He expands and deepens down, the more I contemplate him," Melville had admiringly written of these deeper compulsions of the psyche that Hawthorne was exploring.

As 1836 commenced, Hawthorne was 31 years old, still a resolute bachelor, and still a completely anonymous writer of stories that were appearing in annuals and magazines throughout New England. And here lies a fundamental difference between his and Melville's early development as writers: While Melville would have his name and his own experiences deeply tied to his first published works—walking a tenuous non-fiction/fiction tightrope—Hawthorne still chose to distance himself and his name from his stories or any public existence as "writer," despite modest and growing success. Family, close friends, and publishers (the latter by necessity) knew the author of these tales, but that was it.

The paltry wages of short-story publication were not enough to subsist on, however, and in January 1836 Hawthorne—upon the recommendation of his *Token* publisher Goodrich, with whom he would come to share an ambivalent relationship, at best—was offered a job in Boston as the editor of the *American Magazine of Useful and Entertaining Knowledge*. It was Nathaniel's first proper employment, but it was not to last long. The magazine was a compendium of biographies of significant people, pseudo-intellectual essays, travel pieces, and other varied human-interest writings. Hawthorne did the yeoman's work, producing most of the pieces himself—that is, unless he could convince his ever stalwart sister Ebe to send him material, which she frequently did. Feeding the voracious press soon burned out Hawthorne, as did delays in payment from his employer, the Bewick Company, and housing with strangers, as congenial as his host family may have been. Most importantly, the job ate up all of his time for his own writing. By September, he had resigned and was back in Salem, looking to publish his stories in a book volume, something at which he had failed thus far. He again looked to Goodrich for help, while old college friend, Horatio Bridge—an investor practicing law in Maine at the time and soon to embark on a vaunted Navy career—championed the effort and made financial insurances against any possible loss. It was important, however, wrote Bridge to Goodrich, that Nathaniel not know of his generosity. Bridge's friendship became one of several close relationships that evolved into deep sources of support, patronage, and care-taking. Hawthorne was socially and professionally helpless in many ways, but he always seemed to find someone to bolster him —from his dominant older sister Ebe; to Bridge; to Franklin Pierce, who would appoint him to the consulate in Liverpool, England, upon becoming a U.S. president; to Longfellow; to his wife's sister Elizabeth Peabody; to his overtly and demonstratively worshipful wife herself. Even Melville, who on the surface seemed to have little to offer Hawthorne, became a stanchion in the unfamiliar, lonely, long-wintered Berkshires, and it is doubtful that the mercurial and often fragile Hawthorne would have lasted there as long as he did without the comforting glow of Melville's devotion. This was a relationship dynamic for Hawthorne that would last until his final moments, when he died in his sleep in Plymouth, New Hampshire, in 1864, having been taken on what was supposed to be a restorative journey through the mountains by Franklin Pierce, who— despite having the worldly concerns of a former president — had fully devoted himself to the cause of his friend's health.

Twice-Told Tales, a collection of eighteen reprinted stories, published in March of 1837, marked the writer's transition from anonymity to public recognition of his identity. But in doing so, Hawthorne seemed hesitant to reveal the more compellingly dark, troubling, and risqué elements of his craft; therefore, such harrowing pieces as "Young Goodman Brown," "Roger Malvin's Burial," and "My Kinsman, Major Molineux" were abandoned in favor of lighter fare. He also omitted any story passages that might offend the sensibilities of the public to which he was newly unveiling himself.[31] Abandoned were those probing tendencies that would come to ignite Melville. In what was for him a very forward move, Hawthorne took it upon himself to send a copy of the collection to his old Bowdoin classmate Henry Wadsworth Longfellow, who— after a period of teaching at their alma mater — had recently assumed a post as a professor of modern languages at Harvard. Longfellow was not yet the esteemed national poet who would cement his place in history, though he was known and respected as an academic and a writer, his most recent work having been a European travelogue entitled *Outre-Mer; A Pilgrimage Beyond the Sea* (1835), which consisted of sketches based on the writer's significant European travels. "We were not ... so well acquainted at college that I can plead an absolute right to inflict my 'twice-told' tediousness upon you," Hawthorne wrote on March 7, eight and a half years after the two had graduated together. "I know not whether you are aware that I have made a good many idle attempts in the way of [writing].... The present volume contains such articles as seemed best worth offering to the public a second time; and I should flatter myself that they would repay you in some part of the pleasure which I have derived from your own Outre-Mer."[32] Longfellow took it for what it was, an unspoken request for a review, and he responded in generously grandiose fashion in a July 1837 piece in the *North American Review*. "To this little work we would say, 'Live ever, sweet, sweet book.' It comes from the hand of a man of genius."[33] What Hawthorne did not know was that Longfellow was still deep in the aftershock of tragedy, having lost his wife to a miscarriage during a second European trip that he had taken for purposes of language study in order to achieve his post at Harvard. He was consumed by grief and guilt, and his gesture toward his fellow author was magnanimous. This was not lost on Hawthorne, and Longfellow's oblique reference to his own misfortune (he was not specific) led Hawthorne to be uncharacteristically revelatory; it also prompted him to showcase two warring instincts, his isolative self-obsession and his need to break through that wall toward meaningful human contact. "I can assure you that trouble is the next best thing to enjoyment, and that there is no fate in this world so horrible as to have no share in either its joys or sorrows," he soliloquized. "For the last ten years, I have not lived, but only dreamed of living."[34] He described himself to Longfellow as a shut-in who never left the house until after the sun had gone down. "By some witch-craft or other.... I have been carried apart from the main current of life, and find it impossible to get back again."[35] (Like many of his characters, Hawthorne portrayed himself as one who was at the mercy of larger forces.) The openness and warmth of their early correspondence grew into an enduring closeness over the years.

Longfellow was not the only one to praise Hawthorne's debut collection; the *Salem Gazette* celebrated the "beautiful simplicity and elegance" of Hawthorne's prose and declared him "among the very first of American writers." The *Knickerbocker* magazine proclaimed Hawthorne a writer with "few equals" and with only "eminent exceptions, no superior in our country."[36] Longfellow had also sounded the national battle cry through his review of Hawthorne, praising its New England themes and roots and eschewing of overseas influence. This was a mindset that Longfellow would take forth into his own poetry in future years, as he rose to preeminence as an American writer of the purest sort. (Of course, as discussed in the previous chapter, this issue of an American literature freed from outside influence would also bedevil Melville, who used his own review of Hawthorne in 1850 as a clarion call for literary nationalism — even as he discussed Hawthorne's stories in the context of Shakespeare.) All of this praise for Hawthorne's work did not translate to a financial windfall, however, though his book sales (600 to 700 copies) in the early months were certainly respectable. Of course, the financial panic of 1837 was also drawing to a head. In addition, Horatio Bridge, who never did end up having to cover any losses for Hawthorne, pointed out to his friend that the stories' availability elsewhere (in periodicals) may have dampened the overall reception a bit.

Nevertheless, Hawthorne had made a name for himself. Forged in isolation and anonymity, he had finally entered the world as a public figure. All of the life that he had bemoaned missing when he wrote to Longfellow was now at his fingertips, and he had begun to open himself up to it.

* * *

Melville was only six years old when Hawthorne graduated Bowdoin in September 1825, and by the time he too had reached the age at which his own adulthood beckoned, his father's death, family debts, the financial "panic" of 1837, and an inability to find consistent employment had all compounded to leave him but one viable option: the sea. In June 1839, Melville, not quite 20 years old, made his first ocean voyage as a simple sailor on a merchant ship, the *St. Lawrence*, which was carrying cargo and passengers to Liverpool, England. His most notable voyage followed that one, when he signed with a whaler, the *Acushnet*, in New Bedford, Massachusetts, and set sail for the South Pacific in January 1841. The early part of his life had been defined by constraint and limitations, a series of false starts and unrequited possibilities; now, truly, he had broken free. All societal expectations and familial order fell away as he shipped off for regions he had only imagined, a non-entity at the bottom of the ship's insular community. He was, for all intents and purposes, a blank slate waiting to be filled in with identity and experience. Calling upon this formative period in *Moby-Dick*, Ishmael and Melville speak to the reader in interwoven fashion:

> And, as for me, if, by any possibility, there be any as yet undiscovered prime thing in me; if I shall ever deserve any real repute in that small but high hushed world which I might not be unreasonably ambitious of; if hereafter I shall do anything upon the whole, a man might rather have

done than to have left undone; if, at my death, my executors, or more properly my creditors, find any precious MSS. in my desk, then here I prospectively ascribe all the honor and the glory to whaling; for a whaleship was my Yale College and my Harvard.[37]

Melville could only be all too acutely aware of lost opportunities when he sized himself up against Hawthorne. With Melville's heritage it would have seemed a birthright to have walked academic pathways with the sons of the ruling class, with future presidents, congressmen, and men of letters, as Hawthorne did. But the circumstances of life had sent him to the forecastle, among the crowded ranks of a ship's lower caste. And he had found literary capital there. Having the power of retrospection, as he wrote in his third decade, he could see that this was the one endeavor that had finally *culminated* in something. He had drained that storehouse of experience into his first five books, rolled out in quick succession from 1846 to 1850. And in the midst of tapping into his whaling experience while writing his sixth, many things catalyzed — foremost among them his deep acquaintanceship with Hawthorne and Hawthorne's works — to send him into his deepest and profoundest depths yet.

Because Melville's experiences at sea, like the Hawthorne friendship, are clearly central to understanding both Melville and *Moby-Dick*, they warrant close scrutiny. And it was a series of misfortunes and constantly unraveling circumstances that finally led him there, when it seemed like there was no where else to turn for gainful employment.

Not long after his father's death, in early 1832, both Herman and older brother Gansevoort were no longer students of the Albany Academy, tuition having become an indulgence that the family fortunes couldn't weather. Herman, at 12 years old, became a clerk at the New York State Bank on State Street in Albany (just up the steep slope from the Hudson River), where he filed, copied, and ran various errands. (His uncle Peter Gansevoort was on the board of directors.) The ever industrious, ambitious, and mature Gansevoort Melville, now 16, opened his own fur and cap store, but a fire destroyed the factory in which he kept his inventory in May 1834, inciting him to pull Herman into his employ. Herman, as ever, had no agency over his circumstances or comings and goings; he landed where the tides of misfortune placed him.

Then, of course, came the Panic of 1837, the financial crisis in the United States that would lead to five years of economic depression, unprecedented unemployment, and bank after bank folding. The

Melvilles, already in dire straits, found things unspooling at a frantic rate. Thomas Melville, Jr. was once again falling into tax arrears on the Pittsfield farm, Gansevoort departed for New York City to apprentice at law, younger brother Allan was pulled from school to work with uncle Peter in *his* law office, and Maria made plans to move her family from the three-story brick house at Clinton Square in Albany to an area with cheaper rents.

Herman was sent to work the Melvill family farm during the summer, and as fall came he secured his first teaching gig, at Sikes District School, which lay southwest of Pittsfield. Herman's own education was limited, and his academic acumen questionable, but it would suffice in this rural educational outpost, where, as he wrote to his uncle Peter, his thirty or so students were lacking in even the basics. "My scholars," he wrote ironically, "some of them who have attained the ages of eighteen can not do a sum in addition."[38] He moved from the family farm and boarded with an opinionated, crotchety, and shrewd New Englander in whom he perceived "the perfect embodiment of ... Yankee character."[39] Of the man's twelve children, five were in Herman's thirty-student flock of pupils. The "remote & secluded" habitat was "on the summit of as savage and lonely a mountain as ever I ascended," wrote Herman to his uncle.[40] And the family "burrow[ed] together in the woods—like so many foxes."[41] His writing shows that the Berkshires stay and his authoritative post as a teacher, however marginal, had given him a shot of intellectual confidence and greater self-possession. Away from the scrutiny of family and the comparison to his law-studying brothers, he began to unfold in his own wonderfully idiosyncratic way. Uncle Peter had sent him a book, John Orville Taylor's *The District School*, a scholarly study that reflected Herman's own teaching experience. (Taylor was a major proponent of public support for "common schools.") The volume served as both a gift and as Peter's acknowledgment of Herman's intellectual gains. A little bit of encouragement went a long way with Herman, whose letter soared a bit with a brand of heightened diction and observation that anticipated the flights of *Moby-Dick* (albeit with typically compromised spelling). Of Taylor's observations regarding "Common-Schools," Herman, his own experience reflecting that of the book, could confidently and sternly cry out in prose like clotted cream and in a more pessimistic mode than the author:

> Orators may declaim concerning the universally-diffused blessings of education in our Country, and Essayests may exhaust their magazine of

adje[ctives] in extolling our system of common school instruction, — but
when reduced to practise, the high and sanguine hopes excited by its
imposing appearance in *theory* — are a little dashed.[42]

For the first time, Herman could confidently put in writing that he had
seen and more importantly, *experienced* what most readers had not —
and it would be from this perspective that he would later pen his greatest
works.

Melville's first foray into teaching was short, and by the summer of
1838, he was in Lansingburgh, New York, several miles up the Hudson
River from Albany, where his mother had relocated the family in a large
house on the eastern shore of the river in search of cheaper rent. The
Melville brood consisted of eight children, four boys and four girls. The
oldest, Gansevoort, was born in 1815, and the youngest, Thomas, still a
boy at the time, was born in 1830. This would be the house in which
Melville hammered out his first book, but for now — as ever — he was in
search of gainful employment. Lansingburgh Academy was in a large
brick building just down the street from the family home, and in November 1838 Herman enrolled there to undertake training in surveying and
engineering. The hope was that through his uncle Peter's influence and
connections he could find work on the Erie Canal. This became yet
another failed enterprise — and whether he knew it or not he was being
drawn toward the sea. While dithering in Lansingburgh, Melville did
make his first appearance in print as a writer via a crude, melodramatic,
and pseudonymous two-part story ("Fragments from a Writing Desk")
in the local *Democratic Press* newspaper. There is nothing there to antic-
ipate a literary future, yet it is interesting that Melville, despite inaus-
picious intellectual beginnings and an incomplete formal education, had
begun to perceive himself as a writer before his maiden voyage (to
England).

Redburn, written years later, captures the essence of that trip. In
the first chapter, the book also describes the circumstances that led Herman Melville to ship life: "Sad disappointments in several plans which
I had sketched for my future life; the necessity of doing something for
myself, united to a naturally roving disposition, had now conspired
within me, to send me to sea as a sailor."[43] The merchant ship *St.
Lawrence*, carrying goods and passengers and, among its crew, an impres-
sionable young sailor mistakenly listed on the roster as "Norman
Melville," set sail on June 5, 1839, and returned on September 30. The
crude bustle of the English port city left many impressions upon him

that he would pick up on in *Redburn*, including the site of people dead, or near death and hardly noticed, in the street gutters. Mostly though, the trip whet his appetite for more ship experiences and held sea life out there as a viable option, should his enterprises on land continue to amount to naught. Of course, in retrospect, the merchant service bore none of the glory of whaling. Ishmael enters the first pages of *Moby-Dick* with only merchant ship experience under his belt, and therefore bears the brunt of *Pequod* co-owner Captain Peleg's derision:

> "Dost know nothing at all about whaling, I dare say — eh?"
> "Nothing, Sir; but I have no doubt I shall soon learn. I've been several voyages in the merchant service, and I think that —"
> "Merchant service be damned. Talk not that lingo to me. Dost see that leg?— I'll take that leg away from thy stern, if ever thou talkest of the marchant service to me again. Marchant service indeed! I suppose now ye feel considerable proud of having served in those marchant ships. But flukes! man, what makes thee want to go a whaling, eh?"[44]

Back home from merchanting in Lansingburgh in the fall of 1839, with his mother beseeching her brother Peter for continued financial support, Herman put his head down and tried to do the right thing,

Lansingburgh, New York, house where Melville wrote *Typee* and *Omoo* (author photograph, 2010).

reentering the teaching fold with the hope of offering his mother a steady allowance. He took up a post at the Greenbush and Schodack Academy, across the river from Albany. Befitting his luck, the school closed down by May and didn't pay him the salary they owed him. He then took on a teaching stint in a rural school just east of Lansingburgh, amid the rolling hills of Brunswick, New York. It transpired quickly and came to a similar end. To compound the misfortune, his lawyer brother Gansevoort, now in the patriarchal role and writing to their mother from New York City, continued the family tradition of unfavorably branding Herman, this time with the tag of laziness: "not general laziness by any means," he wrote, "but that laziness which consists of an unwillingness to exert oneself in doing at a particular time, that which ought then to be done."[45] The ocean life, even at its most menial, had provided liberation from such aspersions and suffocating family fortunes — and this was not lost on Herman.

First though, he ventured toward the western frontier (then Illinois), with his friend Eli James Murdock Fly in tow. It was a well-beaten path for young men seeking better circumstances, and Herman's uncle, Thomas (Melvill), was in Galena, having already gotten himself into the kind of financial problems that had dogged him back home in the Berkshires. The young men traveled the Erie Canal and then zipped by steamboats across the Great Lakes and down the Mississippi River. Melville stored these impressions for use a decade later in *Moby-Dick*, in "The Town-Ho's Story" chapter. The bawdy, drinking, and brawling humanity along the banks of the canal clearly left a mark on the young man instilled with firm Calvinistic principles. Melville, as Ishmael, pours out those stored impressions:

> For three hundred and sixty miles, gentlemen, through the entire breadth of the state of New York; through numerous populous cities and most thriving villages; through long, dismal, uninhabited swamps, and affluent, cultivated fields, unrivalled for fertility; by billiard-room and bar-room; through the holy-of-holies of great forests; on Roman arches over Indian rivers; through sun and shade; by happy hearts or broken; through all the wide contrasting scenery of those noble Mohawk counties; and especially, by rows of snow-white chapels, whose spires stand almost like milestones, flows one continual stream of Venetianly corrupt and often lawless life. There's your true Ashantee, gentlemen; there howl your pagans ... so sinners, gentlemen, most abound in holiest vicinities.[46]

Arriving in Buffalo after their canal voyage, Melville and the stalwart Fly hopped a steamer to Toledo then Detroit and Chicago and on downriver Galena. With Uncle Thomas having no prospects for them and having been caught embezzling, the two made the long sweep home, traveling through Pennsylvania. The only record we have of Melville's western trip are scattered references to the Erie Canal, Great Lakes, and Niagara Falls in *Moby-Dick*. Otherwise, the trip exists in the Melville history as yet another failed enterprise that sent him to sea, this time on the multi-year voyage that would become his ultimate muse.

Reading later reflections in *Moby-Dick* (1851) and *Redburn* (1849), one gets the sense of the complicated and vacillating feelings that Melville experienced as a young man with blue-blooded heritage and a dose of education who was now indelibly bound to the lowly servitude of others. He moves between outrage and enduring humility. In *Redburn* he vents spleen at the "Miserable dog's life" of the sailor and spouts indignation at "vulgar and brutal men lording it over me, as if I were an African in Alabama."[47] In *Moby-Dick,* through his consummate mouthpiece Ishmael, he becomes more reflective, understatedly deeming the penury "unpleasant enough." Melville also tips his hand regarding his own bloodline and prior vocation:

> It touches one's sense of honor, particularly if you come of an old established family in the land, the Van Rensselaers, or Randolphs, or Hardicanutes. And more than all, if just previous to putting your hand into the tar-pot, you have been lording it as a country schoolmaster, making the tallest boys stand in awe of you. The transition is a keen one, I assure you, from a schoolmaster to a sailor, and requires a strong decoction of Seneca and the Stoics to enable you to grin and bear it. But even this wears off in time.[48]

By November of 1840, Melville was in New York City (having arrived in late summer), in a kind of horse latitudes of existence. Gansevoort put him up in a boardinghouse and kept him fed, and the ever-anxious, industrious, and genteel older brother wrote to the younger brother Allan that the often wild-looking Herman was in "good health & tolerable spirits" and had "had his hair sheared & whiskers shaved & looks more like a Christian than usual."[49] Fly, still accompanying him, had found copyist work, but Herman was still adrift. Several influences conspired to finally launch Herman on a whale ship in early January 1841. As always, there was his lack of prospects. The sailor's life thus far had been the only paid endeavor that he had seen through from beginning to satisfying conclusion. Additionally, ever under the spell of books, he had not so long ago read James Fenimore Cooper's multicultural sea adventure *The Red Rover* and Richard Henry Dana, Jr.'s, personal narrative of the sailor's life, *Two Years Before the Mast*. He had always held Cooper close through family association: His mother could recall the author playing with her brother Peter at her war hero father's home while waiting for the ice to clear for travel down the Hudson. Dana's memoir, however, cut to the quick with Herman, and he regarded the writer's experience as uniquely tied to his own. The Cambridge, Massachusetts, native Dana — born to a preeminent colonial family and well-educated (counting Ralph Waldo Emerson among his teachers) — had been similarly sent toward the common sailor's life by circumstances beyond his control. Born exactly four years, to the day, before Herman, he also possessed Melville's distinct streak of racial egalitarianism. Melville had devoured the book when it came out in 1840, seeing in it his own, albeit brief experience as a sailor the previous year, and, more importantly, finding in it a template for his conflicting existence as a common sailor from patrician lineage. *Two Years Before the Mast* also framed out the idea of putting such experience into writing. Melville would write to Dana later, after he too had established himself as a writer of firsthand sea experiences, noting that Dana's book had given him the feeling of being "tied & welded to you by a sort of Siamese link of affectionate sympathy."[50] Likely Dana's book also infused a desire to see the Pacific Ocean for himself — to use his Liverpool sailor experience as a jumping off point for a more distant, involved, and perilous journey. This desire emerges in Ishmael, who genuflects in reverie before the "sweet mystery" of the Pacific, before the "hidden soul" of "this mysterious, divine Pacific."[51] It is, he declares, the very "tide-beating heart of earth."[52] And, of course, there was plenty of work in the thriving American whale fishery for an unemployed young man who had menial sea experience. Gansevoort accompanied Herman to New Bedford, eager to find a productive position for his problematical brother and also eager to get him off of his own tab. Soon enough, they located a whaling ship, the new *Acushnet*, and on Christmas Day 1840, Herman signed on as a lowly green hand, with his "lay" — that is, share of the profits — at 1/175th, a strikingly low sum. But Gansevoort had given him a head start with some work clothing, and his food and board would be covered for a few years while at sea. Such were Herman's prospects at the time, and to illustrate the financial futility of the occupation, Melville gives Ishmael the 300th lay (1/300), a sum that "might pretty near pay for the clothing," and not much more.[53]

On January 3, 1841, the *Acushnet*, with Herman Melville on board, sailed out of frigid New England, headed for warmer waters and, eventually, the South Pacific. At the time, the journey, as biographer Andrew Delbanco, characterized it, "might as well have been to the far side of the moon."[54] The occupation itself was hardly fathomable; Melville sailed at a time when men, in hot pursuit of a forty- to sixty-ton animal in its native environment, launched from the ship in small boats, affixed a line to the creature with a thrown harpoon, and then attempted to continually stab it to death. Then, of course, came the more workaday and laborious task of hacking, cutting, and boiling down the mammoth creature to its usable products. Very little went to waste: Whale oil lit up America at night, from lamps to lighthouses, and also lubricated small and large machinery; whale bones were fashioned into countless everyday items; ambergris was refined into perfume; and whale bristles became brooms and brushes. America, by Melville's time, had come to dominate whaling, and the daringness and resourcefulness of it seemed a natural outcrop of the American character. "To produce a mighty book, you must choose a mighty theme,"[55] rhapsodizes Ishmael in *Moby-Dick*, and whaling was such a theme, bundling together extraordinary feat, epic adventure, and American daring and relentlessness. "The whaleship will always remain an American epic symbol," wrote President Franklin Delano Roosevelt well into the next century, asserting that its only comparison was "the prairie schooner" of the westward-pushing pioneers.[56]

There was another quality to whaling that made it remarkable: The cultural and racial diversity of the lower-caste workers on the ship. The forecastle, with barely six-foot ceilings and walls that curved with the forward hull (those of higher-rank and skilled trade slept aft), was an egalitarian space in which widely varying cultures rubbed equal elbow to equal elbow, a quality that Melville emphasizes through the multicultural cast aboard the *Pequod*. The *Acushnet* sailed with men of African American, Portuguese, and Irish heritage, along with the usual collection of young white men from New York and New England. But beyond teeming diversity and adventure lay a grim reality: Men constantly deserting whale ships in distant ports, either unable or unwilling to bear the hardship, penury, and authoritarianism or simply left diseased or dying from maladies such as venereal disease (acquired during land contact along the way). Nearly half of Melville's shipmates, including Melville himself, did not return on the *Acushnet* in 1844. They deserted at points all over the Pacific map — Ecuador, Peru, Maui, Rio de Janeiro, Oahu, the Marquesas Islands (specifically, Nuka Hiva, in Melville's case)—some for combative, anti-authoritarian reasons; some had simply had enough of the danger and penury; others hobbled ashore venereal and/or "half dead." One, a teenager from Maine and shipmate of Melville, was described as "half dead" and "spitting blood."[57]

In the early weeks of the journey, however, with the crew still fresh, Melville's eyes were opened to the world of whaling. First, of course, the *Acushnet* left the slate-like New England winter in its wake as it slipped into the warm latitudes. Melville conveyed the experience in *Moby-Dick*, placing the *Pequod*'s departure around the same time of season. "Now, it being Christmas when the ship shot from out her harbor, for a space we had biting Polar weather," narrates Ishmael, "though all the time running away from it to the southward; and by every degree and minute of latitude which we sailed, gradually leaving that merciless winter, and all its intolerable weather behind us."[58] By the time they were off the Bahamas, the *Pequod* was already in the hunt, and Melville for the first time witnessed the barely comprehensible feat of primitively equipped men slaying the leviathan, a process that started with a cry from a look-out, and then about a half-dozen men each shoving off from the mother ship in whaleboats, which were treacherously small and open craft tapered at each end for speed and maneuverability. The small crews would row in furious pursuit until drawing close, when the goal became stealth and the oars were lifted or paddled lightly. The harpooner then stood in the bow, legs taut and holding a double-barbed iron harpoon above his shoulder, flinging hand tightly wrapped around the sturdy hardwood handle. The harpooner had to be brought close enough to puncture the dense skin and blubber. A successful, attempt, however, was just a beginning. As Melville would write (in a review of *Etchings of a Whale Cruise* in 1847), "[A]ll this is nothing to what follows. As yet, you have but simply *fastened* to the whale: he must be fought and killed."[59] Here were the realities Melville observed firsthand, and which he related to enchanted listeners, including Hawthorne, in coming years: An injured multi-ton whale on an outright run, towing the small craft behind it; the giant, destructive flukes whipping back and forth; the riot of plunging and foaming surf as the leviathan thrashed. A harpooned whale could take a whaleboat on a hair-raising ride—that is, if it hadn't already scattered the crew and dashed the craft with its flukes. A best-case scenario would see the exhausted whale slow down and the boat pull up closely alongside it, whale skin to wood, so that someone could finish it off with a long, sharp lance.[60] This involved plunging the implement deep into the lungs and "churning" it around to cause mortal damage, a feat the second mate Stubb enacts in lingering detail in *Moby-Dick*: "Stubb slowly churned his long sharp lance into the fish, and kept it there, carefully churning and churning, as if cautiously seeking to feel after some gold watch that the whale might have swallowed, and which he was fearful of breaking ere he could hook it out. But that gold watch he sought was the innermost life of the fish."[61] If successful, the fatal lance plunge would culminate in "a geyser of crimson blood"[62] erupting from the whale's blowhole. Then, of course, there was the potential danger of a spasmodic final flurry.

When the great creature finally came to rest and rolled "fin out," a T-shaped toggle with a rope on it was inserted into a punctured fluke, and the wrung-out crew towed their burden back to the ship, where the work had seemingly just begun. And though Melville later claimed to a publisher to have been a harpooneer (a.k.a. boatsteerer, and so named for the forward rowing position), evidence shows that he was likely more engaged in the labors and drudgeries of sailing—and conversing and daydreaming and reading—than anything else.[63] Nevertheless, he was a front-line witness to the spectacle of whale slaughter and the prodigious activity that went into reducing and breaking down the leviathan to its commercial products. The whale ships during Melville's time had become virtual factories, with large "try pots" built into a brick furnace on deck; here, blubber, having been cut from the whale and then into blocks and thin leaves, was heated into oil. Another of the many rigorous procedures involved extracting the waxy spermaceti from the whale's head. All of this manifests itself in the pages of *Moby-Dick*.

Melville was also witness to the Southern Hemisphere. Thus far, the circumference of his travels had been to Liverpool, England, by ship, and to the relative frontier of Illinois to the west. But now the doors of his awareness were being thrown wide open, as he traveled south and then around Cape Horn—and it was the fusing of his imagination with the actual Pacific that essentially made him a writer. In the *Moby-Dick* chapter "The Pacific," the waters become wedded with the very qualities of Melville's literary form, as he extols its "gently awful stirrings" that "speak of some hidden soul beneath." *Moby-Dick*, beyond its elements of adventure and straight facts about whales and whaling, is a book of reverie and meditation, of the duality between that which is apparent to the waking conscious and that which is hidden in the deeper subconscious layers, of "millions of mixed shades and shadows, drowned dreams, somnambulisms, reveries," Melville writes. In this conceptual Pacific, he tells us, "all that we call lives and souls, lie dreaming, dreaming, still; tossing like slumberers in their beds; the ever-rolling waves but made so by their restlessness."[64] Clearly this is not your average ocean rendering, but also a psychological canvas that the writer spreads out before the reader; and Melville was clearly not your average sailor, prone as he was to profound meditation and reverie, even as he kept watch high in the mast. He was, like Ishmael, the kind of sailor he warned ship captains against: "a lad with lean brow and hollow eye; given to unseasonable meditativeness." While high in the mast on lookout for whales, Ishmael describes such a mentality as being

> lulled into such an opium-like listlessness of vacant, unconscious reverie ... by the blending cadence of waves with thoughts, that at last he loses his identity; takes the mystic ocean at his feet for the visible image of that deep, blue, bottomless soul, pervading mankind and nature; and every strange, half-seen, gliding, beautiful thing that eludes him; every dimly-discovered, uprising fin of some undiscernible form, seems to him the embodiment of those elusive thoughts that only people the soul by continually flitting through it.[65]

Melville describes "this tropic whaling life" in *Moby-Dick* as one in which "a sublime uneventfulness invests you; you hear no news; read no gazettes ... you hear of no domestic afflictions; bankrupt securities; fall of stocks; are never troubled with the thought of what you shall have for dinner."[66] And it is the recollection of that experience that induced Melville to stretch his prose toward nearly indescribable sensations, much like Freud's "oceanic feeling": a fused, primordial connection with the outside world, a sense of "eternity" in the individual from which "religious energy" emerges.[67] For Melville, writing in "The Mast-Head" chapter of *Moby-Dick*, it is a sense of egoless wonderment, an "enchanted mood" in which one's "spirit ebbs away to whence it came; becomes diffused through time and space."[68]

Adding to this psychological and imaginative transformation in the young Melville was all that he bore witness to not just in the watery reaches, but on land. In March 1841, while still in the South Atlantic, Herman went ashore at Rio De Janeiro when the *Acushnet* stopped to sell barrels of whale oil. Plunging further south along the South American coastline, the ship passed between Tierra del Fuego and Staten Land, where the dramatic mountains, sharp and bare, rose toward the roof of the world. He would dredge up the experience in *White-Jacket* (1850), the book he wrote immediately before *Moby-Dick*: "On our starboard beam, like a pile of glaciers in Switzerland, lay this Staten Land, gleaming in snow-white barrenness and solitude.... High, towering in their own turbaned snows, the far-inland pinnacles loomed up, like the border of some other world."[69] Not long after passing by these "Flashing walls and crystal battlements" that seemed to him the "diamond watch-towers along heaven's furthest frontier,"[70] the ship rounded Cape Horn in "thick" and "hazy" weather.[71] (Melville earned the mariner distinction of rounding the Horn on April 15, 1841.) In the Pacific, he saw the Galapagos Islands, and years later he would conjure up their volcanic barrenness and resident giant tortoises in the sketch "The Encantadas" (1854). But it was after months upon months of whaling that Melville made his most significant land contact when he deserted in the Marquesan Islands at Nuka Hiva. This was the experience that he would transpose into his first book, *Typee* (1846), a work that would, to his eventual dismay, cause him to be labeled as "the man who lived among the cannibals" and as an American Daniel Defoe. Four years before becoming friends with the author, Nathaniel Hawthorne would assert in the *Salem Advertiser* that "no work ... gives a freer and more effective picture of barbarian life."[72]

As mentioned, desertion was common on such journeys, and Melville was not the first on the *Acushnet* to determine that he had had enough. There is not significant and compelling evidence to show that the *Acushet's* captain, Valentine Pease, was particularly cruel; therefore, Melville's desertion — in the company of a shipboard friend, Richard Tobias ("Toby") Greene, from Rochester, New York — seems to have been motivated simply by the year and a half he had spent sleeping in the crowded forecastle and toiling in the small world of the whale ship. It was time for a change. And the Nuka Hiva Bay in which the ship was anchored offered enough enchantments to suggest something better: celestial, translucent waters; pale sands; and lush mountain greenery rising straight up in a sharp rise of hills out of the sea. Of course, there were also the young Polynesian women, who ceremoniously swam out in groups to greet the many ships (American, French, and British). Herman and his stalwart friend Toby Greene, who would a few years later validate the story told in *Typee*, after charges against its veracity, used the opportunity of a shore liberty to dart into the hills choked with vegetation. Their progress, however, was slowed by the thick growth and by an injury Melville sustained to his leg. Lost, they ended up in the Typee Valley, among the people who made their home there. With Melville's condition worsening, Toby canoed back to the harbor to seek help. Toby, though, ended up departing on a ship, allegedly paying an Irishman to retrieve Melville. This, of course, never came to fruition, and Herman spent weeks healing and lingering among the natives until slipping away and returning on his own to the harbor. His ordeal had made the familiar business of whaling all that more appealing, and he signed up on an Australian ship, the *Lucy Ann*. Whether much of which he described in *Typee* was based in fact—the shipboard orgy between the crew and native women upon first arriving, the romantic and erotic interludes with "Fayaway" in the Typee Valley, the potential threat of being tattooed and eaten—will always remain speculation. This much is clear, however: Herman Melville's Nuka Hivan ordeal had made the familiar—if rigorous and dangerous—business of whaling a better alternative, and he signed up on an Australian ship, the *Lucy Ann*, leaving Nuka Hiva forever.

His second book, *Omoo*, took up as its subject this leg of his journey, which involved a revolt among the crew (after a mere month aboard) and Melville and others being imprisoned in Tahiti as mutineers. Released after a few weeks, Melville ended up on the neighboring island of Eimeo, where he found work in the fields, cultivating sweet potatoes and other produce with which to supply ships. Soon though, he was whaling again, this time for several months on a Nantucket ship, the *Charles and Henry*, which he abandoned in April 1843 in Maui (in what is today, of course, Hawaii). Melville headed to Honolulu, at the time a paradoxical mix of missionaries and prostitution, and found work wherever he could, including time as a pin setter at a bowling alley. By August 1843, however, he had had enough; home beckoned, and signing on as a lowly seaman in the U.S. Navy aboard the *United States*, he made the long sweep home, arriving in Boston, the place of his paternal heritage, in October of 1844.

Thus ended the journey during which Melville the writer was made. From this long, variegated experience he would pull most of the work for which he is known today, including, most importantly, the book that would cement him in history and become his masterpiece, *Moby-Dick*. Where and how that volume would be written, however, is a whole other matter. It incorporates, of course, Melville's whaling experience and all of the books he swallowed whole in the interim. The final catalyst, however, that gave *Moby-Dick* its eventual shape and form was the relation-ship he cultivated in the Berkshire Mountains of western Massachusetts with Nathaniel Hawthorne, whose own works, friendship, and role as a not-so-far off neighbor, fellow writer, conversational companion, and epistolary sounding board inspired Herman Melville to heights and depths that he had never before explored.

It was to Hawthorne, after all, that he would dedicate his greatest work, and the product of all of that voyaging.

FOUR

Annus Mirabilis; or,
The Haunted Mind
and the Whale

The world should recline its vast head on the first convenient pillow, and take an age-long nap. It has gone distracted, through a morbid activity, and, while preternaturally wide-awake, is nevertheless tormented by visions, that seem real to it now, but would assume their true aspect and character, were all things once set right by an interval of sound repose.

> —*passage repeatedly pencil-scored by*
> *Melville in Hawthorne, "The Old Manse"*
> (Mosses from an Old Manse, *Volume 1*)

What a trustful guardian of secret matters fire is! What should we do without Fire and Death?

> —*Hawthorne, in his journal*

We represent a new race of men, living no longer in the past, scarcely in the present — but projecting our lives forward into the future.

> —*Hawthorne, "Old Esther Dudley"*

"Book! you lie there; the fact is, you books must know your places. You'll do to give us the bare words and facts, but we come in to supply the thoughts."

> —*Stubb, in* Moby-Dick

By October of 1850, Melville and his wife Lizzie had left New York City society behind and were permanently settled into the large, drafty farmhouse near the Pittsfield-Lenox line that Melville would dub "Arrowhead." It was in the upstairs study of this house that he would wrestle with his imagination and hash out what Hawthorne would come to dub his "gigantic conception"[1] of the whale. He and Hawthorne would be relative neighbors now, with only six miles of rutted, jolting road between them — a byway over which Melville would often travel in his single-horse drawn pine-box carriage to visit. Hawthorne was not the prime reason for the move (as some apocryphal legends insist); Melville's love for the Berkshires and his family's deep roots there were well-established. Furthermore, he understood that the Hawthornes were interlopers here, renters that would soon outgrow the small, red workman's home in which they had settled after the debacle and tragedy of Salem, where politics had harshly interceded into Nathaniel's life to bounce him from his custom house post, and where he had only recently sat by his mother's death bed, wracked with the loss of his only parent.

Melville, though, was in his glory. For one, he was all afire with his developing book. He was also newly settled into marriage and fatherhood (with a toddler, Malcolm) and had commenced to live the part of author and country gentleman at his new home and farm, turning away from stifling New York City. In addition, he could now call one of the first, truly great American authors his friend and neighbor. No more family tragedies and misfortunes controlled the compass of his life, and no more would he toil at the lower end of the ocean's caste system. He had thrown himself into authorship, and upon the publication of *Typee*, he struck again and again while the iron was hot, and in less than five years he had published five books. There was none of Hawthorne's methodical, decade-long woodshedding, and there was no hiding behind anonymity; Melville's tales were associated with his own adventures. He was all *persona*— the retired sea dog turning toward authorship — while Hawthorne wrote of other people and other times and still endeavored to hide himself (even in plain sight). Melville's sense of himself as a writer only stretched back a little over four years, while Hawthorne's stretched back decades. Melville was a shooting star, a marrow sucker, a train rushing headlong; Hawthorne was deliberate and steadfast. But they quickly became close, despite a difference in capacities and ages, fused by the very "sudden flame of friendship" that Melville would ascribe to Ishmael and Queequeg. It was a friendship spurred to life by mutual admiration and whatever primal attracting forces brought people together; it was also a friendship borne out of their democratic outlook on life — put simply, Melville was Hawthorne's kind of guy; that is, one with few airs. Even as his public reputation grew in Salem (while at the custom house), Hawthorne had preferred the tavern goers and the men of the sea to the aristocracy or highbrow intellectual circles. Prior to that, while living at the Old Manse in Concord, Massachusetts, Hawthorne had ruefully snorted at Emerson and his sacrosanct ilk. With Melville, though, the pull was strong and immediate. Writing to his longtime close confidante Horatio Bridge in mid–August 1850, Hawthorne exclaimed, "I met Melville, the other day, and like him so much that I have asked him to spend a few days with me before leaving these parts."[2] (Melville still called New York City home in August 1850, but not for long.) This was a generous and surprising offer in light of Hawthorne's isolative nature and the recent trouble and tragedy that had befallen him. It had taken years after their college association for Hawthorne to develop closeness with Longfellow; with Melville, it was immediate.

And Hawthorne had traveled a long path to arrive at the publication of his popular and heralded *Scarlet Letter* earlier that year and his defection from Salem to the Berkshires. After finally shedding his anonymity and embracing the world as a known writer, Hawthorne also emerged as a person, engaging more closely with life and love and the rest of it. He continued to acquire influential friends, including John O' Sullivan, the powerful political writer and Democratic figure, who would gain posthumous (and somewhat problematical) fame as the man who penned the idea of "Manifest Destiny." Hawthorne wrote numerous pieces for O' Sullivan's *Democratic Review*, while beginning to acquire the political affiliation through which he would find work and for which he would be eventually tarnished and fired from his Salem Custom House post. He also made the acquaintance of fellow Salemite Elizabeth Peabody, his eventual sister-in-law — a generous, influential, and at times overbearing character who would became yet another strong champion of his work. She was a generative force in the world of education, Transcendentalism, and publishing, and she pulled Hawthorne into her circle. Hawthorne would be romantically linked to her (perhaps falsely), but it would be her shyer, hypochondriacal, and artistic sister, Sophia, that he would eventually marry.

With influential friends pushing for him, he found his first government employment at the Boston Custom House as a measurer of coal and salt. And while he congratulated himself on having a "part to act in the material and tangible business of life,"[3] his writing slipped in the face of his governmental duties. He had also begun cultivating a secretive relationship with Sophia, their romance blossoming through correspondence. In his mid–30s, he finally greeted the world as a writer, romancer, and regularly paid worker; he also (despite his own protestations) began to greet the world politically. In January 1841, after two years on the job — with President Martin Van Buren (Andrew Jackson's Democratic successor) out and the Whigs on their way in — Hawthorne resigned from his Boston post. The following months found him in a curious position, living on Brook Farm, the communal experiment in West Roxbury, Massachusetts, that had been inspired by Transcendentalist ideals. Here, everyone was a joint shareholder and took equal part in the work and profits of the farm. Moving there in April 1841, Hawthorne dutifully did his job, with thoughts of perhaps settling there with Sophia, as he pursued his long-distance engagement with her (a premarital bond that remained a secret to family and friends). Predictably, the communal situation did not work for Nathaniel, who left in November, just before a new two-volume edition of *Twice Told Tales* hit the market to meager sales and lukewarm reviews.

He finally married Sophia on July 9, 1842, five days after his 38th birthday, in a small ceremony at Elizabeth Peabody's bookshop in Boston. (Sophia was 32.) His sisters were miffed at the secrecy of the relationship, though Louisa eventually came around. Soon after, the lovers found themselves in Concord, Massachusetts, a place they dubbed "paradise." Here, in bucolia, with Nathaniel fishing, gardening, and gathering flowers for his wife, they lived out their early married life at the old parsonage that Hawthorne would dub "The Old Manse." He tolerated the occasional parade of visitors, palled around with Henry David Thoreau, and generally steered clear of Ralph Waldo Emerson. His relationship with Emerson would come to be marked by mutual ambivalence, misunderstanding, and potshots at each other's work; Sophia, however, admired the Concord figurehead and his ideas. The truth was likely that they had threatened each other's egos — Emerson collected people to his circle in Concord; it was *his* town. (He had even dispatched his stalwart friend Thoreau to prepare the couple a vegetable garden before their arrival.) But Hawthorne, living in the very house that Emerson's grandfather had built, would not be collected. He had done all of the "joining" he was prepared to do at Brook Farm. Emerson, meanwhile, had drawn the admiration and respect of Sophia, an unacceptable situation that stirred up Hawthorne's inner darkness. Hawthorne became known as somewhat of a misfit in Concord and didn't care; he became a father, was writing prolifically, and was enjoying the romantic love that had once been so alien to him. After three years in Concord, though, he was clearly not making enough money to support Sophia and his first-born, Una. Again, friends petitioned for a government post for him. The influential democrat John O'Sullivan, now godfather to Una, and working on Hawthorne's behalf, exclaimed, "Hawthorne is dying of starvation!"[4] Hawthorne turned to housework in the absence of hired help and waited on Sophia and his daughter. He sold apples and potatoes. Finally, in October of 1845, the family was evicted for lack of payment — although politely and in not so many words.

Hawthorne was 41 years old, and he was forced to move back in with his family at Herbert Street in Salem. He took stock of the sad situation, sitting in the very third-floor room that had once cloistered him from the world as he burgeoned as a young writer. Sophia and Una took a room on a lower floor. The business of being an American writer was not for the faint of heart — here was a lesson that Melville and Hawthorne would learn again and again, throughout their lives. (Perhaps the best one could hope for was posthumous glory.) But, again, it was others that lifted Hawthorne up when he was unable to lift himself. Hawthorne still had a name as a writer, and friends and associates besieged President James K. Polk, the newly elected Democrat, with that name. After a long winter, in March 1846, Nathaniel became surveyor of the Salem Custom House. His collection *Mosses from an Old Manse* also came out in June, representing the fruits of his Concord labors. He also penned a few reviews for the *Salem Advertiser*, and that year the book that piqued his interest the most was *Typee*, the debut from a new American author named Herman Melville. As it always was with Hawthorne, political tides determined his passage through life, and in November 1848 Zachary Taylor, a Whig, ascended to the presidency. Hawthorne was dismissed in June of 1849, and the family lived off of the charity of friends and lampshades that Sophia, using her artistic talents, painted and sold. With the death of his mother, he put Salem behind him and headed toward the mountains of western Massachusetts — but not before he had crafted *The Scarlet Letter*, his first novel, and found yet another champion of his work, the prominent publisher James T. Fields, to send it out into the world. (Fields would remain his publisher for the rest of his life, and, of course, would tromp up Monument Mountain with him and the group the day he met Melville.) Published in March of 1850, it sold out its first printing of 2500 copies in mere weeks. To boot, Hawthorne had painted an insulting portrait of the Salem Custom House and his former colleagues in its prefatory essay. At the end of May, he, Sophia and the children, now including young Julian, moved into the red cottage.

Again, Hawthorne was on the receiving end of charity: Sophia's friend Caroline Sturgis had married the successful New York City broker William Aspinall Tappan, and it was to their property (now the Tanglewood estate and music venue) that the Hawthornes fled. Nathaniel insisted on paying fifty dollars for the rent, though it was offered for free. Good reviews were little succor for the writer packed with his family into the tiny, drafty abode — an actual cottage amidst the magnificent and misnomered "cottages" (large estates, in fact) of the Berkshires elite. He had come here exhausted, disenchanted, and wondering when fortune would smile on him. He was sick of poverty, sick of politics, and sick of most people. It was no wonder that Melville was a breath of fresh air to the aging Hawthorne. Here was a ball of energy, vitality, and intelligence — a gentleman in every respect but one of little pretense who had seen the hard end of life but had not let it beat him down.

Here was another American writer: one he could respect.

* * *

By late 1850, after the first flush of the authors meeting each other, Melville and his family had seen their New York City life give way to country and subsistence-farming life at Arrowhead. The purchase of the Melvill family home (soon to be dubbed Broadhall) by the Morewoods had made Herman even more intent on maintaining his connection to the Berkshires; therefore, he bought the large farmhouse and tract of land roughly adjacent to the Broadhall plot. It was not a cavernous, grand house like the old Melvill home, but it would provide enough room for him and Lizzie and their growing family, as well as for Herman's mother and sisters.

Ever conscious of his persona — and ever conscious of keeping his name on the lips of New York literati, despite his decampment from the city — Melville, once settled, portrayed himself to Duyckinck, who was still the hot center of New York literary society, as the very model of a country gentleman and diligent writer. Melville had exulted in the idyllic Berkshires autumn, waxing to his "Beloved" Duyckinck about the "glowing & Byzantine" days, "ripe & ruddy" heavens, and the "red blasings" of the Maples.[5] As colder days arrived, Melville's world became smaller and more habitual; in fact, his days became caught up in agrarian rhythms. He rose at eight, he told Duyckinck, and fed his horse and cow, taking meditative delight in the animal's deliberate chewing ("she does it so mildly & with such a sanctity," he recorded).[6] Then, his own breakfast over, he ascended to his study, lit his fire, spread the large sheaf of papers that was becoming *Moby-Dick* across his table, and delved inward — summoning sense memories of whaling, summoning influence from Hawthorne and the various books upon which he had gorged himself, summoning the complex and terrible Ahab deep in his own psyche — still inchoate but rising from those depths and into crisper focus all the time. During afternoons, he took his mother or sisters the few miles into town for mail and supplies; while the evenings, he noted, found him in a "mesmeric state," mentally spent and (due to eyesight issues) mostly unable to read in weak light. "Mesmeric" also described the state of mind of a writer who was clearly, to borrow a more contemporary phrase, "in the zone" with his new book; that is, in a state of creative flow and imaginative acuity that he would never recapture in his lifetime. Such was his creative vitality, he joked to Duyckinck, that he needed "fifty fast-writing youths, with an easy style" to help him get down all of his ideas.[7] This "mesmeric" state he describes was also a state of heightened preoccupation, tinged with anxiety in those non-working hours, of striving toward a heightened ideal in his mind that was nonetheless not fully clear to him yet. Melville marked this passage in Hawthorne's "The Birthmark," which clearly resonated for him: "his most splendid successes were almost invariably failures if compared with the ideal at which he aimed."[8] Hawthorne, Shakespeare, Virgil, his own experience, and legends of the whale fishery were all jumping off points. But he was now plunging into blank space.

He and Hawthorne had also fallen into the habits of friendship and an ever-growing closeness cultivated during an Indian summer of dinners, cigars, booze, and long talks that dealt not only with authorship and life but those deeper, hardly fathomable matters of existence: metaphysics, ontology, and other such great mysteries. Melville, of course, had also entered the family fold during an extended stay with the Hawthornes in early September. The cold weather, though, had driven the writers to their labors after that: Melville to his whale book and Hawthorne toward his seven-gabled romance.

Life for Melville had moved quickly since his landing back home from his multi-year ocean voyage and reaching this *annus mirabilis* in the Berkshires. And much in the same manner that Hawthorne had entered finally entered real, tangible life after his long period of sequestering, Melville too entered the world in late 1844, at twenty-five years of age, after his ship came to port in Boston. "From my twenty-fifth year I date my life," he would write to Hawthorne. "Until I was twenty-five I had no development at all."[9] Re-birthed in waters, he returned to Lansingburgh, New York, just north of Albany and on the opposite side of the Hudson River (the east side), to live with his mother and sisters and youngest sibling, Tom, in a large house flush up against the Hudson—the broad, vital expanse of the industrious river maintaining his connection to the waterways of the world and serving as a reminder of his journey and of his new life. He returned home tanned and strong, a whiff of distant worlds emanating from him—and with so many stories to tell. And it was as raconteur that he began his life as an author, enchanting his friends and family with tales and images of whaling, the Pacific, South America, the Galapagos Islands, and of course the Marquesas. It was the latter, his "anxious paradise," as early critic and Melville literary executor Arthur Stedman termed it, living among the Polynesian "cannibals" in Nuka Hiva, which he finally decided to commit to paper. There had been glimmerings of Melville's sense of himself as a writer before he went to sea, but now, with such a rare and wild story to tell, he embarked upon *Typee*. His pre-ocean-dwelling years had seen him tossed on the tides of misfortune, with no agency over his direction, and struggling to locate a vocation. Now, Herman Melville was truly coming to life.

Like Hawthorne, part of this emergence (of truly living and not simply dreaming of living, as Hawthorne had put it to Longfellow in his early author years) also meant finding romantic love and a life partner. The esteemed and revered Bostonian Judge Lemuel Shaw, Chief Justice of the Commonwealth of Massachusetts, had once been engaged to Melville's aunt (Allan Melvill's sister, Nancy), who died shortly before their wedding. (He had also been the executor of Melville's father's estate after Allan's death.) Shaw did eventually marry another woman, Elizabeth, and in yet another tragedy, she died while giving birth to their daughter. He gave that child the same name as her mother. Grown, that young woman, Lizzie Shaw, became friends with Herman's sisters—Helen, Augusta, Kate, and Fanny—and she was ensconced in their close circle when Herman arrived home from his sea travels. Befitting her heritage, she was intelligent and sharp-witted, and to Melville's good fortune saw something in the unemployed adventurer who was just now coming into his own as a writer.

In February of 1846, Melville greeted the world as an author with the opening salvo of his first published book, *Typee*: "Six Months at sea! Yes, reader, as I live, six months out of sight of land; cruising for the sperm-whale beneath the scorching sun of the Line, and tossed on the billows of the wide-rolling Pacific — the sky above, the sea around, and nothing else."[10] This was Melville the author at his youngest and most histrionic, and a world removed from the subtle, cryptic manner with which *Moby-Dick* beckons its readers forth, never tipping its hand at the wonders, terrors, and vastness that lay beyond "Ishmael's" humble greeting and salutation. *Typee* is a bit of chest-beating, Melville quickly laying out the chasm of experience between himself and his readers: "Oh! Ye state-room sailors who make so much ado about a fourteen-days' passage across the Atlantic ... what would you say to our six months out of sight of land?"[11] This is the rookie literary craftsman at his most flamboyant, carving out a mythology of himself behind the persona of "Tommo": part Lotus eater, part Crusoe, part erotic adventurer among the Polynesians. The, latter of course, was in somewhat veiled form (befitting the era), but for the times, Melville displayed a surprising straightforwardness; in fact, as biographer Andrew Delbanco points out, one of the few of his contemporaries who "got close [as Melville] to candor about sexual pleasure was Nathaniel Hawthorne" (particularly in *The Scarlet Letter*).[12] Incidentally, upon *Typee*'s release, and four years before meeting Melville, Hawthorne praised this very quality in his *Salem Advertiser* review: "The author's descriptions of the native girls are voluptuously colored," he wrote. "He has that freedom of view — it would be too harsh to call it laxity of principle — which renders him tolerant of codes and morals that may be little in accordance with our own." But Melville's was, defended Hawthorne, "a spirit proper enough to a young and adventurous sailor."[13] This was the fairly liberal mindset of a Hawthorne who was on the cusp of carving out the risqué predicament of Hester Prynne. And while he would not be able to exercise the "freedom of view" that he affords this young, adventurous sailor — his own milieu being an antiquarian and Puritan Boston — he builds glorious tension through Hester's bottled-up passions. She is, after all, a strikingly sexual figure (though Hawthorne's twisting tensions also allow her to be profoundly chaste). Hawthorne also had praise for other aspects of this debut from a young writer, admiring the patchwork blend of elements — anthropology, detailed facts, and romance — that Melville would build upon and infuse with metaphysics in *Moby-Dick* (a combination that Duyckinck would look askance at as "intellectual chowder" in his *Literary World* review of the whale book in November 1851). Hawthorne estimated *Typee* as "a very remarkable work" with a "skilfully [*sic*] managed" narrative.[14] The author who was soon to leave us with the jarring and indelible image of Ethan Brand's lime skeleton in a kiln also lingered over the macabre flourishes in Melville's debut: "[W]e catch a glimpse of a smoked human head, and the half-picked skeleton of what had been (in a culinary sense) a *well-dressed* man."[15] In a letter to Duyckinck after posting the review, Hawthorne reinforced his admiration, noting that he liked *Typee* "uncommonly well."[16] In reflecting upon the book, Hawthorne was also undoubtedly thinking of his own late father, suspended in the amber of imaginative memory as an eternally "young and adventurous sailor," having died barely known to him in faraway Suriname, and he was mentally yoking Nathaniel Senior's experiences to those of Melville. Far more than just exciting the interest of Hawthorne, *Typee* found a healthy readership, selling 6000 copies in its first two years in print. Walt Whitman, born the same year as Melville, and on the same long (though quite different) path to canonization, also waxed positive about this "strange, graceful, most readable book" in a review in *The Brooklyn Eagle*.[17]

But while Herman was in the ascendant, finally coming into his own, his older brother Gansevoort, the family's once bright star, was in profound trouble. Gansevoort had taken to the law well, and had furthermore gained a reputation as a successful political orator, stumping for the Democratic Party, in particular presidential candidate James K. Polk (the resolute westward expansionist) in New York City. He had also managed to obtain a political appointment for himself in London, as secretary to the American legation. Of course, it was Gansevoort, always the patriarchal figure to his brothers, who had gotten Herman's first book into a London publisher's hands — and who, more importantly, had bent the ear of esteemed American writer Washington Irving, visiting overseas at the time, with passages from the tale. (Irving was confident enough in the material to recommend it to his American publisher, Wiley & Putnam.) This was his last gift and charity to his younger brother; for while "Gans" had been so essential to getting his brother's career off the ground, his own fortunes and health were in jeopardy by 1846. Like his father, his decline was rapid; in April, he wrote from London to Herman to assure him that he had witnessed good reviews for *Typee* and to bemoan his own debt and failing health. He could barely dress himself to go out, his gums were bleeding, he couldn't keep down nourishment, and his eyesight was growing ever dimmer. His tone grew fatalistic, much like his own father's had toward the end: "Man stirs me not, nor woman either," he wrote, paraphrasing *Hamlet*. "I never valued life much — it were impossible to value it less than I do now."[18] By mid–May —coughing up blood, cold to the doctor's touch, and eyes fixed and unseeing — he was on the brink of death; by June, Herman was meeting his older brother's coffin as it arrived in New York Harbor. His brother's death and the weight of family mourning did not slow Herman's literary career, however, and by the spring of 1847, a sequel, *Omoo: A Narrative of the South Seas*, had found its way to the public.

On August 4, 1847, he married Elizabeth Shaw in Boston, and his fame was enough to rouse a *Typee*-referencing notice of the matrimony in a prominent New York City newspaper, which nudgingly declared, "The fair forsaken FAYAWAY will doubtless console herself."[19] The newlyweds wasted no time in moving to New York City, where Herman's name was becoming prominent, setting up house on 4th Avenue, behind Grace Church (in what is now Greenwich Village). From the fall of 1847 to early 1850 became a remarkable period for the writer; he dipped further into his well of ocean reveries to churn out three books—*Mardi*, *Redburn*, and *White-Jacket* — all based on his own experiences, with only *Mardi* dipping into romance and the more imaginative and psychological waters of *Moby-Dick*. During this period, he also embarked upon the initial, tentative stages of his whale book. In addition, he cultivated his friendship with the influential Duyckincks and their circle, which was known as "Young America," a politically vocal and literary group of Democrats whose crucible was New York City. Despite falling in with the literati of that circle, Melville's relationship with the movement was much like Hawthorne's with the more intellectual and heady Transcendentalists— that is, ambivalent and ultimately skeptical. The association with the thin, prim little Knickerbocker Evert Duyckink did yield tremendous benefits beyond literary networking, as Herman voraciously read his way through Evert's personal and extensive library. Between that collection, on Clinton Street, and the New York Society Library, on lower Broadway, Melville was essentially packing away an entire education. This voracious period during the few years leading up to *Moby-Dick* was crucial to that book's eventual shape and spirit. By the time of *Mardi*, he had begun to thickly drop canonical references (Homer, Shakespeare, and Milton, among others) into his work; by the time of *Moby-*

Dick, Ishmael would boldly proclaim, "I have swam through libraries and sailed through oceans."[20] The boast was the author's as well.

* * *

The earliest evidence that Herman Melville had embarked upon *Moby-Dick* came in May of 1850, three months before the initial Hawthorne meeting, in a letter to Richard Henry Dana, Jr., the writer whose own book, *Two Years Before the Mast*, had had such a profound impact upon Melville right before his own whaling voyage — and the writer for whom he felt great kinship in light of their similar family backgrounds and ocean experiences. Dana had written him a complimentary letter regarding his work (*Redburn* and/or *White-Jacket*), and Melville was ebullient, speaking of the "strange, congenial feelings" and "Siamese link of affectionate sympathy" he had felt for Dana after reading his book for the first time.[21] "About the 'whaling voyage,'" Melville continued, "I am halfway in the work, & am very glad that your suggestion so jumps with mine. It will be a strange sort of a book, tho', I fear."[22] This is Melville's first reference to the book (among known and available documents), and it is telling of his mindset at the time. His veracity had been questioned regarding his Marquesan adventures, and his old shipmate and fellow deserter Toby Greene had materialized to support his story, but now he was simultaneously struggling with the essence of "truth"—that is, portraying the "realities" of a whale ship — and moving his work away from himself and into the realm of the fantastical and imaginative. "[B]lubber is blubber you know," he confided to Dana. "[T]o cook the thing up, one must needs throw in a little fancy, which from the nature of the thing, must be as ungainly as the gambols of the whales themselves. Yet I mean to give the truth of the thing, spite of this."[23] The letter to Dana also displayed Melville's seemingly desperate need for affinity, for a friendship link with another writer of books, one whose work he respected. He was, to all appearances, primed for the Hawthorne meeting a few months down the road. (As a side note, his claim that he was "halfway" into the whale book might have been writer-to-writer bluster; or simply illustrative of the shift the work would take in the fall; or it could be that he was anticipating an altogether shorter work than *Moby-Dick*'s was to become. Of course, it could have been a combination of all three as well.)

Soon into Melville's creation of the book, it could be said that Hawthorne, his new affinity, and the spinner of fancy and dark imagination, was sitting on one shoulder, while Dana, his onetime "Siamese link," and the exacting ocean realist and historian, was sitting on the other. But, of course, it was Hawthorne who ultimately spoke to him in the strongest manner as he cut deeper into the work in late 1850. (And it was Dana that he artistically outgrew.) For by then, it was clear that the work was taking an entirely new direction — and that the whale book he had spoken to Dana about had undergone a sea-change, becoming an even "stranger" sort of book than he had first envisioned. He was prepared to make a more committed plunge into the regions he had described in *Mardi* — that is, "the world of the mind; wherein the wanderer may gaze round, with more of wonder than Balboa's band roving through the golden Aztec glades."[24] In *Mardi*, this voice had been inchoate, but under the spell of Hawthorne — as Melville's *Mosses* review shows — and under Hawthorne's appreciative gaze, he was able to crystallize those profounder instincts. "Whether it was reality or a dream, I could never settle,"[25] narrates Ishmael of an uncanny experience he undergoes early in *Moby-Dick*, as upon first waking, he finds Queequeg's arm thrown over him, the harpooneer's patchwork tattoos blending into the patchwork of the quilt. The feeling of Queequeg's arm around him, the blurring of the harpooneer's arm into the quilt, and Ishmael's not-quite-awake state induce him to recall a childhood incident when, sent to his room for hours on end as punishment, he falls into a deep sleep then partly emerges, "half steeped in dreams," to the feel of a "supernatural hand" holding his own and the sense of a "silent form or phantom" at his bedside.[26] Ishmael can't and won't explain the incident; rather, it establishes the glorious *uncertainty* of *Moby-Dick* — the uncertainty of a narrative that, at times, merges dreamworlds and waking, and outer and inner, and that is poised in a borderlands between both.

This is a world with which Hawthorne was already familiar. Ishmael's quandary ("Whether it was reality or a dream, I could never settle") echoes Hawthorne's depiction in "The Haunted Mind" (1834) of partially waking in the middle of the night to find that "the mind has a passive sensibility, but no active strength" and "imagination is a mirror, imparting vividness to all ideas, without the power of selecting them or controlling them."[27] (This piece, appearing in the second edition of *Twice-Told Tales* [1842], which Nathaniel gave him a copy of in early 1851, is something that Melville undoubtedly both read and drew influence from.) Here was the disorienting sense of authorial uncertainty that gave the work of both Hawthorne and Melville such strange power — but the readership of the mid-nineteenth century was not well-prepared for an "author" who would not claim full "authority" (though, of course, ambiguity and a lack of authority could place the two comfortably among the twentieth-century moderns). And much of this powerful authorial uncertainty comes from the effort to represent a conscious/unconscious state, what Melville describes as being "half steeped in dreams" and what Hawthorne deems an only partially awake condition in which "imagination is a mirror, imparting vividness to all ideas, without the power of selecting them or controlling them." Thus, for example, the reader encounters the uncertainty of the mysterious figure's staff in "Young Goodman Brown," which is carved in the image of a snake and that actually appears to "twist and wriggle itself like a living serpent," owing perhaps to an "ocular deception, assisted by the uncertain light."[28] (This, of course, is only one of many uncertainties built into the tale.) And thus we mark Ishmael refusing to tie up or draw a circle around his tale of the night visitor or tell us what we are to glean from it, or even what it has to do at all with the feeling of Queequeg's embrace: "Nay, to this very hour, I often puzzle myself with it," is his inconclusive ending.[29]

Melville had been begun experimenting with ambiguity and uncertainty in *Mardi*, and tying it to psychological explorations (again, that book explores "the world of the mind," as he explicitly tells the reader), but he hadn't yet gotten a firm and deft hand on this tendency. It was the work of Hawthorne that gave him a road map — and in this and other ways he absorbed the tones of Hawthorne then extended them and bent them toward his own purpose, ultimately sublimating the influence into an expression utterly his own. In *Mardi*, the reader encounters a chapter subtitled "They Sail Round an Island without Landing; and Talk Round a Subject without Getting at It,"[30] which is illustrative of Melville's emerging uncertain — and essentially proto-modernist — mode, but here conveyed in a clever, nudge-nudge, and ultimately more ham-fisted manner.

But perhaps the best symbolic examples of Hawthorne's and Melville's powerful ambiguity and uncertainty come in the form of Dimmesdale's revealing of his own stigmatic mark upon his breast in the concluding moments of *The Scarlet Letter* (1850) and in Ahab's nailing of the doubloon (Spanish gold coin) to the mainmast in *Moby-Dick* (1851). Both of these books, coming in 1850 and 1851, illustrate the authorial mindset of the writers around the time of their new friendship, and these two symbols are central to the works in question: the *Pequod* mariners revere the doubloon as "the white whale's talisman"[31] while Dimmesdale's scarlet marking in his actual flesh mirrors Hester's hand-crafted and titular "A." Both are also are keys to understanding Melville and Hawthorne's resistance toward authorial certainty and absolute narrative meaning. Of course, Melville's illustrative passage has not stopped a century's-plus of readers from trying to insist on the whale as representing some-"thing"—besides a white whale, of course. (Conservative pundit George Will perhaps had the final, albeit crankish, word on this, castigating what he saw as a reductive and ideological slant of literary studies in the early 1990s: "Emily Dickinson's poetic references to peas and flower buds are encoded messages of feminist rage, exulting clitoral masturbation to protest the prison of patriarchal sex roles," he sarcastically fumed. "Melville's white whale? Probably a penis. Grab a harpoon!")[32]

That Dimmesdale's own scarlet letter and the *Pequod's* doubloon are central to the respective works—though one degree removed in mirroring Hester's badge and being the white whale's "talisman"—is clear. How to read them is purposefully not so clear, as Hawthorne and Melville swerve both "symbols" toward an exegesis on symbolic ambiguity, toward the idea that, as Richard Ruland and Malcolm Bradbury assert (regarding Melville, specifically, in this case), "any and all meaning must remain uncertain."[33] Melville might have used Ishmael's words during the early, landed stages of *Moby-Dick* to draw the same conclusion: "It is the image of the ungraspable phantom of life; and this is the key to it all."[34] After Dimmesdale's revelation of his scarlet marking, in the high, striking moments of conclusion, Hawthorne uses what F.O. Mathiesson in *American Renaissance* has termed "the device of multiple choice."[35] The spectators to Dimmesdale's unveiling, upon reflecting on what they witnessed, conjure up "various explanations" as to how it came to be, without the author stepping with a definitive explanation—and, of course, Hawthorne unburdened himself from authority in the introductory "The Custom House" by declaring the whole thing to be a found story. "The reader may choose among these theories," Hawthorne writes. He then pulls the rug completely out from beneath the reader, adding that some "highly respectable" spectators, who "professed never to once have removed their eyes from the Reverend ... denied that there was any mark whatever on his breast, more than on a new-born infant's."[36]

This suspension of certainty in Hawthorne's work liberated Melville, who had given himself a crash course in the bulk of the older writer's work during the writing of *Moby-Dick*, and drove him to refine his own tendency toward the compellingly ambiguous. A clear indication of this, as mentioned, is the characters' reactions to the doubloon (Spanish gold coin) which Ahab had ceremoniously nailed to the mainmast as reward to whoever may raise the white whale. The coin becomes then a dominant and central symbol — that is, *physically* it is located at the center of everything, right on the "main"-mast, with all of the action swirling about it. Melville also takes pains to show that the coin came from Ecuador, "a country planted in the middle of the world, and beneath the equator," heightening its centrality and importance to all things.[37] The coin, in being revered by the crew as the whale's talisman, therefore bears connection to the very fate of the *Pequod*. For Melville, the act of "reading" the coin — of reading this most important and central symbol — becomes the act of *reading* and the act of interpretation itself. But, showing even more resistance toward certainty of meaning than Dimmesdale's scarlet letter, Melville *presents* the symbol, *emphasizes* the symbol, and then, by having the characters interpret it variously and to death, reduces it to *nothing* and absurdity. Clearly, this is the kind of multiperspectival and untidy mode that anticipated twentieth century modernism (T.S. Eliot's "The Waste Land," for example) and that frustrated and confused many contemporary readers of the time. The only thing that becomes certain as the various characters "read" the coin and offer up their interpretation of the coin is uncertainty.

For Ahab, of course, interpretation becomes an egotistical act in which "every man in turn but mirrors back his own mysterious self." Therefore, in examining the coin's depictions, he yields up only Ahab: "The firm tower, that is Ahab; the volcano, that is Ahab; the courageous, the undaunted, and victorious fowl, that, too, is Ahab."[38] For the monomaniacal captain, reading means imposing himself on and into the text, much as he imposes his obsession on the entire crew and voyage; for Ahab is not passive, receptive, or open to anything beyond himself and his own drive: "[S]mall gains for those who ask the world to solve them," he asserts, "it cannot solve itself."[39] Through Stubb, Melville takes another, more humorous, jab at those would read into a text what they want to see, imposing their own ego and desires upon it: "Book! you lie there; the fact is, you books must know your places. You'll do to give us the bare words and facts, but we come in to supply the thoughts," he chides, as if admonishing a spaniel.[40] The noble Starbuck, by contrast, offers up a soulful and spiritual reading of the coin's symbols, but one that only highlights his own powerlessness and lack of intellectual scope. "So in this vale of Death, God girds us round; and over all our gloom, the sun of Righteousness still shines a beacon and a hope."[41] For Melville — the endless questioner, skeptic, and ponderer of metaphysics and religion — Starbuck's weakness lies in his faith and therefore in his being a dogged follower with an utter lack of imagination. And Starbuck wants no part of what he might see if he really scrutinizes the doubloon outside the lens of his prescribed doctrines, muttering a paradox as he turns away: "I will quit it, lest Truth shake me falsely."[42] Starbuck, then, is ultimately as foolhardy a reader as Ahab and Stubb. (Melville likely had in mind the harsh, moralistic book reviews he had received because of his critiques of Protestant missionaries, critiques that he based on what he witnessed in the South Pacific and categorized as hypocrisy and cruelty.) The shallow third mate Flask is the blunt, hyper-literal, and unthinking reader who sees nothing beyond the surface: "I see nothing here, but a round thing made of gold, and whoever raises a certain whale, this round thing belongs to him. So, what's all this staring been about?" He sees the sixteen dollars that it is literally worth, which for him means, at two cents a cigar, "nine hundred and sixty cigars ... I like cigars."[43] (Clearly, his math is poor too.) Hidden and observing other mariners reading into the coin, Stubb archly exclaims, highlighting the shifting meanings, "There's another rendering now; but still one text."[44] Ultimately, of course, the unfortunate, mind-addled Pip collapses the whole thing in on itself, underscoring the uncertainty of reading any one thing (or perhaps *anything*) into the doubloon. "I look, you look, he looks; we look, ye look, they look,"[45] he conjugates, speaking, as Andrew Delbanco underscores it, "the candid truth that they all see the world as a reflection of themselves,"[46] and displaying himself, despite his declared idiocy, as the only one with an encompassing enough scale of vision to recognize this. But ultimately, like Macbeth's tale told by an idiot (Melville was steeped in the Bard's plays at the time), Pip too signifies nothing, as his conjugating deteriorates into nonsensical jabber: "and we, ye, and they, are all bats; and I'm a crow, especially when I stand a'top of this pine tree here. Caw! caw! caw! caw! caw! caw! Ain't I a crow? And where's the scare-crow? There he stands; two bones stuck into an old pair of trowsers, and two more poked into the sleeves of an old jacket."[47] Through this lack certainty, and through the multiple voices, Melville creates a narrative in which there is no dominant perspective or meaning — and speaks to the larger infrastructure of *Moby-Dick*, in which the empirical information, the wild adventure tale, the metaphysical disquisitions, the psychological delving, the human drama, and the first-person narrative of Ishmael all compete for space. In fact, is there anything more uncertain than our narrator, Ishmael, who welcomes readers so intimately into the tale and then, at times, recedes from the text completely as we behold scenes and information that only an omniscient eye could have witnessed? By the time of the tellingly titled *Pierre; Or, the Ambiguities* (1852), Melville's experience writing *Moby-Dick* has galvanized a view of the novel that jibes with his worldview. The reader finds out somewhat abruptly (and *in media res*) that title figure is a writer, and through Pierre's character and vocation, Melville lays out an exegesis on uncertainty and ambiguity:

> Like all youths, Pierre had conned his novel-lessons; had read more novels than most persons of his years; but their false, inverted attempts at systematizing eternally unsystemizable elements; their audacious, intermeddling impotency, in trying to unravel, and spread out, and classify, the more thin than gossamer threads which make up the complex web of life; these things over Pierre had no power now. Straight through their helpless miserableness he pierced; the one sensational truth in him transfixed like beetles all the speculative lies in them ... [H]e saw, that not always doth life's beginning gloom conclude in gladness; that wedding-bells peal not ever in the last scene of life's fifth act; that while the countless tribes of common novels laboriously spin veils of mystery, only to complacently clear them up at last; and while the countless tribe of common dramas do but repeat the same; yet the profounder emanations of the human mind, intended to illustrate all that can be humanly known of human life; these never unravel their own intricacies, and have no proper endings; but in imperfect, unanticipated, and disappointing sequels (as mutilated stumps), hurry to abrupt intermergings with the eternal tides of time and fate [Book VII].[48]

Ambiguity and uncertainty: Melville recognized the power in these modes, recognized their relative mastery in Hawthorne, and adapted them toward his own vision. He also recognized that is wasn't an end in and of itself, but at its most powerful arose from the areas where dream and waking or outer and inner both met and blended. This was a relatively organic instinct for him, of course — he had begun to forge into these borderlands before, albeit not as successfully; but the absorption of Hawthorne helped him to coalesce this intention.

Therefore, in late 1851 one gets a sense of Melville squaring up to the task of reentering *Moby-Dick* and employing this influence and inspiration that he had voiced through "Hawthorne and His Mosses." True,

some of the review piece is puffery and a role Melville is playing, behind
the mask of a genteel southerner, but glimpses emerge of what is catalytic
in Hawthorne for Melville, as he speaks of "such manifold, strange and
diffusive beauties" in the work of the older author and surmises that
some of the tales are "directly calculated to deceive — egregiously deceive,
the superficial skimmer of pages."[49] Newly kindled by Hawthorne's imaginative scapes, in "Hawthorne and His Mosses" Melville is still trying to
find the appropriate language to describe what he perceives, and he falls
to the supernatural, describing a "secret sign" and "wondrous, occult
properties," which through "very rare accident ... may chance to be called
forth here on earth." Hawthorne tips his own hand toward this tendency
in the "Custom-House" introduction to *The Scarlet Letter*, when he
describes a condition in which "the Actual and the Imaginary may meet,
and each imbue itself with the nature of the other."[50] (Similarly, Melville
would write in *The Confidence-Man* [1857], "It is with fiction as with
religion; it should present another world, and yet one to which we feel
the tie.")[51] Hawthorne's manifestation of that Actual/Imaginary inter-
penetration emerges in "Young Goodman Brown," which Melville
deemed as "deep as Dante"[52] and which drew his particular attention in
the "Mosses" piece. In "Young Goodman Brown," Hawthorne achieves
stirring effect and great dramatic potential through this ambiguity —
the cloaked identity of the second traveler, for example, who seems to
be at once a "devil" figure and an aspect of Goodman Brown himself
with his "considerable resemblance" to him and their appearing to look
like "father and son."[53] Additionally, things seen and heard in the gloom
of the forest are hypnagogic, hallucinative, and transitory: The strains
of a familiar hymn sung by a choir of recognized voices become a chorus
"not of human voices, but of all the sounds of the benighted wilderness
pealing in awful harmony together."[54] This "blackness" (Melville's term
from the "Mosses" piece) and this borderlands landscape of Hawthorne's
ignited something in Melville. But where Hawthorne will point to the
uncertainty and directly pose the question of whether Brown had "only
dreamed a wild dream of a witch-meeting" — again, as he did with
Dimmesdale's scarlet marking, offering options for the reader — Melville
is up to something less fathomable, less clear, and altogether more complicated in *Moby-Dick*.

Melville not only achieved a similar command and, as F.O. Mathiessen would phrase it, a "realm of emotional forces quite out of
Hawthorne's range,"[55] he in effect (to cite Mathiessen again) conjured

up "a whole extension of consciousness."[56] Again, however, it is important to stress that the very modes of ambiguity and uncertainty that were often perceived as weaknesses in Melville's own time (as was his patchwork narrative structure) are the qualities through which *Moby-Dick* derives much of its psychological power. And although the land-born chapters are less daunting in this respect, one gets a sense of where Melville is headed very early on, in the opening chapter "Loomings," when Ishmael declares, "Yes, as everyone knows, meditation and water are wedded for ever."[57] And it is, of course, once the ship sets sail that Melville delves into his deepest meditations and seems to, at times, sound those subconscious depths. But this is more than just "meditation"; according to Ishmael, we see "that same image" of ourselves "in all rivers and oceans" that Narcissus saw in the fountain before he plunged toward his drowning death: "It is the image of the ungraspable phantom of life; and this is the key to it all."[58] At the simplest level, Ishmael is exploring the mystery of why so many people are drawn to watery shores to gaze outward in "ocean reveries" ("How then is this? ... What do they here?" he asks.).[59] At another level, he is establishing the world of *Moby-Dick*, which is partly the world of the mind — it is that "ungraspable" region where unconsciousness and consciousness meet and "each imbue itself with the nature of the other."[60] Melville is taking the Hawthornian confusion between actual and imaginary and expanding it and deepening it down (to paraphrase his "Mosses" wording) into more profoundly psychological territory. Put in another way, Melville's ambiguity is more ambiguous; he does not pose for the readers any multiple choice solution for events (did Dimmesdale bear a scarlet letter or not? Was Young Goodman Brown's night ceremony experience a dream or reality?) For Melville, the deeper mysteries of existence — of psychology, metaphysics, and ontology ("the phantom[s] of life") are "ungraspable." This is the key to it all, and the key to *Moby-Dick*, which explores deeply but inconclusively. (That is, Melville's key is in fact no key at all for any reader who seeks and needs definitive resolution.) To doubt this is to deny the fact that he subtitled his next book, *Pierre*, "the Ambiguities" or to deny Hawthorne's own wonderment at his friend the last time they would meet, in 1856, in England:

> Melville, as he always does, began to reason of Providence and of futurity, and of everything that lies beyond human ken.... It is strange how he persists — and has persisted ever since I knew him, and probably long before — in wandering to and fro over these deserts, as dismal and monotonous as

the sand hills amid which we were sitting. He can neither believe nor be comfortable in his unbelief.[61]

Fittingly, the two men were sitting by the sea (on dunes, gazing upon the Irish Sea), which Ishmael has forever wedded to meditation. More importantly, though, in this description we see Melville through Hawthorne's eyes—something that the missing side of his correspondence (letters that Melville presumably burned, likely at Nathaniel's request) deprives us of. And what Hawthorne recognizes and describes in Melville's personality is the tendency we experience in *Moby-Dick:* A roving, nomadic, deeply explorative impulse with unwillingness to settle upon a single resolution (often taken up through a psychological mode). The very discomfort that Hawthorne attributes to his friend in this state is the very "discomfort" of reading *Moby-Dick* at times. Hence, the aforementioned scene with Queequeg and Ishmael in bed, lodged somewhere in an inconclusive state between awake and dreaming, conjures a memory of a ghostly and inconclusive night visitation: "I lost myself in confounding attempts to explain the mystery," writes Melville through Ishmael. "Nay, to this very hour, I often puzzle myself with it."[62] In this ambiguous state, "*half*-steeped in dreams" (emphasis mine) Ishmael and Queequeg also seem, for a moment, twinned parts of a single consciousness, with Melville moving in between the conventional or obvious (Ishmael's comical predicament in the embrace of a sleeping Queequeg) and the ambiguous and mysterious—that is, Queequeg rendered ethereal and compared to a "phantom" form and "supernatural" experience in that twilight state between dream and waking. And Melville makes it clear that we are in the inconclusive realm of psychological experience when he writes, "I knew not how this consciousness at last glided away from me."[63]

A more obvious and sustained example of characters blurring into each other to become components of the same psyche emerges through the pairing of Ahab and Fedallah, the Parsee. And in setting this up, Melville again slides back and forth between conventional or conscious narrative elements and that which could be termed ambiguous, unconscious, and dream-like material. This originates in two types of foreshadowing prior to the *Pequod* setting sail. First, of course, there is the more conventional and obvious, rendered in the form of Elijah (a character with clear canonical roots, from the Bible), who suggests that signing with the ship means signing away one's soul and who speaks of an inexorable fate that surrounds Ahab ("it's all fixed and arranged a'ready").[64] But then Elijah's more direct foreboding gives way to Melville's "little lower layer" (to borrow a term from Ahab), when the Parsee and his men slip aboard the *Pequod*. All of this is cast behind a dream-like veil of uncertainty, the figures glimpsed only as shadowy apparitions in a "grey imperfect misty dawn" when it is "too dim to be sure."[65] Later, using the same language he used in the bed scene, Ishmael continually describes them as "phantoms." Then, of course, they disappear, and Ishmael cannot figure out where they have gone to or who or what he has seen. Melville keys us into the fact that we are dealing (at least partly) with a dream state and unconscious concerns through a second, brief encounter with Elijah that occurs simultaneously. Trying to shake off the ominous forecaster, Ishmael asks him to withdraw from his and Queequeg's company, noting, "We are going to the Indian and Pacific Oceans, and would prefer not to be detained."[66] "Ye be, be ye?" cracks Elijah. "Coming back afore breakfast?" Elijah here parallels the *Pequod's* journey to the time elapsed during one night of sleep — and therefore, of course, dreaming. And when Fedallah and his men do finally appear — at the first sighting of sperm whales and the first lowering — Melville uses imagery that would be ascribed to dreams, referring to them as "five dusky phantoms that seemed fresh formed out of air."[67]

As to Fedallah himself, Melville overtly paints him as an aspect of Ahab, particularly noting how when the two stand close together, the "Parsee occupied his shadow; while, if the Parsee's shadow was there at all it seemed only to blend with, and lengthen Ahab's."[68] Much later, as the pursuit of the white whale intensifies, the two are seen to "fixedly" gaze at one another, "as if in the Parsee Ahab saw his forethrown shadow, in Ahab the Parsee his abandoned substance."[69] And when Ahab leans over the rail to stare in the water at his reflection, it is Fedallah's eyes that stare back at him.[70] The most specific language we have to describe Fedallah's orientation toward Ahab is psychological theory, coming in the early twentieth century from Carl Jung, who described a *shadow archetype*, "a dark companion which dogs our steps" and who appears in dreams as a "sinister or threatening figure possessing the same sex as the dreamer" or as an "Evil Stranger."[71] Jung presents this as a counterpoint to the persona; it is the secret, often negative, and repressed parts of our character. And the Parsee and his men are hidden and secreted away on the ship early on, only to emerge as Ahab's true madness begins to emerge. The Jungian take provides a good template for the pairing —

the danger, though, in relying too heavily upon a theoretical context's own logic and arrangement, is that *Moby-Dick* — as was once asserted of Cormac McCarthy's *Blood Meridian* (1985, one of the few clear and worthy descendants of *Moby-Dick*) — "seems designed to elude interpretation, especially interpretation that would translate it into some supposedly more essential language."[72] Even without the benefit of Jung's language, however, one can see how Melville is working in the arena where the conscious and unconscious "meet, and each imbue itself with the nature of the other," to again borrow Hawthorne's language (from the "Custom-House" *Scarlet Letter* preface).

In fact, in the sequence leading up to the first lowering and Fedallah and his men's initial appearance on deck, the reader is thrust into such a condition. "So still and subdued and yet somehow preluding was all the scene," narrates Ishmael as "The Mat-Maker" opens, "and such an incantation of revery lurked in the air, that each silent sailor seemed resolved into his own invisible self."[73] Melville, through a series of sibilances, lulls the reader into the same thick reverie that hangs over the scene, in which "so strange a dreaminess did there then reign all over the ship and all over the sea."[74] And for Melville this is the threshold where one can ponder the ungraspable phantoms (in this case the metaphysical). As he and Queequeg mildly and methodically weave a mat,

> it seemed as if this were the Loom of Time, and I myself were a shuttle mechanically weaving and weaving away at the Fates. There lay the fixed threads of the warp subject to but one single, ever returning, unchanging vibration, and that vibration merely enough to admit of the crosswise interblending of other threads with its own. This warp seemed necessity; and here, thought I, with my own hand I ply my own shuttle and weave my own destiny into these unalterable threads. Meantime, Queequeg's impulsive, indifferent sword, sometimes hitting the woof slantingly, or crookedly, or strongly, or weakly, as the case might be; and by this difference in the concluding blow producing a corresponding contrast in the final aspect of the completed fabric; this savage's sword, thought I, which thus finally shapes and fashions both warp and woof; this easy, indifferent sword must be chance — aye, chance, free will, and necessity — wise incompatible — all interweavingly working together. The straight warp of necessity, not to be swerved from its ultimate course — its every alternating vibration, indeed, only tending to that; free will still free to ply her shuttle between given threads; and chance, though restrained in its play within the right lines of necessity, and sideways in its motions directed by free will, though thus prescribed to by both, chance by turns rules either, and has the last featuring blow at events.[75]

The obvious reference here is the to the Greek Fates, but Melville fashions his own philosophy through the mat-making analogy, representing fate as an interplay between chance, free will, and necessity (undoubtedly resonating the example of his own path through life up to that point). But he is also adapting Thomas Carlyle's *Sartor Resartus*, which he had read recently and deeply. The English writer — with his blends of fact and fiction and wit and probing thought, and his representation of "truth" as slippery and inclusive — appealed directly to Melville's sensibilities and the worldview he was carving out in *Moby-Dick*. In *Sartor Resartus*, Carlyle describes a "Dream-grotto" or the "Canvas (the warp and woof thereof) whereon all our Dreams and Life-visions are painted."[76] His extended metaphor of all of existence as a dream — "This Dreaming, this Somnambulism is what we on Earth call Life"[77] — is one that Melville will adapt to his purpose. In Carlyle's thought, we can only fleetingly glimpse the grand design or the infinite in "rare half-waking moments"[78] — again, that threshold between sleep and waking that both Hawthorne and Melville explore. And just as dreams, as expressions of the unconscious, call into question our sense of time and place, Carlyle uses the dream analogy to question these constructions. In *Sartor Resartus*, "where" and "when" become the "master-colours of our Dream-grotto," or, expressed more bluntly, "there *is* no Space and no Time."[79] (The emphasis is Carlyle's.) All of these ideas in the Carlyle piece emerge from the meditation-prone individual who asks, "Who am I; What is this ME?" much like the stream of thought that arises from Melville's use of the reflection in the water (Narcissus and Ahab), which leads to his central idea early on in *Moby-Dick*: "It is the image of the ungraspable phantom of life; and this is the key to it all."

In Carlyle, Melville finds an infrastructure for his thought — for the dream logic that he will employ in *Moby-Dick*, a "logic" that blows certainty and authority out of the water, even the idea of the individual "self," but in Hawthorne he finds catalytic and literary examples, bolstered by descriptive and imagistic power, more suited to his own mode, and, of course, an undeniably "American" (in Melville's best sense of the word) strain of literary expression. Melville and Hawthorne are both preoccupied with uncertain imagery and events that are outside the locus of control and at the periphery of attention and apprehension. Therefore, their literary efforts often verge into explorations of the unconscious through dream or dream-like situations; dreams being the place where unconscious processes manifest themselves in symbolic and imagistic form. More specifically, they are fascinated with *liminality*— that is, the disorienting, ambiguous threshold where the two (dreaming/awake; unconscious/conscious) blur into each other. In the opening of the "Haunted Mind," Hawthorne brings us straight to this threshold:

> What a singular moment is the first one, when you have hardly begun to recollect yourself, after starting from midnight slumber! By unclosing your eyes so suddenly, you seem to have surprised the personages of your dream in full convocation round your bed, and catch one broad glance at them before they can flit into obscurity. Or, to vary the metaphor, you find yourself, for a single instant, wide awake in that realm of illusions, whither sleep has been the passport, and behold its ghostly inhabitants and wondrous scenery, with a perception of their strangeness, such as you never attain while the dream is undisturbed.[80]

"[T]he personages of your dream in full convocation round your bed," certainly conjures up the sinister ceremonial meeting of "Young Goodman Brown," after which Hawthorne puts it upon the reader to decide whether it was a dream or not. Both writers attempt to translate the liminal experience into literary exploration, and this is where their powerful ambiguity and compelling lack of authority emerges: Melville's ungraspable phantoms and Hawthorne's "passive sensibility" or state of imagination in which vividness is imparted to "all ideas, without the power of selecting or controlling them."[81] To apply the idea to their creative processes, Hawthorne and Melville not only have a sense that their richest creativity as writers comes from both conscious effort and unconscious impulses and that the line between the two can be confusing — they try to represent that very ambiguity on the page. Melville became the Melville of *Moby-Dick* when he was able to sustain the impulse that was scattershot in previous efforts, when, as Mathiessen described it, "the two halves of his experience, his outer and inner life, [became] fused in expression."[82]

Because Melville read Hawthorne deeply and appreciatively, and because he was so affected by that reading experience around the time that he readdressed the *Moby-Dick* manuscript, it is clear that this outer/inner impulse in Hawthorne helped galvanize his own vision. In Hawthorne, he found a writer steeped in dream logic and the sort of sliding consciousness Melville himself would come to master — and one who had built a consistent and fully formed artistic vision around such impulses. "The Haunted Mind" is more of an essay, an artistic manifesto regarding this movement across dream logic, dream thresholds, and dream imagery, but a story such as "The Celestial Railroad" plants itself clearly in this realm in the opening lines: "Not a great while ago, passing through the gate of dreams, I visited that region of the earth in which lies the famous City of Destruction."[83] In this case, it is a heavy-handed announcement and permission to enter the slippery logic of a dream state. In the masterful "The Birthmark," however, the reader is on uncertain ground, sliding along the continuum between the world of waking and dreams without clear markers. In fact, the psychic pairing of Ahab and Fedallah has its roots in "The Birthmark," in the relationship between Aylmer and his "servant," Aminadab. The story, of course, was collected in *Mosses from an Old Manse*, which Melville read around the time of the Hawthorne meeting and which he celebrated in the review "Hawthorne and His Mosses." And Melville's preoccupation with the unconscious and dream manifestations is apparent by two particular passages he marked in "The Birth-Mark" in his own copy of *Mosses from an Old Manse*. The first: "Truth often finds its way to the mind close muffled in robes of sleep, and then speaks with uncompromising directness of matters in regard to which we practise an unconscious self-deception during our waking moments."[84] And the second: "The mind is in a sad state when Sleep, the all-involving, cannot confine her spectres within the dim region of her sway, but suffers them to break forth, affrighting this actual life with secrets that perchance belong to a deeper one."[85] The two passages directly describe states that Melville would apply in *Moby-Dick*.

In "The Birth-Mark," much can be (and has been) made of Aminadab's name, both in its Biblical roots and in its backwards rendering of "bad anima," but the moniker is likely more of a bout of antagonism toward the would-be interpreter, for Hawthorne directly spells out that Aminadab, "With his vast strength, his shaggy hair, his smoky aspect, and the indescribable earthiness ... seemed to represent man's physical nature." And, Aylmer's "slender figure, and pale, intellectual face, were no less apt a type of the spiritual element."[86] One gets a sense that Hawthorne, through Aminadab, is dealing with psychology or human nature because Georgiana never really seems to see or acknowledge him. Additionally, Aminadab is not a fully fleshed-out human character — Hawthorne renders him in the crudest terms, as some kind of shaggy, brutish entity prone to grunts and occasional bouts of soulfulness (as in his questioning of Aylmer's objective to remove Georgiana's birthmark). Even Hawthorne's contemporary critics appreciated his proto–Freudian, psychological plumbings. In 1851, a reviewer, Henry

Tuckerman, praised Hawthorne in such terms, noting, "What the scientific use of lenses—the telescope and the microscope—does for us in relation to the external universe, the psychological writer achieves in regard to our own nature."[87] In retrospect, Hawthorne has been credited with devising a "nascent ... pop psychology for the middle class."[88] At times, however, and unlike Melville (and because he was often working with allegory), the seams of his craft are more apparent and heavy-handed, as when spells it out that Aminadab and Aylmer are two sides of the same nature. What Melville saw in "The Birthmark," however, was a model for the psychological twinning we see in Ahab and Fedallah. Moreover, through Aylmer's destructive pursuit of perfection, Hawthorne presents a template for the type of destructive obsession that is illustrated in Ahab. All of which is not to say that Melville wasn't wrestling with these elements before his protean encounter with Hawthorne and his work, but that the experience of deeply reading *Mosses from an Old Manse* at the exact right time helped crystallize these impulses—and he absorbed and transmuted the Hawthorne influence into his own discrete forms. He had never encountered a writer like Hawthorne; the reading experience was uncanny and transformative. Ultimately, however, Melville was too clever and too seamless for their age; in Hawthorne, at least, the reader encounters clearer signals and markers when entering or when in the uncertain and ambiguous realm of the psychological.

The argument is harder to make regarding the issue of reciprocal influence—of Melville's influence upon Hawthorne—largely because of the absence of Hawthorne's letters to Melville, particularly the letter in which he praised *Moby-Dick* in terms that made the younger writer euphoric (as evidenced by Melville's own letter in response). It is also harder to make because Hawthorne was a writer with decades of publications behind him and in his mid-forties by the time of the friendship. But we do know that Hawthorne made a vehement defense of *Moby-Dick* (vehement for him, at least) against Evert Duyckinck's backhanded review of the book; additionally, as explored in an earlier chapter, we do know, from an 1850 letter to Duyckinck, that Hawthorne intently and appreciatively read all of Melville's pre–*Moby-Dick* books in one stretch, prior to heading into his work on *The House of the Seven Gables*. Hawthorne was a selfish guardian of his craft and a very deliberate writer; and as an older artist, further into his own development, he was less prone to influence and excitement. Nevertheless, one can see, beginning with the *Seven Gables*, an undeniably "Melvillian" strain of prose creeping in, a strain that Mathiessen would characterize as "the two halves of [Melville's] interest: the immediate and the abstract, the concrete event with the thought rising from it."[89] The aforementioned mat-making scene with Ishmael and Queequeg illustrates this, as does the analysis in chapter two of this book of the fall from the yard arm in *White-Jacket*, a scene that was fresh in Hawthorne's mind when he wrote to Duyckinck that "no writer ever put the reality before the reader more unflinchingly" than Melville.[90] The sentiment is extreme for Hawthorne and the praise is of the highest standard (*"No writer"*) and the message is aimed straight at the literary center of New York City (Duyckinck). (By 1850, Hawthorne was certainly aware enough of his own significant literary reputation, and aware enough of the capital of his own praise, to avoid frivolity with words.) By the time he gets deep into the writing of *Seven Gables*, an undeniably Melville-like handling of the "concrete event with the thought rising from it" has crept into his vision. This stopping on a dime and halting narrative movement to interrogate the momentary for metaphysical and/or ontological implications is a distinct tendency in *Moby-Dick*, and a prose strain that one encounters in Melville's next-century stylistic inheritors (William Faulkner, Cormac McCarthy, Toni Morrison). Hawthorne, in the fresh thrall of reading and knowing Herman Melville, was also not immune, as a striking passage in Chapter 18 of *The House of the Seven Gables* illustrates. "Hawthorne halts his story," writes Brenda Wineapple, "as the narrator speaks of life and death and the sure oblivion that opens beneath our feet"[91]:

> There is still a faint appearance at the window; neither a glow, nor a gleam, nor a glimmer, — any phrase of light would express something far brighter than this doubtful perception, or sense, rather, that there is a window there. Has it yet vanished? No! — yes! — not quite! And there is still the swarthy whiteness, — we shall venture to marry these ill-agreeing words, — the swarthy whiteness of Judge Pyncheon's face. The features are all gone: there is only the paleness of them left. And how looks it now? There is no window! There is no face! An infinite, inscrutable blackness has annihilated sight! Where is our universe? All crumbled away from us; and we, adrift in chaos, may hearken to the gusts of homeless wind, that go sighing and murmuring about in quest of what was once a world!
>
> Is there no other sound? One other, and a fearful one. It is the ticking of the Judge's watch, which, ever since Hepzibah left the room in search of Clifford, he has been holding in his hand. Be the cause what it may, this little, quiet, never-ceasing throb of Time's pulse, repeating its small strokes

with such busy regularity, in Judge Pyncheon's motionless hand, has an effect of terror, which we do not find in any other accompaniment of the scene.[92]

Wineapple also claims, regarding this riveting passage, that "this singular novel goes where books have not yet tread, stopping time entirely."[93] Nevertheless, as we have seen — particularly in the scene describing the fall from the yard-arm in Melville's *White-Jacket* (discussed in chapter two of the book you are reading) — this is a mode that Melville was already exploring, and *White-Jacket* was the last among Melville's books that Hawthorne admiringly read and praised to the heavens immediately before embarking upon *The House of the Seven Gables*. This is a strikingly new form for Hawthorne, and a new form of writing in general, but it is one that Hawthorne seems to have adapted, consciously or not, from his reading of Melville. Of course, Hawthorne also began *House of the Seven Gables* shortly after "Hawthorne and His Mosses" appeared in New York City's *Literary World*, and the quality and nature of Melville's praise reverberated through the Hawthorne household. Therefore, in *Seven Gables*, one also finds the writer conjuring up some of his "darkest" and "blackest" episodes yet, seemingly prodded along and encouraged to go even deeper by Melville's assessment and characterization of these very qualities. And where he had painted with more subtle and suggestive blacks in the past, he is now overt, bringing all of his ancestral Salem *sturm und drang* to bear upon the pages of the book. Blood curses, corpses, and ancestral burdens weigh in on the book. Of Hawthorne's tales, Melville had written, "You may be witched by his sunlight, — transported by the bright gildings in the skies he builds over you; — but there is the blackness of darkness beyond." And one half of the writer's "soul," proclaimed Melville, "like the dark half of the physical sphere — is shrouded in a blackness, ten times black."[94] It was, he declared, a "great power of blackness" in Hawthorne that "derives its force from its appeals to that Calvinistic sense of Innate Depravity and Original Sin."[95]

Hawthorne must have cherished the image of his craft as he saw it reflected in Melville's eyes. He didn't gush appreciation, as Sophia did, over the "Mosses" review; rather, he evinced it under a cloak of perhaps feigned, yet typical, humility. He had, he wrote to Evert Duyckinck, read the pieces (it appeared in two parts in August 1850) "with very great pleasure," opining that the reviewer (still unknown to him) was "no common man": "[I]t is good to have bewitched such a man into praising me more than I deserve," wrote Hawthorne. This was no common man and therefore no common review; it was a perspective that Hawthorne took to heart and one that threw new light for him upon his own work. And its points rang even more when he learned that the writer was Melville, the man whose books Hawthorne read closely and appreciatively, asserting that the work contained "depths ... that compel a man to swim for his life."[96] *The House of the Seven Gables*, taken up in the freshness of the Melville friendship, was clearly in many ways a work energized and spurred on by Melville. The "Mosses" review; long days stretched upon the hay gorging on *Typee, Omoo, Mardi, Redburn,* and *White-Jacket*; the penetrating conversations with Melville about writing and all matters of existence — all of these conspired upon Hawthorne as *Seven Gables* began to assume its shape and essence in the low writing room in the upper-floor of the small red cottage in Lenox. Though, of course, there's a traditional, apocryphal strain of thought regarding the relationship that doesn't allow for much degree of counteradmiration and counterinfluence — but it is one that outright ignores or casts aside primary evidence in the face of a tantalizing blank slate imposed by parcel of destroyed letters.

By November 1850, toiling during the early part of the day, only six miles away from each other, the two writers were on parallel paths, deeply immersed in their respective works. *Moby-Dick* had begun to deepen and expand — that is, had begun to assume its multiple facets and unconventional form and had launched Melville into a writing sphere that was entirely uncharted. And it is easy to forget that, in this arena at least — that is, the long-form — Melville was the more veteran of the two, and Hawthorne was the neophyte. Yes, Melville had bolted through his five books in rapid succession and had not, as Hawthorne divined, "brooded long" over them in an effort to make them "a great deal better," but Hawthorne only had one protracted romance (discounting *Fanshawe*) to his credit, *The Scarlet Letter*, and even that had begun its life as a shorter work and was ultimately rather brief for a long-form "romance" (as Hawthorne liked to distinguish his work). Melville's huge, productive gusts of labor were on Nathaniel's mind as he wrote the *House of the Seven Gables*. Hawthorne even framed out his vision of Melville's creative process in *A Wonder-Book for Boys and Girls*, a children's work he published during the summer of 1851: "On the hither side of Pittsfield sits Herman Melville, shaping out the gigantic conception of his 'White Whale,' while the gigantic shape of Graylock [*sic*] looms upon him from his study-window."[97] Hawthorne's own labors were a distinct contrast to this "gigantic conception," the herculean effort he attributed to Melville. Having habituated himself to the precision of his fine-tuned, tightly wound short stories, Hawthorne wouldn't and couldn't reconfigure his patterns to the longer form; he was like Owen Warland from his own tale "The Artist of the Beautiful," working on minute machinery with magnifying glass and delicate instruments. "I write diligently, but not so rapidly as I hoped," he informed his publisher, James T. Fields, in early November (1850).[98] This book, he noted, required a great deal of "care and thought," and much of it "ought to be finished with the minuteness of a Dutch picture."[99] At the other end of the spectrum, Melville seemed to be disgorging himself of everything he contained: life experiences and sensations, diverse readings and influences, encyclopedic facts, and barely fathomable philosophy and ruminations. While working on his new romance, Hawthorne also found time to write a preface for a new edition of his early collection *Twice-Told Tales*, slated for publication in March 1851. In it, he examines his youthful work from the perspective of maturity and fame, looking through the window at the sequestered young writer on Herbert Street and deeming him "the obscurest man of letters in America." But he also now sees the early stories through Melville's eyes, and just as Melville (in "Hawthorne and His Mosses") lauds the turgid, probing reaches of Hawthorne's later stories, which he declares to be "immeasurably deeper than the plummet of the mere critic,"[100] so too does Hawthorne, in that light, find a comparative meekness in his earlier creations. Looking back — and deep into the creation of the dark and turbulent *House of the Seven Gables* — he perceives "the pale tint of flowers that blossomed in too retired a shade." Instead "of passion, there is sentiment," he sighs.[101] (As established, the Melville piece "Hawthorne and His Mosses" undoubtedly had a strong impact on Nathaniel's self-perception as a writer, an impression that he carried into *The House of the Seven Gables*.)

Interestingly, however, Melville actually came to admire the more modest hues of the *Twice-Told Tales* and the different aspect of Hawthorne they conveyed. Having received an earlier, inscribed edition as a gift from Hawthorne early in 1851, and now for the first time reading Hawthorne's earliest stories (after having already lauded his later stories), Melville declared to Duyckinck, "[T]hey are, I fancy, an earlier vintage from his vine. Some of those sketches are wonderfully subtle. Their deeper meanings are worthy of a Brahmin."[102] One should also note Melville's association of the word "vine" with Hawthorne. This anticipates both his later poem *Clarel* (1876), which presents a Hawthorne-like character named Vine, and the reference to "the shyest grape" in his poem "Monody," which many—this writer included—consider to be about Hawthorne. During late 1850 and on into 1851, Hawthorne's tales were flickering among Melville's key influences as he crafted out *Moby-Dick*. One line from "The Gentle Boy" that Melville underlined in his copy of *Twice-Told Tales* particularly stands out and seems to echo in the opening salvo of the whale book: "'Friend,' replied the little boy in a sweet though faltering voice, 'they call me Ilbrahim and my home is here.'"[103]

Enchanted as he was by the works of Nathaniel Hawthorne, Melville struggled with the emotional aloofness of the older writer. Amidst praising *Twice-Told Tales* to the heavens, Herman, writing to Duyckinck, pondered, "Still there is something lacking—a good deal lacking—to the plump sphericity of the man. What is that? ... He doesn't patronize the butcher—he needs roast beef, done rare."[104] But Melville was quick to qualify that, confounding elements of personality aside, "Nevertheless ... I regard Hawthorne (*in his books*) as evincing a quality of genius." (Emphasis via italics is mine; parentheses are Melville's.) As a writer, declared Melville, he was "loftier, & more profound, too, than any other American."[105] Now that the initial glow of their sudden kinship had subsided, Melville could not help but notice that his powerful volleys of affection were not returned with the same ardor, and he had begun to separate Hawthorne the sentient being from Hawthorne the authorial voice. Melville was still inextricably tied to his own works—the readers of his tales perceived the adventures therein to be the adventures of Melville himself (and in many ways, embellishments aside, they were). But Hawthorne did not, and likely could not, exhibit in person anywhere near the emotional range of his own work and was indeed "the shyest grape" Melville would later describe in "Monody"; supposedly even Sophia, as her sister Elizabeth Peabody would relate in later years, declared that Nathaniel's "passions were under his feet."[106]

Hawthorne, of course, remained tucked away and oblivious to such scrutiny in the red cottage on the rim of the Stockbridge Bowl throughout the winter of 1850 to 1851, immersed in work and nestled among his family: the little children, Una and Julian, and Sophia, who was now pregnant with Rose (to arrive on May 20, 1851). Hawthorne, at the advanced age of 46, was deeply settled in the beatific domestic rhythms of a growing family, and though he was inclined to damper his expression of greater joys, Sophia was not so inclined; she was outwardly rapturous, even in the heart of a Berkshires winter, ensconced in the small shabby cottage. In letters, she celebrated "opaline mists" cloaking the morning mountain-views and offered radiant descriptions of the children: "Such clear, unclouded eyes! Such superb cheeks, as come in and out of the icy atmosphere! such relish for dry bread, such dewy sleep, such joyful upris-ings, such merry gambols under pails of cold water [in the fire-warmed bathroom]!" In the early mornings, Hawthorne rose to feed the chickens and have breakfast; then he disappeared upstairs to his cramped study to immerse himself in *The House of the Seven Gables*, wearing a worn, faded purple and gold damask-patterned robe that Sophia had made for him and settling down to a hinged mahogany lap-desk that she had cleaned, polished, and lined with interior velvet upholstery. (As an adult, Julian remembered his father in his dressing gown, and the ink stains on the skirt of the garment, where he had continually wiped his pen.) At noon, he descended to the sound and atmosphere of, in Sophia's words, "great rejoicing throughout his kingdom" as the children were reunited with their father and freed from their morning lessons with their mother.[107] The family dined at sunset, and in the evenings, with the children in bed, the couple enjoyed the privacy and insularity of each other's company, with Nathaniel often reading other authors' works to his wife (Dickens' *David Copperfield*, for example) and acting out all of the characters. He also read aloud to Sophia parts of his work in progress, and at the end of January she reported to her mother that he had read to her his freshly hewn conclusion of *The House of the Seven Gables*. "There is unspeakable grace and beauty in the conclusion, throw-ing back upon the sterner tragedy of the commencement an ethereal light," she wrote, rhapsodizing over the book's "depth of wisdom, its high tone, the flowers of Paradise scattered over all the dark places" in language that mirrored Melville's assessment of Nathaniel's impulses.[108]

Melville was immersed in parallel circumstances of both blissful domesticity and the mental preoccupation of writing, though Lizzie took young Malcolm (just over eighteen months old) to Boston for an extended stay at her father's home from Thanksgiving to just after the New Year. By mid–December, Melville had rounded upon the eighty-fifth chapter of his whale book ("The Fountain"). And while it was clear to Hawthorne that Melville was composing something altogether vaster than his own book, he displayed no sense of being threatened by Melville's "gigantic conception." Hawthorne prided himself on his own tightly controlled craft; plus Melville's literary world was a watery one, far from his own. This, and Melville's undying admiration and respect for Hawthorne kept the literary friendship uncompetitive and non-threatening. Deep into January and with both authors plunged into their respective literary preoccupations, Melville hooked his horse to his sleigh and glided down to the little red cottage on the Lenox-Stockbridge border. "I found [Hawthorne], of course, buried in snow; & the delightful scenery about him, all wrapped up and tucked away under a napkin, as it were," he reported to Duyckinck.[109] The Hawthornes entertained him with conversation and cold chicken, and Melville invited the whole family to come stay at the more spacious Arrowhead in the near future. The turning inward of the deep, dark months of the mountain winter had caused Melville to miss the probing conversations with his fellow writer — fueled as they were with booze, cigars, and the two big minds bouncing off of each other. Melville did not have men such as Hawthorne's old college chums Franklin Pierce, Horatio Bridge, and Longfellow in his past; his path through life had not afforded him such friendships. True, while living in New York City, he had tapped into Duyckinck's circle, but for Melville these were acquaintances who were more socially than intellectually equipped — or, at least, he did not have as strong an affinity or a meeting of the minds with them as he did with Hawthorne. Melville, had known close pals like Fly and Toby Greene, but the affinity between him and each of them was not a deeper one, of hearts and minds, as he perceived his relationship with Hawthorne to be. Melville's path through those years when such lifelong friendships are made was laden with toil and responsibility — a responsibility to his family (as an adolescent) to work at the bank, a responsibility to his brother to help him in his hat and fur store, a responsibility to his small and rural clutch of students, a responsibility to himself and others (in the face of few options) to leave the limits of the land to find gainful and menial employment on the oceans.

Now, settled and seemingly on the rise in both reputation and circumstance, he relished this presence of Hawthorne, and he sought to hold the friendship as close to him as possible as the months wore on — to savor it and to maximize the encounters as long as the Hawthornes, who were clearly temporary lodgers, stayed in the Berkshires. And though both writers were beset by literary obligations and, of course, obligations to their growing families — Sophia was pregnant with the Hawthorne's third child, while Lizzie would become pregnant early in the year and deliver their second son, Stanwix (named after Herman's grandfather's war heroics at that fort)—Melville wanted to make sure that their new friendship was kept aloft. All too aware of Hawthorne's frequent lapses into social skittishness and insularity, Melville drove the relationship as the year turned.

In late January, after Sophia's polite refusal regarding the Arrowhead visit, Herman penned a firm and jovial rejoinder directly to Nathaniel: "That side blow thro' Mrs Hawthorne will not do. I am not to be charmed out of my promised pleasure by any of that lady's syrenisms. You, sir, I hold accountable, and the visit ... must be made."[110] Melville's approach to Hawthorne's reticence was disarming forwardness. And, as if studying the character of his friend, Herman had marked a passage from Hawthorne's sketch "Foot-prints on the Sea-Shore" in which Hawthorne describes his own shy inclinations: "[W]ith an inward antipathy and a headlong flight, do I eschew the presence of any meditative stroller like myself.... From such a man, as if another self had scared me, I scramble hastily over the rocks, and take refuge in a nook which many a secret hour has given me the right to call my own."[111] Melville, however, would let Nathaniel take no such refuge from him; he accepted his role as the aggressor and prime driver of the friendship — and this was a pattern of passivity in relationships that Hawthorne would display again and again throughout his life. Hawthorne's closest friends accepted their role as caretakers and supporters of the writer, and they carried a good portion of the load in fostering and sustaining the relationship. Melville, ever a quick study, learned this quickly and accepted his role, and he would have none of Sophia's polite refusals in Nathaniel's name. "Your bed is already made, & the wood marked for your fire. But a moment ago, I looked into the eyes of two fowls, whose tail feathers have been notched, as destined victims for the table."[112] Melville's invitation also attempts to rekindle for Hawthorne the liquored intellectual interplay of their early meetings: "Mark — there is some excellent Montado Sherry awaiting you & some most potent Port. We will have mulled wine with wisdom, & buttered toast with storytelling & crack jokes & bottles from morning till night."[113] Interestingly, Melville ends the letter by throwing a subtle wedge between the Hawthornes. With Sophia having delivered the cordial refusal of his invitation, Melville suggests that "should Mrs Hawthorne for any reason conclude that *she*, for one, can not stay overnight with us — then you must — & the children, if you please."[114]

In Melville's eyes, Hawthorne was simply a bit house-bound and needed a nudge outward. He was not a near native to the area like Melville and was not in possession of a horse and "chariot" (as Melville called it) to get around the Berkshires environs like Herman did. So on March 12, Melville zipped over the relatively flat six miles from his place to the red cottage, arriving at dusk. ("[L]ike an owl, I steal abroad by twilight," he had written to Duyckinck of his daily patterns while still deeply immersed in the whale book.) How pleased or put off Sophia was by the visit is uncertain — she was very pregnant at the time, which was likely the true reason for her desire not to be shuttled by carriage over six jolting country miles. She wrote in her diary that they entertained Melville "with Champagne foam" — a whipped concoction of that beverage, eggs, and sugar — as well as cheese, butter, and bread. "He invited us all to go & spend tomorrow at his house," she wrote. "My husband concluded to go with Una."[115] A snowstorm buffeted the mountains the next day, as Hawthorne, with Una in tow, paid his promised visit, and the weather kept the two writers mostly indoors — either lounging in the barn or before Melville's great chimney and fireplace, talking "metaphysics," drinking, and smoking cigars. In the great glow of Melville's vitality and hospitality, Hawthorne was at ease and magnanimous. He took the time to write to Duyckinck (ever the watchful agent of the literary friendship) from Arrowhead in the little room just behind Melville's study, where he shared the same northward view that accompanied Melville during the writing of *Moby-Dick*: "I have only to glance my eye aside to obtain a fine snow-covered prospect of Graylock [*sic*]," he noted. He also showed clear evidence of his and Herman's bond of friendship, coupling an invitation as both his and Melville's: "May we not hope for the pleasure of seeing you again in Berkshire, next summer? If you were to see how snug and comfortable Melville makes himself and friends, I think you would not fail."[116] The comment is telling — for clearly the profound affection that he felt for Melville upon their first meeting, the feeling that moved him to uncharacteristically invite him to stay at his home so soon after, has not abated. This is not simply a congenial but relatively formal literary friendship; the men were comfortable in each other's homes, in the heart of their respective growing families. And Hawthorne, in his correspondence to others and in his notebooks, displays what he likes so much about Melville: his verve and warmth and acute mind. Hawthorne and Una stayed several days at Arrowhead, while Julian and Sophia stayed behind at the cottage, and before heading home Nathaniel presented Herman with a gift befitting his affection toward the seafaring author. The 1806 book, titled (in typically wordy, early nineteenth-century fashion) *The Mariner's Chronicle; Being a Collection of the Most Interesting Narratives of Shipwrecks, Fires, Famines, and Other Calamities Incident to a Life of Maritime Enterprise*, had been given to Hawthorne by his beloved uncle Richard Manning. It was a touchingly personal token and one that he saw befitting of a retired mariner and respected sea chronicler. The front inscriptions in the volume tell the story of shifting ownership: "Richard Manning 1814," "Nath Hawthorne, Salem, 1832," and "To H Melville Pittsfield March 14, 1851."[117] (As an aside while on the topic of uncles: Not long after the Hawthorne visit at Arrowhead, Herman's own uncle, Peter Gansevoort, spent an evening in dining and conversation in Albany with his boyhood playmate James Fenimore Cooper, who would die in the fall of that year.)[118]

In early April, as spring peeped forth, life turned to practical matters, with Melville taking on the role of friend and caretaker that so many had previously assumed toward Hawthorne, lugging a bedstead and clock to the cottage. In retrospect — though there is little record of it — the day was a significant one, as Hawthorne's friend John L. O'Sullivan had come to visit and stayed on for dinner. It didn't mean much at the time, but looking back it is remarkable that the man who would put "manifest destiny" on the lips of Americans would cross paths in remote western Massachusetts with the man who wrote the definitive American novel and cautionary tale against such an obsessive, all-encompassing enterprise such as westward expansion. For now, though, it was simply Una's godfather, John O'Sullivan, paying a visit and family friend Herman Melville crossing his path by lugging over some household items for the family. (American history would posthumously do the work of canonizing both men at the heart of nineteenth-century thought.) Hawthorne also presented Melville with a copy of *The House of the Seven Gables*, and several days later, having fully absorbed the new work, Melville penned a congratulatory and celebratory salvo and sent the letter fluttering over the six miles of countryside. In the book, Melville perceived the hallmark dusky tones and antiquities, finding it "like a fine old chamber, abundantly, but still judiciously, furnished with precisely that sort of furniture best fitted to furnish it."[119] The work absorbed him and stimulated him, much as the older writer's other works had: "It has delighted us; it has piqued a re-perusal; it has robbed us of a day, and made a present of a whole year of thoughtfulness."[120] Melville also described it as a paragon of achievement, referring back to the dark-light template for admiration that he had set down in "Hawthorne and His Mosses" (and which Sophia herself adopted): "The curtains are more drawn; the sun comes in more; genialities peep out more.... There is a certain tragic phase of humanity which, in our opinion, was never more powerfully embodied than by Hawthorne."[121] He had spoken of these striking and contrasting lights and darks before, in his essay on *Mosses from an Old Manse*, and he returned to that here, reminding Hawthorne of his very public and very lofty accolades and exultations of a few months prior. Melville also touched upon his previous musings regarding "truth": "We think that into no recorded mind has the intense feeling of the visible truth ever entered more deeply than into this man's."[122] The letter was a *tour de force* encore of the review that had stirred up so many (the Hawthornes, Longfellow, and countless *Literary World* readers) back in August.

Here, though — now that he had become closer friends with Hawthorne — he adapted it toward the new book, personalized it, and made it an expression within their friendship alone: This time it was private praise between friends, in the form of a letter. Last time, it had more obliquely been a personal letter to Hawthorne, but in very public form. Now there was the sense that Melville had Hawthorne to himself: "[I]t has bred great exhilaration and exultation with the remembrance that the architect of the Gables resides only six miles off, and not three thousand miles away, in England, say."[123] And, yet again, here he was conjuring the themes of the "Mosses" review and the nationalistic cry for a truly "American" literature that he had sounded through the achievement of Hawthorne. Still, though, his highest praise of Hawthorne refracted back to himself, for the greatness he saw in the older writer inevitably reflected his own emerging impulses and the mounting whale epic. "There is the grand truth about Hawthorne. He says NO! in thunder; but the devil himself cannot make him say *yes*. For all men who say *yes*, lie."[124] Melville was actually celebrating his own freedom and perversity, and projecting it onto Hawthorne — the freedom and perversity that drove him to write like no one had written before, building, gust by gust, the giant volume that he sensed was quintessentially unsuited for popularity, but that was nonetheless aimed at the rare and "true" perceiver such as Hawthorne (and aimed, of course, at a naissance in American writing). This was the perversity that was deeply ingrained into Melville's mindset at the time; in fact, back in February when his close associate Duyckinck asked for a contribution and a daguerreotype (an image of him that could be engraved) for a new publication of which he had assumed the mantle, *Holden's Dollar Magazine*, Herman inexplicably refused and then launched into a lengthy, passionate, somewhat wrongheaded but ultimately unclear explanation as to why:

> How shall a man go about refusing a man?— Best be roundabout, or plump on the mark?—I can not write the thing you want. I am in the humor to lend a hand to a friend, if I can;—but I am not in the humor to write the kind of thing you need—and I am not in the humor to write for Holden's Magazine. If I were to go on to give you all of my reasons—you would pronounce me a bore, so I will not do that.[125]

His engraved image and small writing contribution in Holden's would not only benefit Duyckinck; it surely would also promote Melville himself, who was soon to launch a new work into the public sphere. Focusing specifically on the daguerreotype, Melville wrote, "The fact is, almost everybody is having his 'mug' engraved nowadays ... and therefore, to see one's 'mug' in a magazine, is presumptive evidence that he's nobody."[126] Melville was being ungracious, and he knew it, but as could be his habit, he couched it in humor. Having already been at the receiving end of blows in reviews and having endured what he perceived as misunderstanding from the critical literati, Melville was at once excited by his own current explorations in the blooming *Moby-Dick* and experiencing anticipatory stress at the future reception of his substantial labors—and he was taking a bit of that out on Duyckinck, a key figure in New York literary circles. As he would confess to Hawthorne in May or June of 1851, "What I feel most moved to write ... it will not pay. Yet, *altogether*, write the other way I cannot. So the product is a final hash, and all my books are botches."[127] *Moby-Dick* was five months from publication and Melville was essentially psyching himself out and preparing himself for its poor reception — though he was sure that he had mustered his absolute best effort and poured all of himself into it.

As the message to Hawthorne shows, nowhere does the contemporary reader see more of Melville's utter humanity, self-doubts, and plain heart than in his confessional and revealing missives to the older writer. Money, however — as the letter also shows — was bedeviling Herman Melville, as it had before and as it would continue to in the coming decades, leading him to question the very vocation through which he had finally made a name for himself. On April 25, 1851, he had written to his publisher, Harper & Bros., to ask for an advance on the book in progress. Harpers' response was swift—sending a copy of Herman's account and noting that, in fact, he still owed them a due balance on past work of nearly seven hundred dollars. The fact of the matter was that Melville was living out the paternal curse of sinking into indebtedness, borrowing from family and friends. (A particular benefactor at this time was an old Lansingburgh, New York, friend, T.D. Stewart, who owned a sugar refinery.) The month of May also brought farming obligations; the fields had to be turned by Melville and his ox, and difficult and time-sensitive labor had to be completed to assure food for family and livestock throughout the year. Additionally, Arrowhead was undergoing renovations, and his mother was arriving on the train with his sister Kate, who was spiritually and emotionally downcast and in need of mountain reinvigoration. Debt, a house full of family (sisters Augusta and Helen were already at the house and often helped him with copying the whale manuscript), a farm and home to work on, and—of course—the neglected manuscript weighed down on Herman Melville; and he expressed his doubts and anxieties to Nathaniel Hawthorne. "[B]ut see my hand!—four blisters on this palm, made by hoes and hammers within the last few days."[128] May was a cruel month for writing; his manuscript having languished for three weeks, he had left the whale, he told Hawthorne, "in his flurry." He was in the home stretch, in other words but needed the time and the space for a final, herculean push—yet so much else was weighing on his mind besides the exhausting mental preoccupation of the book itself, which bore down at all times, pen in hand or not. He was, as Hershel Parker describes, "obsessed with his own need to finish his book" and, ever the autodidact, "obsessed with what he was learning, hour by hour, about human psychology from observing the growth of his own mind."[129] Hawthorne spent his energies on consistency and precision, while Melville came upon a mode of creating with *Moby-Dick* that meant stretching his imagination and resources to their outer limits and filling his coffers with information until near bursting. He had, in Parker's words, "battered his imagination against natural and supernatural hieroglyphics, physical and psychological mysteries, against the puzzles that he compulsively identified and compulsively brooded upon—from the meaning of the painting at the Spouter Inn to the sources of the 'sourceless primogenitures of the gods.'"[130] He was flaring toward both his greatest achievement and utter burnout from mental labors, domestic worries, and quotidian obligations.

It was no wonder that, years later, Herman's wife Elizabeth would remember *Moby-Dick* being written "under unfavorable circumstances." During those periods when he could sequester himself, she recalled him locked away "at his desk all day not eating any thing till four or five oclock."[131] "I have been more busy than you can well imagine," he wrote to Hawthorne," and he wasn't talking about just writing. He described hours spent "building & patching & tinkering away in all directions" and having "crops to get in, —corn and potatoes."[132] He apologized for lack of recent visits, but "in the evening I feel completely done up, as the phrase is, and incapable of the long jolting to get to your house & back."[133] His state of mind was evident and his anxiety and frustration over the book crested in his letters to Hawthorne as May turned to June. "I am so pulled hither & thither by circumstances," he wrote to his fellow writer, who possessed an understanding of such things. "The calm, the coolness, the silent grass-growing mood in which a man *ought* always to compose, — that, I fear, can seldom be mine."[134] He was frank about his financial issues as well: "Dollars damn me; and the malicious Devil is forever grinning in upon me, holding the door ajar."[135] (This also a reference to the "printer's devil"; this is the job title of the apprentice who undertakes tasks such as helping to prepare ink and type.) But it was not just Hawthorne to whom he turned to reveal his anxieties; it was also *in* Hawthorne that he imagined respite, a paradise and higher existence away from all of the quotidian concerns and frustrations. "If ever, my dear Hawthorne, in the eternal times that are to come, you & I shall sit down in Paradise," he rhapsodized, "and if we shall by any means be able to smuggle a basket of champagne there (I won't believe in a Temperance Heaven) ... then, O my dear fellow-mortal, how shall we pleasantly discourse of all the things manifold which now so distress us."[136] All of the rumination on the afterlife also drove Melville to think of his reputation and posterity as a writer — something which his post–*Typee* critical and financial fortunes had prompted him to think of quite blackly — especially when compared to the steadily rising success of Hawthorne. Patience and decades-long, methodical labor had been Hawthorne's practice; Melville had been burning steadily, productively, and impatiently for only half a decade. Having recently made a twenty-four-hour visit to New York City (two days to travel, one day in the city) to arrange for the typesetting of the completed portion of his manuscript at his own expense — in order to increase his bargaining power with the publisher and not fall into further debt — he had seen positive notices of Hawthorne's new book. It was enough to remind him of his own humble literary reputation. He saw "a portrait of N.H.," he told Hawthorne, and had "seen and heard ... many flattering allusions to the 'Seven Gables.'" He also saw announcements for the new edition of *Twice-Told Tales*.[137]

The sensation of leaving the secluded rural margins, arriving in pulsing New York City, and finding his neighbor Nathaniel Hawthorne greeting him again, but this time in reputation, had a strange and unpleasant effect on Melville. Here was his friend, who was in actuality still tucked away in his small cottage back on the Stockbridge Bowl, on the lips of everyone. The utter strangeness of leaving the familiarity of Hawthorne, his tangible friend, behind in the small, humble Berkshires home (where temporality was sounded out by the very clock Melville had brought him), only to encounter another Hawthorne in the form of his fame, sent Melville into deep questioning and doubt. Here was the meditation he had been drawn toward in Carlyle, which he had adapted to *Moby-Dick*, and to which he now addressed himself: "Who am I; What is this ME?" Here before him, again, was the "Canvas (the warp and woof thereof) whereon all our Dreams and Life-visions are painted."[138] "So upon the whole, I say to myself, this N.H. is in the ascendant," he wrote to Hawthorne. Less graciously, he continued, "[T]hey begin to patronize. All Fame is patronage. Let me be infamous: there is no patronage in *that*."[139] Melville's pessimism regarding his coming book was un-dampered, and it was a desperate and peculiar state of mind and position in which he found himself: knowing he had written something remarkable and having exhausted himself and his resources in the process, but — even while holding out hope for success — suspecting it was both unsuited for mass taste and bound to be relegated to failure. Hawthorne's unquestionably growing fame made him dwell upon his own reputation as a writer. "What 'reputation' H.M. has is horrible. Think of it! To go down to posterity is bad enough," he wrote, again revealing his innermost haunts to the older writer. "[B]ut to go down as a 'man who lived among the cannibals!'" Melville had tasted some success with *Typee*, and the returns had since been diminishing, and he had deflating hope that this would change with the whale book. Of the generation that would come after his death, he surmised, "'Typee' will be given to them, perhaps, with their gingerbread."[140] He had little respect for the legacy of *Typee*, a book that was light, sweet fare compared to that which occupied him now. Sizing himself up in yet another way against Hawthorne, particularly his brief writing life against the decades-long plodding and woodshedding of the older writer, he displays uncanny self-realization and premonition. "I am like one of those seeds taken out of the Egyptian Pyramids, which, after being three thousand years a seed and nothing but a seed ... grew to greenness, and then fell to mould."[141] Melville was only approaching his thirty-second year, and truly was at the height of his literary powers, yet he was resigning himself to failure and a premature end to his writing life. Reading the premonition, one wants to reach back through time and throttle him, to show him what *Moby-Dick* has become; but one is also shaken by his frighteningly accurate premonition of his short, intense arc and burnout. The letter to Hawthorne is also an elegy to his writing career, despite the fact that he will continue beyond *Moby-Dick*, ever less successfully for several years before resigning himself to anonymity and the distraction of strict poetic forms. Looking backward, he claims, "Until I was twenty-five, I had no development at all. From my twenty-fifth year I date my life."[142] At the age of twenty-five, in October of 1844, Herman Melville had returned home from his multi-year voyages, arriving on the Navy ship the *United States* and tossing his navy white jacket into Boston's Charles River. That winter, in his mother's home in Lansingburgh, he began writing his first book. This was the beginning of his very life, he felt; he also felt that this, his existence as a writer, was at stake with the soon-to-be-published whale book. This was why he was in New York City having the pages typeset himself at his own expense. Everything hinged on *Moby-Dick*— and yet everywhere he was reminded of Hawthorne's reputation and his own comparatively lesser one. Marking his life at his twenty-fifth year, when he began writing, he notes to Hawthorne, "Three weeks have scarcely passed, at any time between then and now, that I have not unfolded within myself." Melville was alluding to a mere six years— and the remarkable self-education he had undergone during his short life as a writer, swimming through libraries, to paraphrase Ishmael, and voraciously reading and writing his way to a new life and a new identity, leaving sailor's penury and the mainmast behind him forever. But Melville's final assessment of this brief period as a writer that he now terms his "life" is troubling and darkly pessimistic. Standing on the verge of publishing *Moby-Dick*, at the ripe age of nearly thirty two— with five books behind him and his best effort yet to come — he sees himself not in the ascendant, but as having fully arced: "But I feel that I am now come to the inmost leaf of the bulb, and that shortly the flower must fall to the mould."[143] This was a peculiar letter to send to Hawthorne, even if Melville had made him his "father confessor" (as Sophia had characterized Nathaniel's role in the friendship). And surely the older writer, with decades of diligent, painstaking (and often barely compensated) writing behind him, would have a difficult time empathizing with this idea of reaching the "inmost leaf" after six years. Melville seemed hung up on the idea of "reputation"—yet Hawthorne, in his early writing years, had spent nearly twice as long as an *anonymous* writer than Melville had spent has a writer, period. Nevertheless, Hawthorne, at least the epistolary Hawthorne, had become a sounding board against which Melville directed his deepest anxieties and enthusiasms regarding his writing and intellectual life. These were conversations with himself as much as they were messages directed at the older writer; hence, the continually vacillating nature of an inner struggle.

By late June, having perhaps made anxiety-quelling progress on the loose ends of the whale book, Melville reared up positive again, brushing aside the black predictions of a month prior as "crotchety and over doleful chimearas [*sic*]."[144] Like Ishmael, apparently, Herman was merely in his "hypos" for a time, but now the "clear air and open window" and "most persuasive season" of early summer induced him to write to his father confessor in an altogether more lightened spirit. Progress toward completion of his book had unburdened him a bit, as had the season, and in the heat of the summer of 1851 he would make his final rush at the work that was, for now, known as *The Whale*. For now, the literary stagnation and domestic labors of spring having lifted, Melville had found a happy balance between the obligations of outer and inner life; work on the house continued, as did work on the substantial manuscript. "Since you have been here, I have been building some shanties of houses (connected with the old one) and likewise some shanties of chapters and essays," he wrote. "I have been plowing and sowing and raising and painting and printing and praying,—and now begin to come out upon a less bustling time."[145] Having recently spent time overseeing the typesetting of his early finished pages in the "dust of the Babylonish brick kiln of New York,"[146] the oven-like heat and the dirty, teeming streets of the metropolis had made him all that more appreciative of his relatively new home in the Berkshires and his choice to leave behind city life. As to the "shanties" he was building onto the whale epic, this was an apt metaphor for finishing a book while the bulk of its first half was being typeset—and therefore fixed immutably. There would be no wholesale revision regarding the book's essential infrastructure at this point. Thus, Melville introduces one of the most compelling figures in the book, Bulkington, in the third chapter ("The Spouter-Inn") and then, having never sustained him in the narrative at all, at once remembers, reminds us of him, and dismisses him with a dramatic flourish twenty chapters later. At the Spouter Inn, Ishmael keys in on Bulkington, every part the mythic mariner:

> I observed, however, that one of them held somewhat aloof, and though he seemed desirous not to spoil the hilarity of his shipmates by his own sober face, yet upon the whole he refrained from making as much noise as the rest. This man interested me at once; and since the sea-gods had ordained that he should soon become my shipmate (though but a sleeping partner one, so far as this narrative is concerned), I will here venture upon a little description of him. He stood full six feet in height, with noble shoulders, and a chest like a coffer-dam. I have seldom seen such brawn in a man. His face was deeply brown and burnt, making his white teeth dazzling by the contrast; while in the deep shadows of his eyes floated some reminiscences that did not seem to give him much joy.[147]

One can't help but think that *Moby-Dick* would have assumed a different shape had Melville retained this compelling figure — and that Ahab wouldn't have held such sway over the entire crew of the *Pequod*. Bulkington is, as his name suggests, and as Richard Chase asserts "the heroic American," "the Handsome sailor," and "the titanic body of America." Chase argues that "Bulkington disappears from *Moby-Dick* because if he had been more a part of the story it would have been inevitable that he should do what Starbuck can only try to do"— that is, oppose Ahab and save the *Pequod* from its disastrous fate.[148] Of course, though, there are other, more practical reasons as well for Bulkington's disappearance — the primary one being that the book, under the influence of Hawthorne and all that catalyzed as Melville continually "unfolded" within himself, had taken a very different course since the creation of its early chapters. It had grown in such scope and complexity that the more conventional heroic figure embodied by Bulkington could find no purchase within it. Melville, likely due to rushing the early part of book through the printer, did not have the liberty to reconstruct the third chapter, altogether omitting Bulkington; thus, the "Lee Shore" (XXIII) chapter becomes Bulkington's explanation and epitaph — and ultimately his scattering and apotheosis:

> Some chapters back, one Bulkington was spoken of, a tall, newlanded mariner, encountered in New Bedford at the inn.

When on that shivering winter's night, the Pequod thrust her vindictive bows into the cold malicious waves, who should I see standing at her helm but Bulkington! I looked with sympathetic awe and fearfulness upon the man, who in mid-winter just landed from a four years' dangerous voyage, could so unrestingly push off again for still another tempestuous term. The land seemed scorching to his feet. Wonderfullest things are ever the unmentionable; deep memories yield no epitaphs; this six-inch chapter is the stoneless grave of Bulkington.[149]

Indicative of Melville's creative shift, Bulkington moves from a genuine heroic mariner figure, rendered in tangible physical description, to phantasm and idea, before dissipating in a metaphysical spray of salt-water:

But as in landlessness alone resides highest truth, shoreless, indefinite as God — so better is it to perish in that howling infinite, than be ingloriously dashed upon the lee, even if that were safety! For worm-like, then, oh! who would craven crawl to land! Terrors of the terrible! is all this agony so vain? Take heart, take heart, O Bulkington! Bear thee grimly, demigod! Up from the spray of thy ocean-perishing — straight up, leaps thy apotheosis![150]

As July dawned, Melville concerned himself with the final flurry of the book and putting it to rest with a suitable ending. "The tail is not yet cooked," he confided to Hawthorne, but still offered to send him a sampling: "Shall I send you a fin of the *Whale* by way of specimen mouthful?" The substantial tome, not yet titled *Moby-Dick*, had gained much from Melville's contemplation of Hawthorne back in August (in the form of "Hawthorne and His Mosses"); and all of the darkness and "blackness" he had attributed to Hawthorne had inspired him to new depths in his own writing. Ominously alluding to the "hell-fire" in which the book had been "broiled," Herman confided to Nathaniel that its secret motto was "Ego non baptiso te in nomine — but make the rest out yourself."[151] The Latin phrase he tried to tantalize Hawthorne with appears in full form in *Moby-Dick*, ceremoniously uttered by Ahab as he baptizes the harpoon intended for the white whale with the blood of the pagan harpooners: "Ego non baptize te in nomine patris, sed in nomine diaboli!"[152] Melville knew that in Hawthorne he had a kindred creative spirit who would appreciate such intent — the notion of Ahab baptizing his obsessive mission in the name of the devil, not the Father, was right in Hawthorne's literary sweet spot; for few other authors had deliberated upon devilry more eloquently than Hawthorne. Melville was also pulling ever more tightly the circle he had subtly placed around him and his friend in the "Mosses" piece as pioneering American authors. And, as always, Melville's reward to himself for such diligent progress on his book was time spent discoursing and drinking with Hawthorne: "When I am quite free of my present engagements, I am going to treat myself to a ride and a visit to you. Have ready a bottle of brandy, because I always feel like drinking that heroic drink when we talk ontological heroics together."[153] Having in recent weeks sent Hawthorne a probing and morose letter and now, out of his hypos, having zipped off a whimsical and enthusiastic one, Melville confessed, "This is rather a crazy letter in some respects ... ascribe it to the intoxicating effects of the latter end of June acting upon a very susceptible and peradventure [i.e. "perhaps"] feeble temperament."[154] As always, he expressed himself with unchecked freedom to his confidante and ally Hawthorne.

The visits between the two were not regular that summer, however, which could be expected: the Hawthornes had welcomed baby Rose into their lives in May, adding a third to their young brood, while Herman's wife Lizzie was entering the latter stages of her pregnancy with their second child and son, Stanwix, who would arrive in late October. Hawthorne, though, wrote Herman a long letter in July. That he appreciated the friendship and correspondence with the younger writer is clear from Melville's brief note, jotted in response to it. (Though, as ever, the absence of Hawthorne's presumably destroyed letters creates an imbalance that has led to continually inaccurate suggestions that Hawthorne mostly held aloof.) On July 22, Melville wrote back, "I thank you for your easyflowing long letter (received yesterday) which flowed through me, and refreshed all my meadows, as the Housatonic [River] — opposite me — does in reality."[155] Melville was still engaged enough with farm, household, and literary labors to put off a visit, however. It was the "height of the haying season" and Melville and his horse were busy reaping and storing winter food for the livestock. Herman was employing all of the lessons he had learned while taking care of his uncle's farm in the Berkshires as a teenager, and he had transformed himself from cosmopolitan dweller in New York City to gentleman farmer in the space of several months (and, of course, by necessity). It was an impression he loved to convey to friends in letters, particularly Hawthorne, whose own farming experience at Brook farm was limited and brief, and Evert Duyckinck, the city editor and Knickerbocker to whom such an existence was remote. "I am not yet a disengaged man," he wrote to Hawthorne of his present duties, but he proposed they "hit upon some little bit of vagabondism" in the near future, and perhaps climb "Graylock" [sic]. "But ere we start," he tellingly wrote, "we must dig a deep hole, and bury all Blue Devils, there to abide till the last day."[156] The two had become close enough to adopt a code name for their depressive tendencies, and Melville, in the glow of summer and literary achievement, was now sweeping aside his fatalistic musings of the spring. Like Ishmael, he was prone to hypos— both cresting highs and scraping lows— leading 2005 biographer Andrew Delbanco to attribute manic episodes and bipolarity to Melville. And now, as he coasted through the tail end of *Moby-Dick*, aware that the yeoman's labor was behind him, he allowed himself an expansiveness that matched the season — and, more importantly, he allowed himself hope for literary success where doubt had constantly probed and prodded. Showing enthusiasm for his book, Melville signed his letter off with an X, using Queequeg's mark. Any doubt about the psychic pairing of Ishmael and Queequeg as, in some respects, twinned aspects of a single consciousness can be allayed by Melville playing the role of the amiable and affectionate "savage" (instead of his sailor doppelganger Ishmael) in his letter to Hawthorne.

Melville finally came through on his overtures for a visit to the red cottage on his thirty-second birthday, August 1, 1851. At the time, Nathaniel was engaged in a period of bachelorhood, with Sophia having gone east for a three-week visit with family in West Newton, Massachusetts. She had left Julian behind with his father and had taken along Una and the baby, Rose. Nathaniel dutifully kept a journal of his time with his son, calling the collection of passages "Twenty Days with Julian & Little Bunny, By Papa," an allusion to Julian's pet rabbit, a creature that ran free through the house and, in its rompings and soilings, often incited Hawthorne to murderous thoughts. The idyllic title also did not reflect the isolative author's dismay at having the constant company of a bright, talkative, and precocious five-year-old boy. With Sophia in the house running interference, Nathaniel could choose his parenting moments— but also have the inviolate hours of contemplation that suited his personality and vocation. But it was not without a streak of humor that Hawthorne wrote that Julian's constant flow of chatter was more than a "mortal father ought to be expected to endure."[157] "He does put me almost beside my propriety," lamented Hawthorne, "never quitting me, and continually thrusting his word between every sentence of all my reading, and smashing every attempt at reflection into a thousand fragments."[158] The private and contemplative Hawthorne also weathered several visits during his time without Sophia and his daughters. The English author G.P.R. James, who was living in Stockbridge at the time, made two tedious pop-ins, subjecting Hawthorne (during the first visit) to a mortifying monologue of observations regarding *The House of the Seven Gables*, and then, another time, seeking shelter in the cottage with his family during a thunderstorm while out for a ride. A young Quaker woman and Hawthorne admirer, Elizabeth Lloyd, made a more discreet visit, limiting her compliments of his work and mercifully choosing to talk with Hawthorne of other writers, such as her friend John Greenleaf Whittier and Hawthorne's friend Herman Melville (who still enjoyed some fame), while Julian climbed and rolled over his father's lap.

As to Melville, he saw no better way to spend his 32nd birthday — August 1, 1851— than with a surprise visit on horseback. He had a chance encounter with Hawthorne and Julian on the way to the cottage; having walked to the post office, the two had settled in a woody grove on the way home so that Nathaniel could read his newspapers. Spying them, Melville raised a greeting in Spanish, but it wasn't until he greeted them a second time that Hawthorne realized who the horseman was. He was surprised and happy to see Melville. It was a welcome visit in a season of unwelcome visits. Melville hoisted a delighted Julian onto the back of the horse and they strolled back to the cottage for afternoon tea and then supper. And then, with Julian asleep, the two took in a late evening in deep conversation, smoking cigars in the sitting room (an indiscretion typically forbidden by Sophia) and discoursing, according to Hawthorne, "about time and eternity, things of this world and of the next, and books and publishers and all possible matters."[159] (Later, incidentally, Hawthorne appreciatively wrote in his journal that Julian claimed "he loved Mr. Melville as well as me and as mamma and as Una.") Several days after the visit, the Duyckinck brothers returned to the Berkshires—a year had passed quickly — and they and Melville swung by the cottage to scoop up Hawthorne and Julian for a picnic and then a visit to the Shaker village in Hancock, about ten miles away. Perhaps reflecting his malcontented state of mind at the time — as he contemplated an escape from the Berkshires— Hawthorne was repulsed by the local Shakers. Contradictorily, he found the sparse neatness of their large residence constraining and painful to look at, but he condemned their meager washing facilities and sleeping arrangements as dirty and disgusting. (Men slept with men in narrow cots in a crowded dormitory.) To him, the men seemed overly severe and humorless and the women wan and sickly. "They are certainly the most singular and bedevilled set of people that ever existed in a civilized land," he recorded in his journal.[160]

The condemnatory and peevish tone was par for the course as fall came upon the Berkshires. As was his wont, Hawthorne had again become unsatisfied to the point of agitation with his geographical surroundings. "This is a horrible, horrible ... climate," he railed. "[O]ne knows not, for ten minutes together, whether he is too cool or too warm." In his unhappiness, he seemed to regress to childish tantrums in his notebooks: "I detest it! I detest it!! I detest it!!! I hate Berkshire with my whole soul, and would joyfully see its mountains laid flat." The little cottage that Sophia had worked hard to make as comfortable and palatable as possible now became "the most inconvenient and wretched little hovel that I ever put my head in."[161] During the previous year-plus, Sophia had fallen in love with the area and waxed admiringly over its natural beauty; now, surrendering to Nathaniel's reality of blaming the landscape for his mental and physical vexations, she too came to the conclusion that she had had enough. Hawthorne didn't want to go back to Salem, but he longed for sea air — something that Melville and his ocean aura only made him long for more. Compounding (and possibly driving) his dissatisfaction, the Hawthornes had a peevish showdown with their landlords, the Tappans, over the harvest in the nearby orchard. The family had been enjoying the fruit, thinking that they had tacit permission to do so. But Caroline Tappan sent Sophia a frosty missive suggesting that they were being presumptuous — noting that, though she would be glad to grant them such a kindness, they should have asked for it rather than simply taken it. Hawthorne applied his formidable writing talents to a stuffy and polished reply. He preferred a "small right to a great favor," he sniffed, pointing out that the year before "no question of this nature was raised; our right seemed to be tacitly conceded, and if you claimed or exercised any manorial privileges, it never came to my knowledge."[162] The already frayed thread binding the family to western Massachusetts would not hold much longer. Melville or not, the time was coming for Nathaniel Hawthorne and family to move on.

Hawthorne's fit of pique regarding Lenox, Stockbridge, and the surrounding areas seems to be a sudden fit of discontent brought on by a collision of factors — a desire for sea air, the crumbling relationship with the Tappans, the thought of another formidable Berkshires winter (in a letter to Duyckinck he claims to have fled the advancing season) — for if one traces his relationship with the area in his notebooks during the time of the Melville friendship, there is a sense of lovely wonderment at this natural, hermetic world he and Sophia had established. In mid-September 1850, not long after Melville's stay at the cottage, he describes himself lying by the lake on a bright day "while the waves and sunshine were playing together on the water, the quick glimmer of wavelets ... perceptible through my closed eyelids."[163] Hawthorne only occasionally infuses emotional colors into his empirical natural descriptions, but he invests much care and descriptive energy into them, and they become the most prominent feature of his personal writing during this time. Back in October, 1850, with his first Lenox fall in full radiance, he wrote of the autumn hues, and of Monument Mountain rising "like a headless sphinx, wrapped in a rich Persian shawl"[164] and of a giant bank of mist filling the entire valley, leaving only the peak of the mountain visible. (Surely, only a boy raised in the exotic merchant paradise of Salem would reach for such a description of the natural world.) "This mist reaches almost to my window, so dense as to conceal everything, except that near its hither boundary a few ruddy or yellow tree-tops appear, glorified by the early sunshine, as is likewise the whole mist cloud."[165] Even in February (1851), with the temperatures brutally hovering around and below zero, Hawthorne is drawn to private natural spectacles rather than complaint. He and Una, bundled in layers and in their India-rubber footwear, trudge across the frozen lake and through the woods, where a rain had melted much of the snow. Hawthorne records "partridge berries frozen, and outer shells of walnuts, and chestnut-burrs, heaped or scattered.... The walnut-husks mark the place where the boys, after nutting, sat down to clear the walnuts of their outer shell." Nearby, there is an oak tree, "with all of its brown foliage still rustling on it."[166] He celebrates February sunsets, which are "incomparably splendid, and when the ground is covered with snow, no brilliancy of tint expressible by words can some within an infinite distance of the effect.... The sunset sky, amidst its splendor, had a softness and delicacy that impart themselves to a white marble world."[167] Seasonal streams, shooting down the surrounding mountains during the same month, also held an empirical fascination for Hawthorne, becoming "most interesting objects at this time ... some that have an existence only at this season, — Mississippis of the moment."[168] The final labors of *The House of the Seven Gables* behind him, he spent much of his time tromping the surrounding land, solo or with a child or two in tow.

Without bustling Salem and the fascination of its pedestrians and its taverns just beyond his door, he becomes attuned to the progression of the seasons, as glimpsed through the lens of its minutest spectacles.

For example, a little brook in steadily warming late March, having not "cleansed itself from the disarray of the past autumn and winter ... is much embarrassed and choked up with brown leaves, twigs, and bits of branches"; nevertheless, it pulses "merrily and rapidly, gurgling cheerfully, and tumbling over the impediments of stones with which the children and I made little waterfalls last year." He notes as well "small basins of pools of calmer and smoother depth ... in which little fish are already sporting about."[169] By late May, his mindset still seems a world removed from the conditions that will cause him to leave Melville and the Berkhires

Nathaniel Hawthorne, undated, likely late 1840s or early 1850s (Library of Congress).

later that same year. "I think the face of nature can never look more beautiful than now, with this so fresh and youthful green, — the trees not being fully in leaf, yet enough so to give airy shade to the woods. The sunshine fills them with green light."[170]

The landscape narratives in his notebooks sometimes call to mind the paradisiacal early married years in Concord, but now Sophia and Nathaniel have all of their children around them. On the same day as the previous passage, he records, "This is a very windy day, and the light shifts with magical alternation. In a walk to the lake just now with the children, we found an abundance of flowers, — wild geranium, violets of all families, red columbines, many others know and unknown, besides innumerable blossoms of the wild strawberry."[171] Even Julian, as an adult, would come to recall his father's utter geographical restlessness, but for a time he seemed to have merged in a sublime manner with his Berkshires surroundings—which he will soon claim to detest and wish the very mountains that he now celebrates laid flat. His autumn 1851 entries denote the shift, as his time to leave nears. On October 29, on a hike with his old Concord friend and neighbor, the Transcendentalist poet

Ellery Channing, whose works made a cameo in Hawthorne's "Earth's Holocaust," he still displays his wonderful empiricism, bringing alive the natural world of Lenox. (Channing himself had a reputation as great aficionado of the natural world, having shown his friends Emerson and Thoreau the most unnoticed and intimate recesses of the Concord woods and becoming, in the 1870s, Thoreau's first biographer with *Thoreau, the Poet-Naturalist.*) "[W]e found a wild strawberry in the woods, not quite ripe, but beginning to redden," he writes, also conjuring up the images and sounds of apple harvesting: "the cider-mills have been grinding apples. Immense heaps of apples lie piled near them, and the creaking of the press is heard as the horse treads on. Farmers are repairing cider-barrels; and the wayside brook is made to pour itself into the bunghole of a barrel, in order to cleanse it for the new cider."[172] A mere few days later, as October changed to November, Hawthorne eked out an artless and hollow description: "The face of the country is dreary now in a cloudy day like the present. The woods on the hill-sides look almost black, and the cleared spaces a kind of gray brown."[173] Even in coldest February, he had seen something of particular interest or even something that induced wonderment, and it had inspired him to marvelous prose. Now, the entry reflected his state of mind: He was done with the Berkshires. Hawthorne's writing relationship with his natural environment reflected his shifting internal shades, and in late November, he wrote the flat, colorless entry that would serve as an epitaph to his time with the region: "We left Lenox Friday morning, November 21, 1851, in a storm of snow and sleet, and took the cars at Pittsfield, and arrived at West Newton that evening."[174] Julian remembered looking backward at the sorrowful sight of their housecats left behind as they pulled away from the cottage — then he recalled being in the last car on the train, with the spires of Pittsfield, hazy in the snow, receding out of view in the rear glass. They had been offered the house of Horace Mann, during his term in Congress, and Mary Peabody Mann (Nathaniel's in-laws) in West Newton, just outside of Boston, and leaped at the opportunity to return to more familiar civilization. Here, he would finish his in-progress book, *The Blithedale Romance*, which used as raw material Hawthorne's experience in the communal environs of Brook Farm. He had started the literary labors at the Red Cottage, and for all of his eventual enmity for the Berkshire Mountains, it was there that that he had rallied his last prolific burst (taking into account *The House of the Seven Gables*). But now that was behind him. Hawthorne could never stay in one place for long; in fact, five years later (in England), he would brood over the effect this transitory life in his notebooks: "I do not know what sort of character it will form in the children, — this unsettled, shifting, vagrant life, with no central home to turn to except what we carry in ourselves."[175]

As to Melville, his dogged friendship was the one aspect that Hawthorne would surely miss from his time in the Berkshires, and he and Sophia saw to it that they stayed in touch with the younger author, who had his own familial obligations to attend to, not the least of which was an infant son, Stanwix, who had been born on October 22. Melville had presented Nathaniel with a just-published copy of *Moby-Dick* in mid–November, before the family's flight eastward. Harper & Brothers had delivered the first copies of the book to Melville on the 14th, and that same day he met with Hawthorne at the hotel in Lenox to present him with a copy — and, of course, to unveil the dedication page, a touching tribute, centered and stanza-like in a sea of white space: "IN TOKEN / OF MY ADMIRATION FOR HIS GENIUS, / THIS BOOK IS INSCRIBED / TO / NATHANIEL HAWTHORNE." It was a proper farewell for a year-plus period of closeness and friendship. Hawthorne read it in the following few days, in the midst of packing and preparing to leave and sent a deeply complimentary letter that, like the others, has been lost to time. Nevertheless, we can trace its fossil-like impression in Melville's emotional response in his reply to Hawthorne's letter, a document that Hawthorne biographer James R. Mellow has rightfully called "one of the most extraordinarily intimate letters one author ever sent another."[176] Melville was never swerved from his outpourings and declarations by Hawthorne's less effusive personality — and there *was* enough in Hawthorne's now long-disappeared and unseen letters to encourage him to maintain this intimate mode of communication. Here, with *Moby-Dick* between them, it reaches its zenith. Hawthorne likely proposed that he write a favorable review of the new book; this certainly would repay the favor of "Hawthorne and His Mosses," which many of Hawthorne's close associates saw as a crucial piece leading toward the kind of national recognition the Salem writer deserved. But Melville, ever perverse and always drawing the circle ever more intimately around their friendship, resisted. "Don't write a word about the book," Melville beseeched. "That would be robbing me of my miserly delight."[177] Ever since his public, albeit masked, outpouring of admiration in the "Hawthorne and His Mosses" piece after their initial meeting, Melville had been ever more miserly regarding the relationship, seeking to make it ever more personal and ever less public. (Hence, his review of *The House of the Seven Gables* in letter form and for Nathaniel and Sophia's eyes only.) And the message that Melville hammers home in the letter is that Hawthorne's private appreciation for *Moby-Dick* means more to him than critical or commercial fortune. "[Y]our appreciation is my glorious gratuity," wrote Herman. "In my profound humble way, — a shepherd-king, — I was lord of a little vale in the solitary Crimea; but you have now given me the crown of India."[178] The evening before, he had been on his way to visit the Morewoods, the owners and residents of Broadhall (the old Melvill family home), when he was stopped by the delivery person and handed Hawthorne's "joy-giving and exultation breeding letter." He hastily opened it there on the road and read it:

> Had I been at home, I would have sat down at once and answered it. In me divine maganimities [*sic*] are spontaneous and instantaneous—catch them while you can. The world goes round, and the other side comes up. So now I can't write what I felt. But I felt pantheistic then — your heart beat in my ribs and mine in yours, and both in God's. A sense of unspeakable security is in me this moment, on account of your having understood the book. I have written a wicked book, and feel spotless as the lamb. Ineffable socialities are in me. I would sit down and dine with you and all the gods in old Rome's Pantheon. It is a strange feeling — no hopefulness is in it, no despair. Content — that is it; and irresponsibility; but without licentious inclination. I speak now of my profoundest sense of being, not of an incidental feeling.[179]

Perhaps most remarkable in the letter is Melville's sense, long before the book has even had a chance to resonate with the public, that it was not suitable for mass appreciation. This is not a trifling observation, Melville has banked his career and his family security on this book — but, as he told Hawthorne in a letter months before, "What I feel most moved to write, that is banned, — it will not pay. Yet, altogether, write the *other* way I cannot."[180] And one gets a true, visceral sense of the depth of admiration he has for Hawthorne when he declares in this letter, "A sense of unspeakable security is in me this moment, on account of your having understood the book."[181] Melville also anticipates all of the critiques that will be aimed at the book's patchwork construction and lack of traditional narrative arc. "You were archangel enough to despise the imperfect body, and embrace the soul," writes Melville in his letter. "Once you hugged the ugly Socrates because you saw the flame in the mouth, and heard the rushing of the demon, — the familiar, — and recognized the sound; for you have heard it in your own solitudes."[182] From Melville's comment regarding the "imperfect body" we can ascertain that he is all too aware of the "problem" of the book's multiperspectival and inconsistent larger infrastructure, and when Melville claims to have written "a wicked book," he is not only referring to the hellfire in his thematic matter, but his complete disdain for traditional narrative form or "rules" (deliberating, for example, across an entire chapter, on the notion of "whiteness"). Melville took seriously his own conch-shell call in the "Mosses" essay for a distinctly American strain of writing separated from the English writers and the writers of the past — and he was fully aware that he was out beyond the pioneering edge of the pale (particularly for 1851) with *Moby-Dick*. He has also consummated the "blackness" he attributed to Hawthorne's vision — in as much as the "Mosses" review served as a reflection of his own development and intentions as he wrote the whale book — and what he somewhat vaguely and suggestively refers to as "blackness" is now a shared quality between him and Hawthorne: uniquely American writers working in unremittingly dark and turgid tones. This is the "flame in the mouth" and "rushing of the demon" that he claims is so familiar to Hawthorne precisely because, he tells him, you have "heard it in your own solitudes."

It is no mistake that the medium of this most intimate letter of all is a discussion of *Moby-Dick*: that is, Hawthorne's appreciation of it and the recognition of its alliance with Hawthorne's own dark vision. For the friendship was above all a literary kinship: It was the writing published and discussed between them that drove the relationship — that fueled the intellectual intimacy that Melville here declaimed to the heavens. There was personal affinity undoubtedly; but the raw material of the friendship was that which drove both men's lives: an intensity of commitment to their respective literary occupations and lifestyles. Here was where both of their passions lay and where the two intersected. It is this that drives Melville to his most unyielding declarations yet — declarations driven by the culmination of *Moby-Dick*, Hawthorne's deeply complimentary letter regarding it, and the dawning awareness that Hawthorne is leaving the small cottage only six rutted miles away from Arrowhead and slipping away from Melville. Reflecting back on the previous year, it is amazing to Melville that Hawthorne arrived at all, almost literally on his doorstep and out of nowhere. "Whence come you, Hawthorne?" he asks. "By what right have do you drink from my flagon of life? And when I put it to my lips—lo, they are yours and not mine. I feel that the Godhead is broken up like the bread at the Supper, and that we are the pieces. Hence this infinite fraternity of feeling."[183] It can't be overstated how much Nathaniel Hawthorne influenced *Moby-Dick*. It may not have emerged on the pages in a way that was recognizably "Hawthorne," filtered as it was through Melville's unique — and uniquely idiosyncratic — expression, but the absorption of Hawthorne's sensibilities, through both his work and his person, had a catalytic effect on the thematic impulses in the whale book; therefore, the dedication of it to "the genius of Nathaniel Hawthorne."

In the letter, Melville is also rallying his all for the powerfully appreciative and emotional farewell to Hawthorne. "I shall leave the world, I feel, with more satisfaction for having come to know you," he intones. "Knowing you persuades me more than the Bible of our immortality.... The divine magnet is on you, and my magnet responds. Which is the biggest? A foolish question they are *One*."[184] The process, begun in "Hawthorne and His Mosses" and continued in this letters of pulling the circle ever more intimately around him and Hawthorne finally culminates here. As kindred artists, they are not merely intimates, shut off from the rest; they are now — with the publication of *Moby-Dick* — one. What Hawthorne thought of such extreme declarations will never be known, though his own words in his English notebooks, five years later — after a Melville visit in Liverpool (the Southport suburb, more specifically, in a temporary Hawthorne home near the Irish Sea) — show that he held Melville in the absolute highest regard, one that he reserved for very few: "he has a very high and noble nature," wrote Hawthorne of his friend, "and is better worth immortality than the most of us."[185] If one is looking for a Hawthorne response to Melville's soaring letter of November 1851 — in which Herman declares, "Knowing you persuades me more than the Bible of our immortality" — here it is: Melville, in Hawthorne's eyes, is better worth that immortality than most. What better could be said of *anyone*? Any readers who still question the depth of *mutual* admiration between the two need look no further than this unalloyed sentiment in primary documents.

Now, however, in Pittsfield, Massachusetts, the 32-year-old Herman Melville contemplated both the commercial arrival of *Moby-Dick*, the book that represented his most herculean effort, and the departure of his friend Nathaniel Hawthorne. As to Hawthorne: looking backward after leaving the Berkshires, he waxed reflectively and philosophically in his journal, with the sage accumulation that came from 47 years living:

Happiness in this world, when it comes, comes incidentally. Make it the object of pursuit, and it leads us a wild-goose chase, and is never attained. Follow some other object, and very possibly we may find that we have caught happiness, without dreaming of it; but likely enough it is gone the moment we say to ourselves, "Here it is!" like the chest of gold that treasure-seekers find.[186]

Melville had held true happiness on the nighttime road in Pittsfield, in those very first moments it took to read and first absorb Hawthorne's appreciative remarks about *Moby-Dick*. That, however, was likely the best he was to feel in his own lifetime toward the whale book.

Before November 1851, the month of the book's release, was even over, the reviews were showing up in prominent journals and newspapers. A few negative and prominent reviews had already appeared in England (where the book was known as *The Whale* and where a crucial publishing lapse had botched Melville's ending), and those sentiments began to find echoes across the pond. Melville had been elated that Hawthorne had "understood" the book, but that was not so for everybody. And the tide of derision showed that the book — particularly in its mixture of elements (facts, romance, natural history, digressions) — was in fact largely misunderstood by the public. America had more than its share of unimaginative critics with little breadth of knowledge who nonetheless had influential platforms, and many of those critics were also Christian moralists who were put off by anything that they deemed irreverent. One writer in New Haven, Connecticut, complained that the conversation between the sailors often contained "a little more irreverence and profane jesting than was needful to publish, however true to life the conversations may be."[187] Melville had endured character assaults from conservative congregationalists earlier in his career, and now he bore the jabs anew. The New York *Independent* used the opportunity of a new Melville work to condemn a "primitive formation of profanity and indecency that is ever and anon shooting up through all the strata of his writings."[188] Even Evert Duyckink, writing in the same New York *Literary World* that Melville had served so well with various pieces (particularly "Hawthorne and His Mosses"), took a high moral ground — though in perhaps gentler, less condemning terms. He wrote, "We do not like to see what, under any view, must be to the world the most sacred associations of life violated and defaced."[189] Duyckinck was far from completely dismissive, however, and unlike other reviewers, his second installment on *Moby-Dick*, published on November 22, 1851, shows that he had actually read and considered the work deeply. He found it "reckless at times of taste and propriety" and presented it early in the piece as a "most remarkable sea-dish — an intellectual chowder of romance, philosophy, natural history, fine writing, good feeling, bad sayings." Compliments regarding Melville's craft, however, were scattered throughout. Evert noted evidence of the author's "keen perceptive faculties" and "salient imagination," as well as his "acuteness of observation" and "freshness of perception."[190] And knowing all that one knows about *Moby-Dick* now, Duyckinck — in the freshness of reading the book just as it emerged to the public — also provides an unintentionally but genuinely humorous moment for later generations of readers when he describes the crew of *The Pequod* as being "more or less spiritual personages talking and acting differently from the general business run of the conversation on the decks of whaler." Then, the punch line: "They are for the most part very serious people, and seemed to be concerned a great deal about the problem of the universe."[191]

The damage to the public view of the work was done, however. A handful of positive reviews did appear, most prominently one in the December *Harper's* from George Ripley, Hawthorne's old Transcendentalist pal from the Brook Farm days. But Ripley was too late to help salvage *Moby-Dick* in the public eye. The initial sales of *Moby-Dick* amounted to merely 1500 copies; from that point, they would drop off into oblivion and Melville would not be able to dig himself out of debt to his publisher. (In December of 1853, the surplus of unsold copies of *Moby-Dick* was destroyed in a warehouse fire, killing any remaining glimmers of hope for the book.) Though it was harder and harder to see himself as an author in the face of all of this, he would soldier on for the next few years, publishing the books *Pierre; Or, the Ambiguities* (1852), *Israel Potter: His Fifty Years of Exile* (1855), and *The Confidence-Man: His Masquerade* (1857), as well as such remarkable shorter works as "Bartleby the Scrivener" (1853), "The Encantadas, or Enchanted Isles" (1854), and *Benito Cereno* (1855).

Evert Duyckinck's review of *Moby-Dick*, as fair-handed and reasonable as it sought to be in tone, had been one of the death knells for the work, and Hawthorne knew it. Moreover, Hawthorne flat out disagreed with a good portion of Duyckinck's assertions and felt strongly enough about it to act aggressively and out-of-character. On December 1, 1851, he wrote to the diminutive Knickerbocker. It was a short letter; therefore, its purpose was clear, delivered unflinchingly at its conclusion, thus ending with a coldness that was unmistakable — though Hawthorne, ever the gentleman, casually made his way to his point with pleasantries. He is even careful to refer to the review obliquely, as if unaware that Duyckinck was the very author:

My Dear Sir,

I have run away from the Berkshire winter.... It was one of my regrets in leaving Lenox, that I should no longer be benefitted by your visits to our friend Herman Melville; but then it is not impossible you may come to Boston — in which case (having good store of bedrooms) I shall hope to have you for my own guest. We are less than half an hour's ride (by rail-road) from the city.

What a book Melville has written! It gives me an idea of much greater power than his preceding ones. It hardly seemed to me that the review of it, in the *Literary World*, did justice to its best points.

Truly Yours,
Nathl Hawthorne.[192]

Melville may have failed in the eyes of those critics for whom he had little respect, but to have succeeded in the eyes of a writer and person of Nathaniel Hawthorne's caliber was something he could take to heart and carry with him. Here was something to keep him from giving up the pen just yet. Long before the disappointing notices, Melville had wisely and reflectively posed to Hawthorne that no one "who is wise, will expect appreciative recognition from his fellows."[193] Therefore, the compliments from Hawthorne regarding the whale book were the "good goddess's bonus over and above what was stipulated for ... I say your appreciation is my glorious gratuity."[194] Melville knew all too well that it was enough to have found in this lifetime one true reader and one true appreciator of Nathaniel Hawthorne's fiber. And, ledgers be damned, this would be enough to keep him going for now.

By the time Hawthorne's letter of subtle admonishment reached Duyckinck, Melville was deeply at work in Pittsfield on his next book, the ill-fated *Pierre*. "Leviathan is not the biggest fish," he had suggestively confided to his friend Nathaniel in his most intimate letter, after receiving the older writer's praise of *Moby-Dick*. "I have heard of Krakens."[195]

FIVE

Monody

Sailor or landsman, there is some sort of Cape Horn for all. Boys! beware of it; prepare for it in time. Graybeards! Thank God it has passed.

—Melville, White-Jacket

The Past is, in many things, the foe of mankind; the Future is, in all things, our friend. In the Past is no hope; the Future is both hope and fruition.

—Melville, White-Jacket

I can see you now, your face, shaded by your hand, — glowing in the ruddy light, and full of changeful expression, as the flickering fire burns brighter or subsides; —changeful, yet continuous, like the notes of an Irish melody; while Lizzie looks up at intervals from her sewing or her book, to recall by a tone and look of love, the musing wanderer from his enchanted Isles.

—John C. Hoadley, picturing the scene at
Arrowhead while writing to Melville, 1854

[A]t my years, and with my disposition ... one gets to care less and less for everything except downright good feeling. Life is so short, and so ridiculous and irrational (from a certain point of view) that one knows not what to make of it, unless— well, finish that sentence yourself.
—Melville to his brother-in-law John C. Hoadley, 1877

The last close hours that Melville and Hawthorne would spend in each other's company came in England in November 1856, where Hawthorne was serving as U.S. Consul in Liverpool. Nathaniel's years of dedicated friendship to Franklin Pierce — who had risen through the military (as a general in the Mexican War), the Senate, and who had finally experienced unlikely ascension to the American presidency — had paid off with this well-paying government post abroad. Pierce, a Northerner who consistently appeased Southern interests, would go down in history as one of the weakest of all American presidents, and his views were anathema to the set of people who surrounded the Hawthornes in Concord. (As a side note, Melville had made a trip to Concord in December 1852 to visit the Hawthornes, over a year after their flight from Lenox.) Nathaniel, however, as his admonishment of the *Literary World* review of *Moby-Dick* had illustrated, was unremittingly faithful to his close friends. During Pierce's campaign, Hawthorne had written a promotional biography of the candidate that glowingly supported Pierce's public image and, of course, sanded down or outright omitted his weaker points. The Abolitionists that surrounded Hawthorne in Massachusetts questioned his close association with this appeaser of Southern interests; that, and Hawthorne's own soft stance against Abolitionism, caused many — including his own sister-in-law Elizabeth Peabody — to question his ethical fiber. His fidelity had paid off, however, with a respected post and a consistent paycheck (though any literary efforts would now be on the back burner). Upon the election of Pierce, Herman Melville's brother Allan, now deep into his law career, had sought out Hawthorne to see if he could sway Pierce toward a job for his brother. Nothing came of it, and Melville's family continued to worry about his lack of a lucrative career and the mental toll that his substantial — and substantially unrequited — literary labors were exacting upon him.

However, in late 1856, Melville decided that it was high time to air himself out around the world again, and he took a voyage to the Holy Land. It was a fitting journey for a seeker such as he — for a fierce questioner and adamant non-believer who nonetheless sought a belief system of some sort. As always, conversation turned to such mysterious spiritual matters as the two sat among sand dunes and tall brown grass on the coast of the Irish Sea near the Hawthornes' current home in Southport, a Liverpool suburb. "Melville, as he always does, began to reason of Providence and futurity, and of everything that lies beyond human ken," wrote Hawthorne in his journal, giving us a remarkable record of the personality of Herman Melville and filling in a perspective lost to time by his destroyed letters to the younger author. According to Hawthorne, Melville "informed me that he had 'pretty much made up his mind to be annihilated'; but still he does not seem to rest in that anticipation; and, I think, will never rest until he gets hold of a definite belief." And, here, for the first time, we get a firsthand and unmistakable sense in the primary record of Nathaniel's awe-tinged admiration of his friend:

It is strange how he persists — and has persisted ever since I knew him, and probably long before — in wondering to-and-fro over these deserts, as dismal and monotonous as the sand hills amid which we were sitting. He can neither believe, nor be comfortable in his unbelief; and he is too honest and courageous not to try to do one or the other. If he were a religious man, he would be one of the most truly religious and reverential; he has a very high and noble nature, and better worth immortality than most of us.[1]

Hawthorne displayed admiration at other characteristics of his friend as well, noting for example that it was little "wonder that [Melville] found it necessary to take an airing through the world, after so many years of toilsome pen-labor and domestic life, following up so wild and adventurous a youth." Besides still holding a sense of awe regarding the essence of brine and faraway places on the onetime mariner, Hawthorne also admired Melville's autonomy and self-reliance: Departing for the Holy Lands after a three-days visit with Nathaniel, Herman left his trunk at the consulate and took only a carpetbag. This mode of travel, Hawthorne recorded, "is the next best thing to going naked; and he wears his beard and moustache, and so needs no dressing case — nothing but a toothbrush — I do not know a more independent personage. He learned his travelling habits by drifting about, all of the south Sea."[2] A more humorous interlude regarding this quality came when Hawthorne described Melville's initial arrival on his doorstep, carrying "by way of baggage, the least little bit of a bundle, which, he told me, contained a night shirt and a tooth-brush." Hawthorne's conclusion was that despite being "a person of very gentlemanly instincts in every respect" Melville was "a little heterodox in the matter of clean linen."[3]

These journal descriptions written by Hawthorne are a touching last look at and acknowledgement of the friendship — as well as a clear indicator of his depth of admiration and affection for the younger author. It also marks the last time that the two authors — who were destined to be canonized together in the top tier of American Literature after death — experienced any degree of closeness. (There is little evidence that Hawthorne and Melville shared much more than a hasty goodbye and the conveyance of a trunk during Herman's return trip.) They had maintained a regular correspondence after the Hawthornes' flight from the Berkshires, and Melville had even offered up a story idea for Hawthorne's use that the older writer politely refused. But England truly marks the end. What had held them together was a literary kinship and the search for new terrain back during a prolific time for both when they were sending their respective plummets into uncharted darkness and psychological depths. Hawthorne, at age 52, had now passed this prolific peak, however, and was currently sidelined from serious literary endeavors altogether due to his government duties. After his consul position ended, he had one more full-length romance in him, *The Marble Faun: Or, The Romance of Monte Beni* (1860), which he would begin writing in 1858, inspired by his extended stay in Italy. Melville was already a bruised and battered writer looking at retirement by the time he visited Hawthorne in northern England. He had just dropped *The Confidence-Man* off at his publisher in New York City before his voyage over to Glasgow by steamer. The novel would represent another critical and commercial failure — and it would be his last. No long-form prose publications would emerge from Herman Melville until the unfinished novella *Billy Budd* (1924), which was written in his very last years, hit the public 30-plus years after his death. Reviews in the intervening years since *Moby-Dick* had been continually harsh. *Pierre* (1852), the follow-up to the whale book had been savaged; in fact, one review (in the *New York Day Book*) had appeared with the headline "HERMAN MELVILLE CRAZY."[4] Similarly, the *American Whig Review* deemed his imagination and muse "diseased."[5] Melville certainly didn't help matters by having at the center of the land-bound tale an incestuous passion between Pierre and his half-sister. All in all, Melville was essentially through as an author by the time he crossed paths with Hawthorne in Liverpool. To capitalize on his ever-shrinking fame, he would turn to lecturing for a time, finding his themes and his delivery similarly out of touch with audiences in that medium. Then he would turn to poetry, publishing poems about the Civil War in *Harper's* after the monolithic conflict had ended, and then compiling them in book form as *Battle-Pieces and Other Aspects of the War* (1866). The taut discipline of verse occupied his time and satisfied his need for creativity, but like much of his work the volume never found an appreciative audience. A review by William Dean Howells (soon to become a noted literary critic and author) in *The Atlantic* suggested that the poems had little to do with the actual reality of war and more to do with the perturbation of "Mr. Melville's inner conscious" by the conflict.[6]

Nevertheless, poetry became Herman Melville's prime creative distraction for years. Continued financial failures had prompted him to move to New York City from Pittsfield, switching residences with his brother Allan in 1863 and settling into a house on East Twenty-Sixth Street in Manhattan. Nevertheless, during the last month of 1866,

Hawthorne having died more than two years prior, Melville's search for gainful and steady employment with the government finally paid off, and at 47 years old he became Deputy Inspector No. 75 of the United States Custom Service. (Melville's small badge that he wore each day is currently on display at the Berkshire Athenaeum in Pittsfield.) He was now the provider for four children — Malcolm, Stanwix, Elizabeth, and Frances — and in September of 1867 tragedy struck, when the oldest, 18-year-old Malcolm (or "Mackie," as his father called

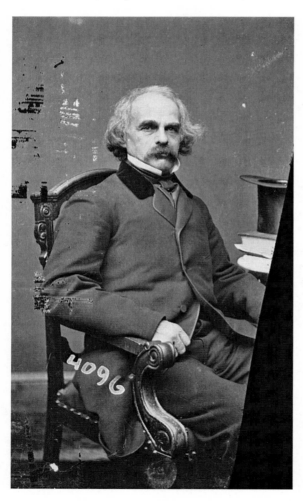

Nathaniel Hawthorne in the 1860s (Library of Congress).

him), shot himself, either accidentally or in an act of suicide, with a pistol in his bed. It was the worst that a parent could endure, and in heartbreaking prose, Melville wrote to his brother-in-law after the funeral, "I wish you could have seen him [in his coffin] as he lay in his last attitude, the ease of a gentle nature. Mackie never gave me a disrespectful word in his life, nor in any way ever failed in his filialness."[7] There has been, for decades, some debate among scholars whether the short poem "Monody" (the term, rooted in the Greek, meaning a poem that laments death) is about Malcolm or Hawthorne. It is not clear when Melville wrote "Monody," and it wasn't published until 1891:

To have known him, to have loved him
  After loneness long;
And then to be estranged in life,
  And neither in the wrong;
And now for death to set his seal —
  Ease me, a little ease, my song!
By wintry hills his hermit-mound
  The sheeted snow-drifts drape,
And houseless there the snow-bird flits
  Beneath the fir-trees' crape:
Glazed now with ice the cloistral vine
  That hid the shyest grape.[8]

However, the reference to "cloistral vine" and "shyest grape" point directly to a pattern of Melville's descriptive association with Hawthorne. Reading Hawthorne's earliest story collection in 1851, Melville had written to Duyckinck that the stories were "I fancy, an earlier vintage from his vine. Some of those sketches are wonderfully subtle. Their deeper meanings are worthy of a Brahmin."[9] Melville would also present a character, "Vine," based on Hawthorne in his epic poem *Clarel: A Poem and Pilgrimage in the Holy Land* (1876). (The epic poem used the raw material his 1856–57 trip, which included his last meeting with Nathaniel Hawthorne.) These lines from "Monody" also seem to reflect the Hawthorne friendship: "To have known him, to have loved him / After loneness long; / And then to be estranged in life, / And neither in the wrong." "After loneness long" suggests Melville's hunger for the type of friendship that Hawthorne offered — a meeting of the minds, a literary kinship. It is not, however, a sentiment that seems to fit an ode to a son. "[T]o be estranged in life, / And neither in the wrong" certainly reflects the eventual fading of the relationship — that is, this is simply one of those things that sometimes happens in friendship: a drifting apart due to the pressing circumstances of life and family.

Melville worked at his epic poem *Clarel* for a good decade, beginning after Malcolm's death, before it was finally self-published in 1876. Like *Moby-Dick*, it was a work of gigantic conception and great ambition; appearing in two volumes, stretching to 18,000 lines, and divided into 150 cantos, it was longer than *Paradise Lost, The Aeneid,* or *The Odyssey.* Melville once joked in a letter that it was "a metrical affair, a pilgrimage or what not, of several thousand lines, eminently adapted for unpopularity."[10] Numerous critics have pointed out the similarity between the character Vine and Nathaniel Hawthorne. In fact, in placing a character very similar to himself, "Rolfe," in the poem as well, Melville presents a dialectic between himself and Hawthorne — and the two appear nearly antithetical. Vine has all of Hawthorne's reputed qualities: his reclusiveness, his mysteriousness, his shyness, and his unique gifts. In the 1930s, Walter E. Bezanson saw the casting of the two characters against each other as "tournament of merits" between Hawthorne and Melville.[11] This is a compelling suggestion, as Melville was surrounded at the time of the poem's composition by his old friend's posthumous fame, even as his own anonymity became more and more solidified during the workaday drudgery of his custom-inspector duties. His private plying away at his epic poem usually consisted of eking out about five lines a night over the course of a decade, after spirit-wearying days at the docks.

For two decades, beginning in 1866, he worked the New York City piers—first, downtown, at the Battery; later, at 79th Street and the East River — securing mail, verifying cargo lists, and collecting fees. This was not labor ideally suited for an individual of Melville's imaginative and intellectual scope, but it was in many ways a return to the intentions of his youth, when fiscal realities drove the course of his life. After years of financial uncertainty, steady work and pay became the priority, as writing became a low-profile avocation. Melville also found his spirits disheartened by the low forms of malfeasance that surrounded him; it was a world in which all but the most ethically resilient were on the take. By all accounts, Melville resisted bribes for special consideration, which were the order of the place and time. Nevertheless, he was not immune to more legitimized forms of extortion: A small percentage of his and others' salaries was automatically funneled into the governing party's state committee as a measure to ensure protection and security to maintain his employment — that is, protection from the very entity that would threaten his position. Here was yet another link between Melville and Hawthorne: political bedevilment while in the employ of the custom-house. At what Andrew Delbanco asserts was possibly a late point in life, Melville marked a salient passage in his copy of Schopenhauer's *Studies of Pessimism*: "If he has a soul above the common, or if he is a man of genius, he will occasionally feel like some noble prisoner of state, condemned to work in the galleys with common criminals; and he will ... try to isolate himself."[12]

He finally published the labors of his off-hours vocation, *Clarel* — a monster of an epic poem at 20,000 lines— in 1876 with money provided by his uncle Peter Gansevoort, to whom he dedicated the work. Herman clearly had no capital left with any publishers at this point in his life. Herman's wife, Lizzie, privately (that is, away from her husband) referred to it as "this dreadful *incubus* of a *book*," due to the strain it put upon Herman. As Lizzie helped him prepare his proofs, she wrote to a cousin, "Herman, poor fellow, is in such a frightfully nervous state, & particularly now with such an added strain on his mind, that I am actually *afraid* to have anyone here for fear that he will be upset entirely, & not be able to go on with the printing."[13] *Clarel*, she claimed in unchecked expression, had "undermined all our happiness." Once the literary effort "gets off Herman's shoulders," she wrote, "I do hope he may be in better mental health."[14] The book was met with very few reviews—about seven in all—upon publication, and what praise there was for it was understated, though, in 1970, the poet, critic, and Pulitzer-Prize-winning novelist Robert Penn Warren would size up Melville's achievement with *Clarel* as forecasting Thomas Hardy, Ezra Pound, and T.S. Eliot, particularly the latter's groundbreaking "*The Waste Land, Ash Wednesday*, and *Four Quartets*."[15]

Of the Melville-Hawthorne friendship, however — to what can one attribute its quiet and hardly dramatic dissolution? Those looking for a great story to explain the eventual distance between these great storytellers will come up empty if adhering strictly to the primary record. There was no "explosive secret" as the ever-unreliable Julian Hawthorne would have it, a view that Andrew Delbanco also promotes in his excellent 2005 biography and critical reading, *Melville: His World and Work*. There was no clear antecedent or cause, but rather interceding circumstances that swept aside the possibility of picking up the threads and renewing the friendship during Hawthorne's final years. First, as mentioned in this book's introduction, there was Melville's periodic quest for a government post to pull him out of the financial quagmire into which a foundered literary career had submerged him — and the liability to that pursuit of a close association with Hawthorne, who had become a political pariah in Massachusetts due to his crankish conservative bent and his undying devotion to his friend Franklin Pierce. (Hawthorne's campaign biography of Pierce had been, at best, a political tool; at worst it was influential and clearly distortive political propaganda.) Melville's last visit with Hawthorne was in early May 1857, on the way back from the Holy Lands and Europe, as he grabbed his trunk that he had left with Nathaniel in Liverpool and headed home. There is little record of the last encounter, and it was, one can assume, cursory and without incident.

When Hawthorne's consul post expired that year, he would relocate to Italy with his family, the experience he drew upon for *The Marble Faun*. The Hawthornes existence touring and living in Europe put any possibility for the friendship out of mind and at a great geographical distance. By the time the family returned to the United States, in 1860, after seven years abroad, and a few years after the authors' last farewell, Melville was again on the verge of seeking a governmental post — this time from the newly installed Republican administration of Abraham Lincoln.

His brother Allan Melville took the lead on this, fueled by the family's continual concerns regarding Herman's mental and physical health, which they felt had been plagued by too many years in the thickets of solitary mental labor. His prodigious output, marked by ever-diminishing critical and financial returns—from the initial excitement of *Typee* in 1846 to *The Confidence-Man*'s stagnated arrival in 1857 — along with a few years after that on the lecture circuit, another failed enterprise into which he had poured himself, had left Herman Melville, at the age of 41, depleted and looking towards a life beyond and well outside of literature. Allan, a well-appointed New York City lawyer, used his network of connections to push for a consulship for his older brother, first in the Sandwich Islands and then, more fixedly with more seriousness of purpose, in Florence, Italy (where, in fact, the Hawthornes had stayed for much of 1858). Herman's brother-in-law John C. Hoadley (the husband of Catherine "Kate" Gansevoort Melville), who was elected as a Republican member of the Massachusetts legislature in 1858, petitioned his good friend Massachusetts Senator Charles Sumner. Several prominent Pittsfield citizenry signed a recommendation and sent it to Abraham Lincoln, and eminent lawyer Alexander W. Bradford, with whom Herman had stayed in 1839 before shipping out on the *St. Lawrence* to England, offered his support. Melville did get an audience with Sumner in Washington in March of 1861, and he witnessed Lincoln with his own eyes, as Hawthorne would months later, but the Florence post was already filled. Herman offered a follow-up request to be positioned in Glasgow, Scotland, but this was not to be either. These endeavors are rarely looked at in the context of the Hawthorne friendship, but Melville clearly could not afford to rekindle the association with the well-known older author, who was recently reinstalled at the Wayside in Concord, as he plowed this tenuous political path on the eve of the Civil War — which broke out mere weeks after his Washington visit.

The distraction of war, both authors' compromised health, and

Hawthorne's further political marginalization of himself in influential Concord became another barrier. And all in all, the two writers' respective attentions were elsewhere. The world had drastically since the early 1850s, when the two could put aside all concerns to talk together lengthily and earnestly about their respective literary vocations, metaphysics, and all matters at the margins of human understanding. For Melville, the winter of 1860 and 1861 which preceded the war became a "sad arch between contrasted eras," as he would describe it in *Clarel* (part 4, Canto 5). In Pittsfield that spring, two volunteer companies trailing guide colors made of Chinese silks tromped off to battle; in Concord, 45 young men gathered at the depot and were hailed off with a speech and a cannon salute. Hawthorne, early on, doubted the purpose of war and furthermore doubted that the country had ever been a "Union" in the first place, in the truest sense of the word. His peevish conservatism and his even more exacerbated tendency toward reclusiveness threw him out of step and company with the progressively activist spirit of the Concord intelligentsia. He condemned the bloody fanaticism of John Brown and proclaimed the abolitionist's hanging to be an act of proper justice. In July 1862, he published a piece in the *Atlantic Monthly*, "Chiefly About War Matters," based on an official excursion through Washington, D.C., and southern war zones. His unflattering portrait of Lincoln and sympathetic slant toward Confederate prisoners pushed him even further out of step with his neighbors' unchecked zeal, idealism, and sense of divine mission. He avoided visitors at the Wayside and was known to bolt out the back door to pace among the pines on the ridge if any but the most welcome approached his door. So Hawthorne spent his final years until his death in the spring of 1864. He was still, however, a public figure — he did accept an invitation into Boston's Saturday Club, a monthly gathering of Boston's intellectual elite, including Oliver Wendell Holmes, Emerson, Longfellow, and the elder Henry James. But by all accounts Hawthorne was not an engaging member during his brief tenure, and he mostly kept his head pointed toward his plate. (Charles Sumner, whom Melville had petitioned for sponsorship, was a frequent guest at the Club too, and a full-fledged member by 1862. He would have been all too aware of Hawthorne's lack of sociability and political "incorrectness.") Melville, however, was not much of a public or literary figure anymore, and he remained sequestered by the mountains and his evershrinking reputation out in far western Massachusetts. Anyone that he petitioned for a government post would have needed to be reminded, or even flat out informed, of his past achievements in order to be aware that the candidate was a once-known man of letters. This too deepened the divide between Hawthorne and Melville. If the friendship were to be renewed in any way, it would be Melville who pursued it — and there were simply too many mitigating circumstances in the way. There was no way back to the companionable tides of the 1850s. In a relatively short time, the world — and the two men — had changed.

Hawthorne, who despite the ever-deepening distance was still very much prominent in Melville's thoughts, died in Plymouth, New Hampshire, on May 19, 1864. He was nearly sixty and had been in poor health for some time; in fact, he died in the company of his old friend, and now former U.S. president, Franklin Pierce, who had hoped that a trip through the spring mountains of New Hampshire would prove restorative. Hawthorne had remained loyal to his Bowdoin College friends, Pierce and Horatio Bridge, until the end and they to him. Hawthorne had dedicated *Our Old Home* to Pierce in 1863, six years after the end of Pierce's highly criticized presidency, and against the protests of his publisher and other people around him. (Pierce did nothing to improve his reputation with northerners by voicing empathy for the Confederacy during the Civil War.) According to Pierce, Hawthorne possessed limited use of his hands and had difficulty even walking during that last trip, and he died peacefully in his sleep in an adjoining room to Pierce's at Pemigewasset House, the large Plymouth, New Hampshire, boarding residence in which they were staying. Hawthorne's funeral and burial were in Concord, where he lived at the Wayside, the home he and Sophia had bought from Bronson Alcott in March 1852, not long after his Berkshires period, and the house he would return to after his duties and travels in Europe. Pierce, who would die a mere five-and-a-half years later of liver cirrhosis, due to alcoholism, found himself quite out of place at the Concord funeral among the ardent liberalism of the many Transcendental Abolitionists.

Hawthorne had rallied for one last romance late in life, *The Marble Faun* (1860), and of his full-length works, it is clearly the most Melvillian. In its inconclusiveness, its digressive dissertations on art and travel, and in its expansiveness of language, it bears out the freedom from constraints he had witnessed and absorbed in his friend's *Moby-Dick*. In fact, in his American Book Award-winning biography of Hawthorne, James R. Mellow asserts that "much of the travel-guide aspect of [*The Marble* Faun] ... was intended to serve as Melville's technical discussions of whaling had served in *Moby-Dick*, as a kind of ballast for the allegorical nature of the story."[16] Additionally, Hawthorne's unspooling and constantly cresting language describing Rome in *Marble Faun* (presented in the introductory chapter of the book you are reading) is worth reexamining in this context. This unharnessed language is not a form we have seen before from Hawthorne, who had been away from the public as a writer for seven years; but it *is* the wheeling, associative, inward-plumbing prose that he, as *Moby-Dick*'s earliest appreciative reader, had been impressed with in that book in November 1851. And it is with great gusts of spleen that he lays out his repulsive sensations of Rome, only to arrive at the idea that he feels heartfelt attachment to the city and all that it embodies. An unbound language is the only language that can express such an emotional paradox. Exit the former hallmarks of control and restraint (what the *Literary World* had called his "marvelous self-control")[17]; enter a mode of writing from Hawthorne in *The Marble Faun* that would not be out of place in *Moby-Dick*:

> When we have once known Rome, and left her where she lies, like a long decaying corpse, retaining a trace of the noble shape it was, but with accumulated dust and a fungous growth overspreading all its more admirable features; — left her in utter weariness, no doubt, of her narrow, crooked, intricate streets, so uncomfortably paved with little squares of lava that to tread over them is a penitential pilgrimage, so indescribably ugly, moreover, so cold, so alley-like, into which the sun never falls, and where a chill wind forces its breath into our lungs; — left her, tired of the sight of those immense, seven-storied, yellow-washed hovels, or call them palaces, where all that is dreary in domestic life seems magnified and multiplied, and weary of climbing those staircases, which ascend from a ground-floor of cookshops, coblers' [*sic*] stalls, stables, and regiments of cavalry, to a middle region of artists, just beneath the unattainable sky; — left her, worn out with shivering at the cheerless and smoky fireside, by day, and feasting with our own substance the ravenous little populace of a Roman bed, at night; — left her, sick at heart of Italian trickery, which has uprooted whatever faith in man's integrity had endured till now, and sick at stomach of sour bread, sour wine, rancid butter, and bad cookery, needlessly bestowed on evil meats; — left her, disgusted with the pretence of Holiness and the reality of Nastiness, each equally omnipresent; — left her, half-lifeless from the languid atmosphere, the vital principle of which has been used up, long ago, or corrupted by myriads of slaughters; — left her, crushed down in spirit with the desolation of her ruin, and the hopelessness of her future; — left her, in short, hating her with all our might, and adding our individual curse to the Infinite Anathema which her old crimes have unmistakably brought down; — when we have left Rome in such a mood as this, we are astonished by the discovery, by-and-by, that our heart strings have mysteri-

ously attached themselves to the Eternal City, and are drawing us thitherward again, as if it were more familiar, more intimately our own home,
than even the spot where we were born![18]

Melville read *The Marble Faun* during the year of its release, in the midst
of a voyage around Cape Horn to California on a clipper ship (a type of
vessel known for its speed), *The Meteor*, that his youngest brother,
Thomas, was commanding. Herman's neighbor Sarah Morewood, who
lived in the old Melvill home, now known as Broadhall, had given him
a copy of Hawthorne's romance as a going-away gift. Whether he ever
commented on Hawthorne's creative shift in *The Marble Faun* is not
known, and his annotations in the book certainly don't tell the tale,
though he did question Hawthorne's assertion in chapter 12 that the Ital-
ian Renaissance painter Perugino was devout — drawn (as Herman
always was) to issues of belief and non-belief. His own reading, he noted,
of *Lives of the Painters*, had led to his understanding that the painter
scoffed at religion in general. Melville had also already turned to poetry
by this time; therefore, his once keen interest in the creative energies
behind prose was latent.

Nevertheless, one must wonder at Melville's reaction to a very
different Hawthorne in *The Marble Faun or, the Romance of Monte
Beni* (published in England as *Transformation; or, the Romance of Monte
Beni*). Was he nagged, like many critics, by its lack infrastructural
arrangement, or did he see how this criticized aspect recalled the very
jabs thrown at *Moby-Dick*? Writing a decade and a half after Hawthorne's
death, English novelist Anthony Trollope, who Hawthorne had come
to admire toward the end of his own life, addressed "The Genius of
Nathaniel Hawthorne" in an essay in *The North American Review*. In
detailing his admiration for the Hawthorne canon, and the divide
between his own well-known dogged realism and the American's supernatural and imaginative bent, he describes the qualities that bring
Hawthorne and Melville together: "Something of the sublimity of
the transcendent, something of the mystery of the unfathomable, something of the brightness of the celestial."[19] To complete the canon-span-
ning piece, Trollope leaves himself just enough room to address, lastly,
The Marble Faun — and, even as he admires the novel's sheer aesthetic
pleasures, he casts criticism toward its construction in language that may
as well be directed toward *Moby-Dick*. While allowing that the writer
who "soars into the supernatural need not bind himself by any of the
ordinary trammels of life ... there must be some plot," and the "great

Herman Melville, seated, and his youngest brother, Thomas, 1860 (courtesy Berkshire Athenaeum, Pittsfield, Massachusetts).

fault" of *The Marble Faun*, in Trollope's mind, "lies in its absence of arranged plot"[20]:

> In "The Marble Faun," as in all Hawthorne's tales written after "The Scarlet Letter," the reader must look rather for a series of pictures than for a novel. It would, perhaps, almost be well that a fastidious reader should cease to read when he comes within that border, toward the end, in which it might be natural to expect that the strings of a story should be gathered together and tied into an intelligible knot. This would be peculiarly desirable in regard to "The Marble Faun," in which the delight of that fastidious reader, as derived from pictures of character and scenery, will be so extreme that it should not be marred by a sense of failure in other respects.[21]

Trollope, writing in Victorian 1879, is describing an element that was also critiqued in *Moby-Dick* during the mid-nineteenth century. Of course, it was an also an aspect of the whale book that literati would come to celebrate as proto-modernistic in the twentieth century. Hawthorne had read and deeply digested and understood *Moby-Dick* like few others upon its arrival, and he had an insider's view of its creation through his intimate conversations and letters with Melville. He therefore had a perspective on the book that *no one* else had or would ever have, and his praise for it was unquestionable. Hawthorne seems to have never forgotten Melville's sense of narrative liberation and soaring aesthetics in the novel — and those are the very qualities that rear up at the reader in *The Marble Faun* as well. There is no other clear explanation for his sudden stylistic shift and throwing off of narrative constraints; there is no other evidence of a clear model or inspiration for this other than his close association with the creation of the very book that bore a dedication to him. *The Marble Faun*, as 2003 Hawthorne biographer Brenda Wineapple asserts, "was so modern it baffled many of its first readers"[22] This could be a verbatim assessment of *Moby-Dick* as well. For his return to writing after a long lapse — and in deference to a new age — Hawthorne chose a Melvillian mode in order to break from his past forms and introduce himself anew. Another modernist element of *The Marble Faun* that baffled readers was its inconclusive ending. Hawthorne was very deliberately bucking the expectations of the contemporary novel reader, tipping his hand in chapter fifty: "The actual experience of even the most ordinary life is full of events that never explain themselves, either as regards their origin or their tendency."[23] Here, in even more heightened form, was that engaging uncertainty and ambiguity that he and Melville shared. In a chapter tellingly marked "Fragmentary Sentences," Hawthorne also tipped his hand to the fragmentary nature of his narrative, showing that, un-visionary critics be damned, it was fundamental to his infrastructure:

> In weaving these mystic utterances into a continuous scene, we undertake a task resembling in its perplexity that of gathering up and piecing together the fragments of a letter which has been torn and scattered to the winds. Many words of deep significance, many entire sentences, and those possibly the most important ones, have flown too far on the winged breeze to be recovered. If we insert our own conjectural amendments, we perhaps give a purport utterly at variance with the true one. Yet unless we attempt something in this way, there must remain an unsightly gap, and a lack of contin-

uousness and dependence in our narrative; so that it would arrive at certain inevitable catastrophes without due warning of their imminence.[24]

Words scattered. Conversations and images in fragments and pieces: The pre-bellum Hawthorne was pioneering away at terrain that modernists such as T.S. Eliot, James Joyce, and Ezra Pound would claim for themselves in the second decade of the next century. And the patchwork merging of the book's elements—plot, characterization, travel guide, and rumination—calls to mind Melville's construction of *Moby-Dick*. (Substitute the intricacies and technicalities of whaling for Hawthorne's travel discussions.) Hawthorne read *Moby-Dick* in November 1851, furnished with a freshly minted copy from Melville. He was well into *The Blithedale Romance* (1852) by then and had a full handle on his intention and infrastructure, so that work wouldn't have borne out much influence from that reading experience—and he was quite specifically exorcising an earlier chapter in his life related to Brook Farm. The very next book he produced (after a period of dormancy), and his last, was *The Marble Faun*, which arguably bears the influence of Melville's crowning novel. Published about four years before Hawthorne's death, it shows him breaking away from old forms and even from the setting of his native New England. Some, though, saw past the book's unconventional structure and into the heart of it, just as Hawthorne had admired *Moby-Dick*, despite its era-challenging idiosyncrasies. "You were archangel enough to despise the [book's] imperfect body, and embrace the soul," wrote Melville to Nathaniel after the latter's complimentary letter in 1851. And so too did *The North American Review* see to the heart of *The Marble Faun*, and past the experiments in form, upon its publication: "As a work of art we are inclined to place it above either of his previous books. Its style has a harmony and beauty of expression and a warmth of coloring which are seen in none of his other writings."[25]

To break literary constraints, to be misunderstood, but to have precious few truly behold their achievement: this was Melville and Hawthorne's last link. And though the two authors had drifted apart during the intervening years—eight, to be exact, since the Liverpool visit—Melville's wife reported that Herman was "much shocked" when he learned of Hawthorne's death in late May 1864. Melville's mother, Maria, reported to her brother Peter Gansevoort, himself a lifelong friend of James Fenimore Cooper until that writer's death in 1851, "Herman was much attached to him & will mourn his loss. He staid [sic] with him a few days in Liverpool, & I believe [sic] has not seen him since."[26] And, in the decade-plus after Hawthorne's death that Melville, as Hershel Parker put it, "worked out his feelings about Hawthorne in *Clarel*,"[27] he witnessed Hawthorne's posthumous star rising higher and higher. Melville would have to spend a thousand dollars to get his epic poem *Clarel* published and out to the public in 1876 (after a decade of toil), where it created only a minor ripple, and in the decades after the older writer's death, he primarily became, when he was remembered or mentioned at all, a footnote: He was the Pittsfield sea writer who had once been friends with Hawthorne.

As if to punctuate that fact, Julian Hawthorne, now 37, called upon Melville at his twenty-sixth street home in Manhattan on August 10, 1883. The individual who, as a boy in Lenox, had declared to love Herman Melville as much as anyone in his immediate family, was writing a book about his parents called *Hawthorne and His Wife* and had in his possession the ardent letters Melville had written to Julian's father over three decades prior. Julian's accounts of the meeting changed a bit over the years, particularly as Melville's posthumous fame grew in the third decade of the new millennium and as the teller became more and more abstracted by time from the experience. But in his earliest (and likely *more* reliable — if not entirely reliable) telling, he recalled Melville opening his door on the placid side street appearing "pale, somber, nervous, but little touched by age," despite his advancing years. Julian also described him, in his nervousness, constantly rising to open and shut again a window facing a courtyard.[28] (Based on such a description, they likely met in the parlor, not the more private sanctum of his twenty-sixth street study.) Julian was interested in the letters that his father had sent Melville but learned during the visit that they were long gone — and most likely destroyed. Julian also claimed that the aging writer was, at first "disinclined to talk, but finally he said several interesting things." The "most remarkable," claimed the younger Hawthorne "was that he was convinced Hawthorne had all his life concealed some great secret, which would, were it known, explain all the mysteries of his career." And this would explain all of the "gloomy passages in his books."[29] The statement, in its simplicity of interpretation and cliff-hanging drama, is suspect and doesn't resonate with Melville's more complex line of thinking regarding Nathaniel Hawthorne. Julian, who, having published several novels, was already "something of a literary posturer," in Andrew Delbanco's estimation, would eventually be charged with stock fraud in 1913 and sent to prison for a year in Atlanta.[30] Julian had attached his formidable last name to a friend's scheme in which over three-million shares of stock were sold against a non-existent silver mine. Julian, as an old man, retold his Melville story numerous times as Melville's posthumous fame grew in the 1920s, and the younger Hawthorne died at the age of 88 in 1934.

Melville, of course, never lived to see his name become foremost in the canon of American literature. In 1919, Raymond Weaver, a Columbia University professor, began researching the first biography of Herman Melville, and Eleanor Melville Metcalf, Herman Melville's granddaughter, then living in New Jersey, granted the scholar access to all of the surviving papers of the late author. Eleanor was Herman's youngest child, Frances,' daughter. Herman's second oldest, the star-crossed Stanwix, had struggled throughout life to find a lucrative career, and then died, childless and 35, of tuberculosis in San Francisco in 1886, the same year that his father was able to retire from customs work due to a financial inheritance of Lizzie's. Herman and Lizzie's third child, the sickly Elizabeth ["Bessie"], did not have any children, either. As early as the 1880s, Melville had been corresponding with English admirers, and was aware that he had garnered somewhat of a literary reputation across the pond. It was less so in his own country, until Weaver's eventual 1921 biography, *Herman Melville: Man, Mariner, and Mystic*. Among the papers that Weaver received from the Melville grandchild was also the remarkable, unpublished, and incomplete *Billy Budd*, which Weaver, initially unimpressed, transcribed hastily; nevertheless, the hackneyed and incorrect nature of the first edition aside, the work was highly heralded, first in England, by D.H. Lawrence, among other notables, and then in America. Melville had likely begun the work after his retirement in 1886 and spent the final half-decade of his life tinkering with it, in a wonderful return to the prose form. Other significant academics took up the resurgence of Melville, and by the late 1920s, Herman Melville — long after death — had found literary fame.

Decades before, in a world away in the Berkshire Mountains of Massachusetts, Melville had written "Hawthorne and His Mosses" in the fresh bloom of encountering both Nathaniel Hawthorne and the writings of Nathaniel Hawthorne. And while the piece sounded his admiration for the writer's genius (as would his dedication to him in *Moby-Dick*), it also made the case for uniquely American writers to emerge and establish a body of work distinct from the widely popular and universally respected English literature. The materialization of this in the next century saw him and Hawthorne finally brought together as equals. In their friendship, Melville had been the young author underling, constantly showing tribute to the master, while also earning Hawthorne's deepest respect as a person and as a writer. After their friendship drifted, Melville witnessed Hawthorne's reputation rise higher and higher, as he himself became ever more forgotten for his formidable literary labors. Melville had lived an extraordinary life, stretched out over an extraordinary time, born in the republic's infancy in 1819 and then seeing technological advancement after advancement change the world around him until his death, in 1891, on the brink of the twentieth century. He had visited the "frontier" of Illinois as a young man, then had seen the westward expansion of the country to the Pacific Ocean, he had seen wave upon wave of industrialism change the faces of cities and towns. He had also seen the troubling undersides of both expansionism and industrialism. He had seen slavery, the monstrous death tolls of the Civil War, and the abolition of slavery. He had come into a world lit by whale oil, was forty when petroleum was discovered in America, and then late in life he had seen Manhattan illuminated by Edison's electric lights. In fact, he had lived virtually another lifetime after his friend Hawthorne's death in 1864.

Ultimately, however, it was the future fate of Herman Melville and Nathaniel Hawthorne to be spoken of in the same breath, as two of the foremost giants in nineteenth-century literature — and, of course, as friends. In the "Mosses" review, Melville had held up Shakespeare as the exemplar of all literature, while the future would see *Moby-Dick* held aloft as an American *Hamlet*. (The book, of course, became like the doubloon that Ahab fastened to the main-mast, something in which readers have seen and perceived countless things.) The closest time of their friendship saw the men bedeviled by quotidian elements: a dispute with landlords, a brutal winter, babbling young children, crops to get in, home improvements to hammer away at, a lack or surfeit of brandy and cigars, rigorous literary labors, ebbing finances — and six miles of muddy, jolting, and rutted road. This was what the flesh-and-blood friendship consisted of, besides (of course) the relationship synergy between two writers. However, as the writer and literary critic Leslie Fiedler would declare in 1969, "To be an American (unlike being English or French or whatever) is precisely to *imagine* a destiny rather than to inherit one; since we have always been, insofar as we are Americans at all, inhabitants of myth rather than history."[31] Fiedler, in the first part of this compelling statement, certainly encapsulates Herman Melville's impulse in "Hawthorne and His Mosses," and in his own work, Melville sought to find new literary frontiers through the drive of his imagination. But it is in that myth that Fiedler speaks of—abstracted from the flesh and blood lives of the two writers—that Herman Melville and Nathaniel Hawthorne were fused together forever.

Chapter Notes

Chapter One

1. Herman Melville, *The Letters of Herman Melville*, ed. Merrell R. Davis and William H. Gilman (New Haven: Yale University Press, 1960), 143. This extremely well-presented collection is rivaled only by *The Melville Log* in its resourcefulness for those just embarking upon an understanding of the life and mercurial mindset of Herman Melville. This is the definitive collection of letters that had been both previously published and unpublished prior to 1960.

2. Herman Melville, *Moby-Dick*, 150th Anniversary Edition (New York: Signet Classic, 1998), 526.

3. Barbara Epstein and Robert B. Silvers, *The Company They Kept* (New York: New York Review Books, 2009), 103.

4. Malcolm Bradbury and Richard Ruland, *From Puritanism to Postmodernism: A History of American Literature* (New York: Penguin, 1991), 149–151.

5. Louis Menand, *The Metaphysical Club: A Story of Ideas in America* (New York: Farrar, Straus and Giroux, 2001), x.

6. Andrew Delbanco, *Melville: His World and Work* (New York: Knopf, 2005), 175. For the reader first entering the biographical world of Melville, Delbanco's book is a good starting point. His movement between biography and eloquent interpretation of the writer's works is highly readable and insightful. Nevertheless, the serious researcher should note the occasional factual lapse. In one example, on page 42, Delbanco claims that Melville deserted the *Acushnet* "after six months at sea," which is far off the mark of Melville's ocean reality. He set sail from New Bedford, Massachusetts, at the beginning of January 1841 and deserted in late June or early July of 1842, a period of about 19 months. This information can be quickly gleaned by following the chronology in *The Melville Log*. Delbanco is long on insight, however, and only occasionally short on facts.

7. Nathaniel Hawthorne, *The Complete Works of Nathaniel Hawthorne, Volume XXII* (Boston: Houghton Mifflin, 1883), 218.

8. Nathaniel Hawthorne, *The Letters*, ed. Thomas Woodson and L. Neal Smith (Columbus: Ohio State University Press, 1985), XVI, 156.

9. Hawthorne, *The Letters*, XVI, 624.

10. Nathaniel Hawthorne, *The English Notebooks*, ed. Randall Stewart (New York: Russell & Russell, 1962), 88.

11. Brenda Wineapple, *Hawthorne: A Life* (New York: Random House Trade Paperbacks, 2003), 232. Wineapple's fairly recent biography is astute, readable, and engaging. This is a perfect starting point for knowledge of Hawthorne's life and work, and though long on readability it is far from short on depth of insight and analysis.

12. Ibid., 381.

13. Leonard Woolf, *Downhill All the Way: An Autobiography of the Years 1919–1939* (London: Hogarth Press, 1967), 9.

14. Melville, *Moby-Dick*, 102.

15. Melville, *The Letters of Herman Melville*, 138.

16. Hawthorne, *The Letters*, XVIII, 271.

17. Wineapple, 224.

18. Carl Gustav Jung, *The Spirit in Man, Art, and Literature: Collected Works of C.G. Jung, Volume 15*, trans. Gerhard Adler and R.F.C. Hull (Princeton: Princeton University Press, 1966), 88.

19. John Updike, "Late Works," *Due Considerations: Essays and Criticism* (New York: Ballantine, 2007), 66.

20. Herman Melville, *Mardi: And a Voyage Thither*, eds. Harrison Hayford, G. Thomas Tanselle and Hershel Parker

(Evanston, IL: Northwestern University Press, 1970), 557.

21. Nathaniel Hawthorne, *The Scarlet Letter*, in *Hawthorne: Collected Novels* (New York: Library of America, 1983), 293.

22. Nathaniel Hawthorne, "The Birthmark," in *Mosses from an Old Manse*, Volume X of Works (Columbus: Ohio State University, 1974), 40.

23. Nathaniel Hawthorne, *The Scarlet Letter*, 325.

24. Nathaniel Hawthorne, "The Haunted Mind" in *Twice-Told Tales*, Volume I (Boston: Houghton Mifflin, 1884), 62.

25. Lewis Mumford, *Herman Melville* (New York: The Literary Guild of America/Harcourt, Brace, 1929), 145. Clearly, the earliest biographies of Melville pale against later works, as knowledge about, and sources regarding, the writer materialized throughout the twentieth century. Mumford's book is still a joy to read for its high emotional tenor and apparent adoration of its subject.

26. Nathaniel Hawthorne, *The English Notebooks*, 432.

27. Andrew Delbanco, *Melville: His World and Work* (New York: Alfred A. Knopf, 2005), 211.

28. *The Selected Poems of Herman Melville,* ed. Robert Penn Warren (New York: Barnes & Noble, 1998), 334.

29. *John Keats: Selected Letters*, eds. Robert Gittings and Jon Mee (Oxford: Oxford University Press, 2002), 41.

30. Herman Melville, 1856 passport application, housed in the Berkshire Athenaeum (Pittsfield, Massachusetts). This library in Melville's hometown for a good portion of his life has an invaluable trove of research resources, including definitive images (daguerreotypes, etc.) of the writer. The Melville Room, as of this writing, also has on display such items as the desk that Herman used late in life, a letter from Gansevoort, Melville's customs inspector badge — and a host of other materials related to the writer and whaling. There are many photos of Melville descendents and their milieu as well. This should be a first stop for the would-be biographer.

31. Nathaniel Hawthorne, *The English Notebooks*, 433.

32. Ibid.

33. Jana L. Argersinger and Leland S. Person, eds., *Hawthorne and Melville: Writing a Relationship* (Athens: University of Georgia Press, 2005), 15. This admirable publication is a collection of essays with widely diverging themes and intentions and not necessarily a cohesive work regarding the two writers.

While offering compelling new critical interpretations it does not add to the informed reader's biographical understanding of the relationship — and that is certainly not its intention.

34. Julian Hawthorne, *Nathaniel Hawthorne and His Wife: A Biography*, Volume 1 (Boston: Houghton Mifflin, 1884), 422.

35. Jay Leyda, *The Melville Log* (New York: Harcourt, Brace, 1951), 394. This compendium of pieces from widely ranging primary sources, edited and arranged to present a life chronology, is the foremost item in the Melville biographer's toolkit.

36. Hershel Parker, *Herman Melville: A Biography, Volume I (1819—1851)* (Baltimore: Johns Hopkins University Press, 1996), xii. Parker's massive and meticulous two-volume set is the definitive word on Melville's life. Nevertheless, it is not necessarily receptive to the reader seeking an introduction. The consequential and less consequential as well as the directly pertaining and not-so-directly pertaining are sometimes rendered thoroughly as equals. Parker's research is unrivalled, however, and his attention to less acknowledged and less known primary documents is exhaustive.

37. Sophia Hawthorne to Elizabeth Peabody, August 8, 1850. Berg Collection of English and American Literature, New York Public Library, New York. Nathaniel Hawthorne's wife's perceptive and colorful writing in her letters provides the reader with not only the most fleshed-out descriptions of Herman Melville during the time of the Hawthorne friendship, but some of the most compelling and human portraits of Melville, period. Her sensitivity and acuity prove her to be a great writer in her own right.

38. Herman Melville, "Hawthorne and His Mosses," *The Portable Melville*, ed. Jay Leyda (New York: Viking, 1952), 407.

39. Melville, *Moby-Dick*, 507.

40. J.M. Coetzee, *Boyhood: Scenes from Provincial Life* (New York: Viking, 1997), 140.

41. Mumford, *Herman Melville*, 92.

42. Melville, "Hawthorne and His Mosses," 408.

43. Melville, *Moby-Dick*, 416.

44. Melville, "Hawthorne and His Mosses," 417.

45. Melville, *The Letters of Herman Melville*, 142.

46. D. Michael Quinn, *Same-Sex Dynamics Among Nineteenth-Century Americans* (Champaign: University of Illinois Press, 2001). Quinn's work is aimed at Mormon culture; nevertheless, it offers up plenty of consideration for nineteenth-century culture in

general. In fact, the book's *modus operandi* as the author states in the introduction, endeavors to avoid the familiar approach of "seeing the Mormon experience in isolation," while "emphasiz[ing] cross-cultural comparisons and the American social context."

47. Melville, *The Letters of Herman Melville*, 111.

48. Quinn, *Same-Sex Dynamics among Nineteenth-Century Americans*, x.

49. Melville, *Pierre; Or, the Ambiguities*, 295.

50. Anthony Storr, *Solitude: A Return to the Self* (New York: The Free Press, 1988), 130. Beyond Storr's salient remarks on male friendship, Storr's work offers a fascinating psychological study of solitude and the creative individual that would be a fitting context for authors such as Melville and Hawthorne. Storr goes a long way to show creative solitude as a path to fulfillment rivaling intimate relationships, and not a pathology or inability to form human bonds. He doesn't specifically mention Melville and Hawthorne, but does analyze the lives of several literary figures, including Kipling, Tennyson, Saki, and Wodehouse.

51. Nathaniel Hawthorne, *Selected Letters of Nathaniel Hawthorne* (Columbus: Ohio State University Press, 2002), 147.

52. Ibid.

53. Newton Arvin, *Herman Melville* (New York: William Sloane Associates, 1950), 138.

54. Laurie Robertson-Lorant, *Melville: A Biography* (New York: Clarkson N. Potter, 1996), 618. Like many others, Robertson-Lorant is also diligent is separating nineteenth-century social context from contemporary assumptions and insinuation. As she also posits in this same set of passages, "Men and women in Melville's America regularly employed erotic tropes when addressing intimate same-sex friends, perhaps because the language of passionate friendship was not construed as an invitation to sexual consummation, as it is today."

55. Ibid., 619.

56. Ibid.

57. Quoted in Arlin Turner, *Nathaniel Hawthorne: A Biography* (New York: Oxford University Press, 1980), 217.

58. Jay Leyda, *The Melville Log* (New York: Harcourt, Brace, 1951), 386.

59. Ibid., 422.

60. Wineapple, 69.

61. Nathaniel Hawthorne, *Our Old Home and English Note-Books, Vol. 1* (Boston: Houghton Mifflin, 1884), 116.

62. Perry D. Westbrook, *A Literary History of New England* (Bethlehem, PA: Lehigh University Press, 1988), 197.

63. Quoted in *The Writings of Herman Melville: Correspondence, Volume 14* (Evanston, IL: Northwestern University Press, 1993), 184.

64. Nathaniel Hawthorne, *Our Old Home and English Note-Books, Vol. II* (Cambridge: Printed at the Riverside Press, 1883), 374.

65. Arvin, 137.

66. Quoted in Wineapple, 226.

67. Wineapple, 220.

68. Leland S. Person, *The Cambridge Introduction to Nathaniel Hawthorne* (Cambridge: Cambridge University Press, 2007), 67.

69. Joel Myerson, *The Selected Letters of Nathaniel Hawthorne* (Columbus: Ohio State University Press, 2002), 137.

70. The original house and land deeds to Arrowhead; Berkshire Athenaeum in Pittsfield, Massachusetts; Herman Melville Room.

71. James R. Mellow, *Nathaniel Hawthorne in His Times* (Baltimore: Johns Hopkins University Press, 1998), 313. This American Book Award-winning tome is the most assiduous of Hawthorne biographies, by a late and revered giant in the world of literary biography. In reviewing the book in the *New York Times* upon its initial release, Alfred Kazin devoted a good portion of his September 21, 1980, piece to the Hawthorne-Melville friendship, writing, "When Melville met Hawthorne in the Berkshires in 1850 and began to read him with rapture, he felt for the first time in his life as an author that another could help him out of his isolation. He had begun with best-selling adventure tales like "Typee,' but going on to struggle with 'Moby-Dick,' he experienced a sense of headlong personal growth that was frightening to him."

72. Henry James, *Hawthorne* (Ithaca: Cornell University Press, 1879), xiii. After reading James' penetrating book about his father, Julian Hawthorne noted in his diary that the effort was better than his own attempt at a biography of the older Hawthorne. In language that echoed his father's regarding Melville's *Mardi*, he noted that it was not only better than his work, but that James took "more pains to make it so."

73. Attributed to Nathaniel Hawthorne, quoted in *Critical Approaches to American Literature, Volume 1* (New York: Crowell, 1965), 214.

74. From original letter. Gansevoort Melville to Allan Melville, January 1841; in Herman Melville Room at Berkshire Athenaeum; Pittsfield, Massachusetts.

75. Ibid.

76. Nathaniel Hawthorne, *Our Old Home and English Note-Books, Vol. II* (Cambridge: Printed at the Riverside Press, 1883), 374.

77. *Moby-Dick*, 89.

78. Julian Hawthorne, *Hawthorne and His Circle, Volume 3* (New York: Harper & Brothers, 1903), 33.

79. *Letters of Herman Melville*, 121.

80. Ibid.

81. Julian Hawthorne, "The Salem of Hawthorne," *The Century Magazine*, 28, no. 1 (May 1884), 6.

82. Nathaniel Hawthorne, quoted in Julian Hawthorne, *Nathaniel Hawthorne and His Wife: A Biography, Volume One* (Boston: James R. Osgood & Co., 1885), 347.

83. Nathaniel Hawthorne, *The Scarlet Letter*, 273.

84. Melville, "Hawthorne and His Mosses," 417 (in *The Portable Melville*, ed. Jay Leyda, 1952).

85. Thomas Wentworth Higginson, "Short Studies of American Authors," *The Literary World*, January 18, 1879, 25.

86. Review, Evert Duyckinck, "Melville's Moby-Dick; Or, The Whale. / Second Notice," *The Literary World*, November 22, 1851. 403.

87. *Moby-Dick*, 112.

88. Wineapple, 21.

89. Letter from Thomas Melville, Jr., to Lemuel Shaw, January 1831. Quoted in Hershel Parker, *Herman Melville: A Biography, Volume I (1819—1851)*.

90. Edward Charles Wagenknecht, *Nathaniel Hawthorne: Man and Writer* (New York: Oxford University Press, 1961), 50. Wagenknecht's book purports to be a "psychography" of the writer; therefore, one should not expect a chronological biography. Wagenknecht often expressed his preference for this kind of approach in books dealing with individuals. He described the methodology as being that of a character portrait.

91. Frank Preston Stearns, *The Life and Genius of Nathaniel Hawthorne* (Philadepphia: J.B. Lippincott, 1906), 332.

92. Delbanco, 146.

93. *The Letters of Herman Melville*, 143.

94. Delbanco, 146.

95. Ibid., 161.

96. Nathaniel Hawthorne, campaign biography of Franklin Pierce. Quoted in Wineapple, 263. Franklin Pierce was in the midst of a public relations debacle when Hawthorne swooped to his defense with the *Life of Franklin Pierce*, and the future president benefitted much from Hawthorne's reputation and credibility. Wealthy political supporters saw to it that the volume was widely distributed in order to offset Whig attacks on Pierce's character. The candidate bore accusations of an inglorious military record (as a general in the Mexican War), cowardice, and alcoholism. Pierce's death of cirrhosis would confirm that latter, but the other matters were more complicated—and the result of embellishment and mischaracterization. Nevertheless, Hawthorne's book on Pierce also sacrificed truth in order to inaccurately glorify and lionize the candidate. If there were any doubts about Hawthorne's awareness of his complicity in political propaganda, they were allayed by his demands to his publisher upon announcement of the work. "I think you must blaze away a little harder in your advertisement," he beseeched Ticknor. "Go it strong.... We are politicians now; and you must not expect to conduct yourself like a gentlemanly publisher." This epoch is more fully laid out in James R. Mellow's Hawthorne biography, 412–416.

97. William Butler Yeats, "The Second Coming," *The Collected Poems of W.B. Yeats* (Ware: Wordsworth Editions, 2000), 158.

98. Sigmund Freud, *An Outline of Psychoanalysis* (New York: W.W. Norton, 1949), 38.

99. Delbanco, 126.

100. *Moby-Dick*, 214.

101. Ibid.

102. *The Centenary Edition of the Works of Nathaniel Hawthorne*, ed. William Charvat et al., 23 vols. (Columbus: Ohio State University Press, 1962–94), Volume 8, 448.

103. *The Letters of Herman Melville*, 128.

104. Ibid.

105. Herman Melville's markings and marginalia in his copy of Hawthorne's *Mosses from an Old Manse* (New York: Wiley and Putnam, 1846, 2 v. in 1). Houghton Library, Harvard College Library. Hershel Parker dates the markings to May 1865.

106. Ibid.

107. Hershel Parker, *Herman Melville: A Biography, Volume 2 (1851—1891)*, (Baltimore: Johns Hopkins University Press, 2002), 680.

108. Ibid., 632.

109. *The Letters of Herman Melville*, 130.

110. Hershel Parker, *Herman Melville: A Biography, Volume 2 (1851—1891)*, 803.

111. Elizabeth Shaw Melville to Catherine Lansing, February 2, 1876, in *The Melville Log*, II, 747.

112. Herman Melville, letter to an English correspondent (fan); quoted in *The Selected Poems of Herman Melville*, ed. Robert Penn Warren, 47.

113. Hershel Parker, *Herman Melville: A Biography, Volume 2 (1851—1891)*, 684.

114. Nathaniel Hawthorne, *The Marble Faun; Or, the Romance of Monte Beni*, Volume II (Boston: Ticknor and Fields, 1860), 120–121.

115. *The Letters of Herman Melville*, 144.

Chapter Two

1. Malcolm J. Rohrbough, *Days of Gold: The California Gold Rush and the American Nation* (Berkeley: University of California Press), 156. Rohrbough's book is the first fully encompassing history of the Gold Rush, and sheds light on much of the individual human complexity and motivations behind this massive movement of American people.

2. Louis Menand, *The Metaphysical Club: A Story of Ideas in America* (New York: Macmillan, 2002), 4. This Pulitzer Prize-winning work serves as a remarkable intellectual history of America during the period of Melville and Hawthorne's adulthood. Reviewing *The Metaphysical Club* for the *New York Times* in June 2001, Janet Maslin writes, "Mr. Menand has undertaken nothing less than an explanation of the social, historical, economic and spiritual forces that caused American thinking to change radically from the period leading up to the Civil War to the advent of pragmatism in the early 20th century." Oliver Wendell Holmes, who made the trek up Monument Mountain with the writers on the day that Hawthorne and Melville met (and who, as a young man, wrote a poem about Melville's paternal grandfather), is a central figure here. Maslin singles out this quote by the diminutive Supreme Court Justice, which is germane to not only the Civil War, but to world history and our current age: "[T]he lesson Holmes took from the war can be put in a sentence.... It is that certitude leads to violence" (61). Melville and Hawthorne bear scant mention here, however. The one reference to Melville picks up on his *Battle-Pieces* description of radical abolitionist John Brown as the "meteor of the war" in "The Portent." Hawthorne gets a few references due to his late-life membership in the Saturday Club in Boston — though Hawthorne never really approached these gatherings with much enthusiasm. Nonetheless, the intellectual context Menand provides is invaluable to an understanding of the world of ideas and forces surrounding these two creative minds.

3. Herman Melville, *Pierre; Or, the Ambiguities, The Writings of Herman Melville*, Vol. 7 (Chicago: Northwestern-Newberry Edition, 1971), 253.

4. Cited in Edward Charles Wagenknecht, *Nathaniel Hawthorne: Man and Writer* (New York: Oxford University Press, 1961), 86.

5. Ibid.

6. Leland S. Person, *The Cambridge Introduction to Nathaniel Hawthorne* (Cambridge: Cambridge University Press, 2007), 67.

7. Newton Arvin, *Hawthorne* (Boston: Little, Brown, 1929), 228.

8. Julian Hawthorne, *Nathaniel Hawthorne and His Wife: A Biography*, Volume 1 (Boston: Houghton Mifflin Company, 1884), 96.

9. Jay Leyda, *The Melville Log* (New York: Harcourt, Brace, 1951), 391.

10. Ibid., 384.

11. Ibid., 382.

12. Malcolm Bradbury and Richard Ruland, *From Puritanism to Postmodernism: A History of American Literature* (New York: Viking, 1991), 157. While there is not ample room for a full discussion of Hawthorne and Melville in Bradbury and Ruland's daunting undertaking, which launches a discussion of literature spanning from Captain John Smith's first recordings of the "New World" in the Jamestown settlement to the late modernism of the twentieth century, there is much to glean here regarding the two writers' accomplishments. In eloquent analysis, the book ties together Melville and Hawthorne in all of their obscurities, uncertainties, and (to borrow Melville's term from "Hawthorne and His Mosses") "blackness."

13. *Melville Log*, 384.

14. Ibid., 383.

15. Ibid., 384.

16. Ibid.

17. Herman Melville, "Hawthorne and His Mosses," *The Portable Melville*, ed. Jay Leyda (New York: Viking, 1952), 409.

18. *Melville Log*, 384.

19. Ibid.

20. Ibid.

21. Ibid.

22. Ibid.

23. Hershel Parker, *Herman Melville: A Biography, Volume I (1819–1851)* (Baltimore: Johns Hopkins University Press, 1996), 746.

24. *Melville Log*, 384.

25. Herman Melville, *Moby-Dick*, 150th Anniversary Edition (New York: Signet Classic, 1998), 449.

26. *Melville Log*, 385.

27. NH to Zachariah Burchmore; June 9, 1850. *The Centenary Edition of the Works of Nathaniel Hawthorne*, ed. William Charvat et al., 23 volumes (Columbus: Ohio State University Press, 1962–94), Volume 16, 340.

28. *Melville Log*, 385–386.

29. Sophia Hawthorne to Elizabeth Peabody, August 8, 1850. Berg Collection of English and American Literature, New York Public Library, New York.

30. *Melville Log*, 393.

31. Sophia Hawthorne to Elizabeth Peabody, August 8, 1850. Berg Collection of En-

glish and American Literature, New York Public Library, New York.

32. Hershel Parker, *Herman Melville: A Biography, Volume I (1819 — 1851)*, 754.

33. Ibid., 755.

34. Laurie Robertson-Lorant, *Melville: A Biography* (New York: Clarkson N. Potter, 1996), 250.

35. Brenda Wineapple, *Hawthorne: A Life* (New York: Random House Trade Paperbacks, 2003), 225.

36. Herman Melville, "Hawthorne and His Mosses," *The Portable Melville* (New York: Viking, 1952), 417.

37. Ibid., 416.

38. Ibid., 413.

39. Ibid., 414.

40. Ibid., 411.

41. Ibid., 409.

42. Herman Melville, *Moby-Dick*, 150th Anniversary Edition (New York: Signet Classic, 1998), 456.

43. Herman Melville, "Hawthorne and His Mosses," *The Portable Melville*, ed. Jay Leyda (New York: Viking, 1952), 401.

44. Herman Melville, *The Letters of Herman Melville*, ed. Merrell R. Davis and William H. Gilman (New Haven: Yale University Press, 1960), 129.

45. Herman Melville, "Hawthorne and His Mosses," *The Portable Melville* (New York: Viking, 1952), 404–405.

46. Ibid.

47. Ibid., 408.

48. Ibid., 407.

49. *Moby-Dick*, 186.

50. Herman Melville, "Hawthorne and His Mosses," *The Portable Melville*, 407.

51. Ibid., 415.

52. Nathaniel Hawthorne, "Young Goodman Brown," *Hawthorne's Short Stories* (New York: Vintage Classics, 2011), 201.

53. *Moby-Dick*, 423.

54. Ibid., 505.

55. "Hawthorne and His Mosses," *The Portable Melville*, 407.

56. Nathaniel Hawthorne, "Young Goodman Brown," *Hawthorne's Short Stories*, 202.

57. Hershel Parker, *Herman Melville: A Biography, Volume I (1819–1851)*, 768.

58. NH to Evert Duyckinck; August 29, 1850. *The Centenary Edition of the Works of Nathaniel Hawthorne*, ed. William Charvat et al., 23 vols. (Columbus: Ohio State University Press, 1962–94), Volume 16, 362.

59. Ibid.

60. Ernest Hemingway, *Death in the Afternoon* (New York: Simon & Schuster, 1999), 12.

61. T.S. Eliot in *The Criterion*, April 1933. Quoted in Jeffrey Meyers, *Hemingway: A Biography* (Boston: Da Capo Press, 1999), 220.

62. F.O. Matthiessen, *American Renaissance: Art and Expression in the Age of Emerson and Whitman* (London: Oxford University Press, 1941), 390. Matthiessen's discussion of Melville remains relevant for its attentive and attuned close reading of Melville's evolving craft. Matthiessen singles out the *White-Jacket* scene as a milestone in the writer's development that can be distinguished from "all of Melville's previous recording of events. This is no longer an external description, but the evocation of an immediate moment," Matthiessen writes. In examining this passage, the critic also notes Melville's beginning mastery of "the life of the senses" (though the comparison to Keats in this regard seems reductive or at least incompatible), rhythm (the "most subtly varied movement of his prose"), and "elaborate" and "organic" simile. Regarding the latter, Mathiessen addresses the use of "frost-work" in the falling passages, which conveys "the strange feeling of remoteness, where the coldness of fear itself was only shifting tracery. Melville's use of whiteness for such an image had already become instinctive" (pages 390–391).

63. Herman Melville, *White-Jacket; Or, The World in a Man-of-War* (New York: Library of America, 1983), 762.

64. Matthiessen, 390.

65. Herman Melville, *White-Jacket*, 763.

66. *Melville Log*, 391.

67. Sophia Hawthorne to Elizabeth Peabody, August 1850. Berg Collection of English and American Literature, New York Public Library, New York.

68. Sophia Hawthorne to Evert Duyckinck; *The Centenary Edition of the Works of Nathaniel Hawthorne*, ed. William Charvat et al., 23 vols. (Columbus: Ohio State University Press, 1962–94), Volume 16, 361.

69. *Melville Log*, 391.

70. Leyda, *Melville Log*, supplement, 924–25.

71. Ibid.

72. *Melville Log*, 393–94.

73. *The Letters of Herman Melville*, 133.

74. "Hawthorne and His Mosses," *The Portable Melville*, 407.

Chapter Three

1. James R. Mellow, *Nathaniel Hawthorne in His Times* (paperback edition, Baltimore: Johns Hopkins University Press, 1998), 14. Mellow also points out here that though Hawthorne often talked about his paternal ancestors, and saw in them raw material for his

work, he showed a "marked reticence" or "perhaps, reverence" when it came to discussing his father. The senior Nathaniel is pretty much absent from letters and journals, though of course, the "unresolved paternity" that Mellow discusses can be seen in much of the author's creative works. And while there is no clear evidence, one has to wonder if the topic of fathers— that is, the early losses that both writers experienced — ever came up between Hawthorne and Melville. It clearly was a significant, character-shaping situation that both writers underwent.

2. Brenda Wineapple, *Hawthorne: A Life* (New York: Random House Trade Paperbacks, 2003), 20.

3. Quoted in Hershel Parker, *Herman Melville: A Biography, Volume I (1819—1851),* (Baltimore: Johns Hopkins University Press, 1996), 35.

4. Ibid., 48.

5. Allan Melvill, quoted in Andrew Delbanco, *Melville: His World and Work* (New York: Knopf, 2005), 23.

6. Jay Leyda, *The Melville Log* (New York: Harcourt, Brace, 1951), 50.

7. Ibid., 51.

8. Ibid.

9. Herman Melville, *Redburn: His First Voyage* (New York: Library of America, 1983), 16.

10. Herman Melville, *Pierre; Or, the Ambiguities, The Writings of Herman Melville,* Volume 7 (Chicago: Northwestern-Newberry Edition, 1971), 70.

11. Robert Booth, *Death of an Empire: The Rise and Murderous Fall of Salem, America's Richest City* (New York: Macmillan, 2011), xxii. The "witch city" is so often spoken about in dusky, antiquarian tones or for its history of persecution — even when addressing Nathaniel Hawthorne. But Hawthorne's depictions of Puritan Salem came from research. An equally or even more compelling Salem greeted his senses at his birth. In fact, a multicultural world spilled into the city's small streets due to the success of the Salem sea captains and business agents in the areas adjacent to the Indian Ocean. Booth claims here that Salem's East India vessels approached distant shores without the attitude of "arrogance and exploitation that were typical of Europeans," steering clear of the colonizing, nation-building impulse to impose politics and values on their hosts. He also describes a successful method of commerce that involved dressing down, speaking the lingo, eating native food, and blending as much as possible with the culture. Booth also claims that most Salem merchants opposed the idea of sending missionaries to the Far East.

12. Ibid., xiii.

13. Ibid., xi.

14. Delbanco, 18.

15. Wineapple, 35.

16. Ibid., 39.

17. Hershel Parker, *Herman Melville: A Biography, Volume I (1819—1851),* 115.

18. *Melville Log,* 383.

19. Quoted in Wineapple, 28.

20. Ibid., 33.

21. Ibid., 35.

22. Ralph Waldo Emerson, *Journals of Ralph Waldo Emerson,* 529.

23. John Neal, *American Writers: A Series of Papers Contributed to Blackwood's Magazine,* ed. Fred Patee (Durham: Duke University Press, 1937), 10, 200. Hawthorne took early inspiration from Neal, despite the older writer (1793–1876) being such a different writer and individual from him-self. Neal is arguably one of the most colorful literary figures of nascent America, and the first great literary "persona" in the country. Born in Maine, into a Quaker community, he came to be known for his feminist ideals and as an advocate for physical health as a foundation for political and social well-being. Beyond his literary and law activities, he introduced the German-form of gymnastics in the United States and was a box-ing and wrestling instructor. He also promoted younger writers such as Edgar Allan Poe and John Greenleaf Whittier. Poe never forgot Neal's generosity and later remarked that this was the first true encouragement he ever remembered receiving as a writer. He wrote in a great range of forms, but became most known well into the twentieth century as a penner of short stories and as embodying an early form of the literary masculinity later represented by writers such as Hemingway.

24. *Hawthorne As Editor,* ed. Arlin Turner (Baton Rouge: Louisiana State University Press, 1941), 195.

25. Quoted in Wineapple, 61.

26. Wineapple, 75.

27. Mellow, 48.

28. Ibid., 57.

29. Ibid., 55.

30. Ibid.

31. Ibid., 77.

32. *The Centenary Edition of the Works of Nathaniel Hawthorne,* ed. William Charvat et al., 23 vols. (Columbus: Ohio State University Press, 1962–94), Volume 15 (The Letters), 249.

33. Mellow, 80.

34. *The Centenary Edition of the Works of Nathaniel Hawthorne,* Volume 15 (The Letters), 251.

35. Ibid.
36. Quoted in Mellow, 81.
37. Herman Melville, *Moby-Dick*, 150th Anniversary Edition (New York: Signet Classic, 1998), 112.
38. *Melville Log*, 71.
39. Ibid., 72.
40. Ibid.
41. Ibid.
42. Ibid., 73.
43. Herman Melville, *Redburn: His First Voyage* (New York: Library of America, 1983), 7.
44. *Moby-Dick*, 71.
45. Quoted in Hershel Parker, *Herman Melville: A Biography, Volume I (1819—1851)*, 160.
46. *Moby-Dick*, 248–49.
47. Herman Melville, *Redburn*, 78.
48. *Moby-Dick*, 6.
49. *Melville Log*, 110.
50. Herman Melville, *The Letters of Herman Melville*, eds. Merrell R. Davis and William H. Gilman (New Haven: Yale University Press, 1960), 106.
51. *Moby-Dick*, 483.
52. Ibid.
53. Ibid., 75–76.
54. Delbanco, 37.
55. *Moby-Dick*, 456.
56. Franklin D. Roosevelt in introduction to Clifford W. Ashley's *Whaleships of New Bedford* (Boston: Houghton Mifflin, 1929), vi.
57. Parker, *Herman Melville: A Biography, Volume I*, 188.
58. *Moby-Dick*, 123.
59. Herman Melville, review of *Etchings of a Whale Cruise* (1847). In *Piazza Tales and Other Prose Pieces, 1839–1860: Volume Nine*, Scholarly Edition (Chicago: Northwestern-Newberry Edition, 1987), 210.
60. Eric Jay Dolin, *Leviathan: The History of Whaling in America* (New York: W.W. Norton, 2007), 49–50. Dolin's book is undoubtedly the gold standard of works about whaling and is exhaustive in its historical breadth and details. Much of the details about whaling in the volume you are reading were gleaned from Dolin, who is also generous in his discussions about Melville, who more than anyone in history has mythologized this pursuit and industry.
61. *Moby-Dick*, 286.
62. Dolin, 50.
63. Parker, *Herman Melville: A Biography, Volume I*, 234.
64. *Moby-Dick*, 482.
65. Ibid., 159.
66. Ibid., 156.
67. Sigmund Freud, *Civilization and Its Discontents* (New York: W.W. Norton, 1989), 11.
68. *Moby-Dick*, 159.
69. Herman Melville, *White-Jacket; Or, The World in a Man-of-War* (New York: Library of America, 1983), 469.
70. Ibid.
71. *Melville Log*, 116.
72. Brian Higgins and Hershel Parker, eds., *Herman Melville: The Contemporary Reviews* (Cambridge: Cambridge University Press, 2009), 22.

Chapter Four

1. Nathaniel Hawthorne, *A Wonder-Book for Girls and Boys* (Chicago: Rand, McNally, 1913), 251.
2. Jay Leyda, *The Melville Log* (New York: Harcourt, Brace, 1951), 389.
3. Nathaniel Hawthorne to Sophia Hawthorne, April 3, 1840. *The Centenary Edition of the Works of Nathaniel Hawthorne*, ed. William Charvat et al., 23 vols. (Columbus: Ohio State University Press, 1962–94), Volume 15 (The Letters), 434–35.
4. Quoted in Brenda Wineapple, *Hawthorne: A Life* (New York: Random House Trade Paperbacks, 2003), 185.
5. Herman Melville, *The Letters of Herman Melville*, ed. Merrell R. Davis and William H. Gilman (New Haven: Yale University Press, 1960), 114.
6. Ibid., 117.
7. Ibid.
8. Marking on 44, "The Birthmark" in Herman Melville's his copy of Hawthorne's *Mosses from an Old Manse* (New York: Wiley and Putnam, 1846. 2 v. in 1), Houghton Library, Harvard College Library.
9. *The Letters of Herman Melville*, 130.
10. Herman Melville, *Typee: A Peep at Polynesian Life* (New York: Library of America, 1982), 11.
11. Ibid.
12. Andrew Delbanco, *Melville: His World and Work* (New York: Knopf, 2005), 69.
13. Brian Higgins and Hershel Parker, eds., *Herman Melville: The Contemporary Reviews* (Cambridge: Cambridge University Press, 2009), 23.
14. Ibid., 22–23.
15. Ibid., 22.
16. *Melville Log*, 211.
17. Ibid.
18. Gansevoort Melville, quoted in Delbanco, 90.
19. Ibid., 91.
20. Herman Melville, *Moby-Dick*, 150th Anniversary Edition (New York: Signet Classic, 1998), 32.

21. *The Letters of Herman Melville*, 106.

22. Ibid., 108.

23. Ibid.

24. Herman Melville, *Mardi: And a Voyage Thither*, eds. Harrison Hayford, G. Thomas Tanselle and Hershel Parker (Evanston, IL: Northwestern University Press, 1970), 557.

25. *Moby-Dick*, 25.

26. Ibid., 26.

27. Nathaniel Hawthorne, "The Haunted Mind," *Twice-Told Tales* (Columbus: Ohio State University Press, 1974), 306.

28. Nathaniel Hawthorne, "Young Goodman Brown," *Hawthorne's Short Stories* (New York: Vintage Classics, 2011), 195.

29. *Moby-Dick*, 26.

30. Herman Melville, *Mardi: And a Voyage Thither*, 491.

31. *Moby-Dick*, 431.

32. George Will, "Literary Politics," *Newsweek*, 22 April 1991, 72.

33. Malcolm Bradbury and Richard Ruland, *From Puritanism to Postmodernism: A History of American Literature* (New York: Penguin, 1991), 161.

34. *Moby-Dick*, 5.

35. F.O. Matthiessen, *American Renaissance: Art and Expression in the Age of Emerson and Whitman* (London: Oxford University Press, 1941), 276.

36. Nathaniel Hawthorne, *The Scarlet Letter* (Ohio State University Press, 1978), 259.

37. *Moby-Dick*, 431.

38. Ibid.

39. Ibid.

40. Ibid., 433.

41. Ibid., 432.

42. Ibid.

43. Ibid., 433.

44. Ibid., 434.

45. Ibid.

46. Andrew Delbanco, *Melville: His World and Work* (New York: Knopf, 2005), 160.

47. *Moby-Dick*, 435.

48. Herman Melville, *Pierre; Or the Ambiguities* (New York: Harper & Brothers, 1852), 191–192.

49. Herman Melville, "Hawthorne and His Mosses," *The Portable Melville*, edited by Jay Leyda (New York: Viking, 1952), 418.

50. Nathaniel Hawthorne, *The Scarlet Letter* (Ohio State University Press, 1978), 36.

51. Herman Melville, The Confidence-Man: *His Masquerade* (London: John Lehmann, 1948), Chapter XXXIII, 219.

52. Herman Melville, "Hawthorne and His Mosses," 418.

53. Nathaniel Hawthorne, "Young Goodman Brown," *Hawthorne's Short Stories* (New York: Vintage Classics, 2011), 195.

54. Ibid., 201.

55. F.O. Matthiessen, *American Renaissance*, 265.

56. Ibid., 284.

57. *Moby-Dick*, 4.

58. Ibid., 5.

59. Ibid., 4.

60. Nathaniel Hawthorne, *The Scarlet Letter*, 36.

61. Nathaniel Hawthorne, *The English Notebooks*, ed. Randall Stewart (New York: Russell & Russell, 1962), 433.

62. *Moby-Dick*, 26.

63. Ibid.

64. Ibid., 93.

65. Ibid., 98–99

66. Ibid., 98.

67. Ibid., 216.

68. Ibid., 328.

69. Ibid., 538.

70. Ibid., 545.

71. Anthony Stevens, *Jung: A Very Short Introduction* (New York: Oxford University Press, 1994), 64.

72. Dana Phillips, "History and the Ugly Facts of McCarthy's *Blood Meridian*" (*American Literature*, volume 68, number 2, June 1996), 434. Cormac McCarthy's novel about the historical west owes much to *Moby-Dick*, and the writer has placed the work among his few favorites. In his 2000 book, *How to Read and Why* Eminent literary critic Harold Bloom claimed that the "fulfilled renown of *Moby-Dick* and of *As I Lay Dying* is augmented by *Blood Meridian*, since McCarthy is the worthy disciple of both Melville and Faulkner" (page 254). In my own previous book, *Cormac McCarthy: A Literary Companion* (McFarland, 2010), I note not only how the elevated Shakespearean and biblical language of *Blood Meridian* echoes *Moby-Dick*, but how the multicultural band of scalpers recalls the crew of *The Pequod* and how the pivotal character in McCarthy's work, Judge Holden, represents a conflation of Ahab and the whale itself. Additionally, the kid (though never a narrator) moves in and out, from forefront to obsolescence in the narrative, much as Ishmael, so prominent at the outset, fades into the background at times.

73. *Moby-Dick*, 214.

74. Ibid.

75. Ibid., 214–15.

76. Thomas Carlyle, *The Best Known Works of Thomas Carlyle: Including Sartor Resartus, Heroes and Hero Worship and Characteristics* (Bethesda, MD: Wildside Press, 2010), 29. In volume one of his Herman Melville biography, Hershel Parker places Carlyle, particularly *Sartor Resartus*, among the prominent

influences on *Moby-Dick*—that is, he places it among those influences that "indisputably made their presence obvious in parts of *Moby-Dick*" (699–700). In his Melville biography, Andrew Delbanco sees the influence of Carlyle on the overboard and rescue incident involving Pip, who afterward seems to both simultaneously lose his mind and attain an elevated state of wisdom that recalls the Fool in *King Lear* (as does his suddenly close orientation to Ahab). For Delbanco, Pip's losing of himself and his coming to feel "indifferent as his God," display Melville's reading of Carlyle's *Sartor Resartus*, particularly Carlyle's "'centre of indifference' as a stage to wisdom" (Delbanco, page 160). In her biography of Melville, Lorant-Robertson, in noting that there were some positive British reviews of *The Whale*, wrote, "British critics who recognized the influence of their own metaphysical writers," including Carlyle, praised the book (Lorant-Robertson, 289).

77. Ibid.

78. Ibid., 28.

79. Ibid., 29.

80. Nathaniel Hawthorne, "The Haunted Mind," *Twice-Told Tales* (Columbus: Ohio State University Press, 1974), 304.

81. Ibid., 306.

82. F.O. Matthiessen, *American Renaissance*, 390.

83. Nathaniel Hawthorne, "Young Goodman Brown," *Hawthorne's Short Stories* (New York: Vintage Classics, 2011), 234.

84. Herman Melville's markings and marginalia in his copy of Hawthorne's *Mosses from an Old Manse* (New York: Wiley and Putnam, 1846. 2 v. in 1). Houghton Library, Harvard College Library. "The Birthmark," 36.

85. Ibid.

86. Nathaniel Hawthorne, "The Birth-Mark," *Hawthorne's Short Stories* (New York: Vintage Classics, 2011), 183.

87. Henry Tuckerman, 1951. Quoted in *The Cambridge Companion to Nathaniel Hawthorne* (Cambridge: Cambridge University Press, 2004), 40.

88. Ibid.

89. F.O. Matthiessen, *American Renaissance*, 388.

90. Nathaniel Hawthorne, *The Letters*, ed. Thomas Woodson and L. Neal Smith (Columbus: Ohio State University Press, 1985), XVI, 362.

91. Wineapple, 236.

92. Nathaniel Hawthorne, *The House of the Seven Gables* (New York: Library of America, 1983), 589.

93. Wineapple, 236.

94. Herman Melville, "Hawthorne and His Mosses," 406.

95. Ibid.

96. *Melville Log*, 391.

97. Nathaniel Hawthorne, *A Wonder-Book for Girls and Boys* (Chicago: Rand, McNally, 1913).

98. Nathaniel Hawthorne, *The Letters*, ed. Thomas Woodson and L. Neal Smith (Columbus: Ohio State University Press, 1985), XVI, 371.

99. Ibid.

100. Herman Melville, "Hawthorne and His Mosses," 406.

101. Nathaniel Hawthorne, *Twice-Told Tales* (Columbus: Ohio State University Press, 1974), 5.

102. *Letters of Herman Melville*, 106.

103. *Melville Log*, 403.

104. Ibid., 406.

105. Ibid.

106. Quoted in Brenda Wineapple, *Hawthorne: A Life* (New York: Random House Trade Paperbacks, 2003), 240.

107. Sophia's domestic descriptions are quoted in James R. Mellow, *Nathaniel Hawthorne in His Times* (Baltimore: Johns Hopkins University Press, 1998), 355–56.

108. Ibid., 355.

109. *Letters of Herman Melville*, 121.

110. *Melville Log*, 403.

111. Ibid.

112. *Letters of Herman Melville*, 119.

113. Ibid.

114. Ibid.

115. *Melville Log*, 407.

116. Ibid., 408.

117. Archibald Duncan, *The Mariner's Chronicle Being a Collection of the Most Interesting Narratives of Shipwrecks, Fires, Famines, and Other Calamities Incident to a Life of Maritime Enterprise.* Autographed by Herman Melville. Houghton Library, Harvard College, Sealts number: 194.

118. *Melville Log*, 408.

119. *Letters of Herman Melville*, 124.

120. Ibid.

121. Ibid.

122. Ibid.

123. Ibid.

124. Ibid., 125.

125. Ibid., 120.

126. Ibid., 121.

127. Ibid., 128.

128. Ibid.

129. Hershel Parker, *Herman Melville: A Biography, Volume I (1819—1851)* (Baltimore: Johns Hopkins University Press, 1996), 833.

130. Ibid.

131. *Melville Log*, 412.

132. Ibid.

133. Ibid.

134. Ibid.
135. Ibid.
136. *Letters of Herman Melville*, 128.
137. Ibid., 129.
138. Thomas Carlyle, *The Best Known Works of Thomas Carlyle: Including Sartor Resartus, Heroes and Hero Worship and Characteristics* (Bethesda, MD: Wildside Press LLC, 2010), 29.
139. *Letters of Herman Melville*, 129.
140. Ibid., 130.
141. Ibid.
142. Ibid.
143. Ibid.
144. Ibid., 132.
145. Ibid.
146. Ibid.
147. *Moby-Dick*, 15–16.
148. Richard Volney Chase, *Melville: A Critical Study* (New York: Macmillan Co., 1949), 58. The Chase comments were originally ascertained from a reading of William Spanos' *The Errant Art of Moby-Dick: The Canon, the Cold War, and the Struggle for American Studies* (Durham, NC: Duke University Press, 1995), 154. A course taught by Professor Spanos at Binghamton University during the time of the publication of that book (and while I was a student there) first stimulated my thinking regarding Melville's processes while writing *Moby-Dick*.
149. *Moby-Dick*, 106.
150. Ibid., 107.
151. *Letters of Herman Melville*, 133.
152. *Moby-Dick*, 489.
153. *Letters of Herman Melville*, 133.
154. Ibid.
155. *Letters of Herman Melville*, 135.
156. Ibid.
157. Quoted in James R. Mellow, *Nathaniel Hawthorne in His Times* (Johns Hopkins University Press, 1998), 376. In a more contemporary age, the idea of Nathaniel Hawthorne as a solo father dealing with a host of mishaps would make for a good sitcom. Mellow also describes in this section how Julian was stung by a bee during a walk, causing his leg to swell alarmingly. In addition, there was a bed-wetting episode not long after Sophia's departure. What Hawthorne was most nonplussed about, however, was the stream of chatter from his young son. Stretching out beneath an apple tree to do some reading, for example, Hawthorne dealt with Julian, above him in the tree, soliloquizing about his desire to live in a tree forever.
158. Ibid.
159. Ibid., 377.
160. Julian Hawthorne, *Nathaniel Hawthorne and His Wife: A Biography, Volume 1* (Boston: James R. Osgood & Co., 1885), 421.

161. Ibid., 412.
162. James R. Mellow, *Nathaniel Hawthorne in His Times*, 380.
163. Nathaniel Hawthorne, *The American Note-Books*, (Newcastle upon Tyne: Cambridge Scholars), 206.
164. Ibid.
165. Ibid., 207.
166. Ibid., 209.
167. Ibid., 210.
168. Ibid., 211.
169. Ibid., 212.
170. Ibid., 213.
171. Ibid.
172. Ibid., 215.
173. Ibid.
174. Ibid.
175. Nathaniel Hawthorne, *Our Old Home and English Note-Books, Vol. II* (Cambridge" Printed at the Riverside Press, 1883), 364.
176. James R. Mellow, *Nathaniel Hawthorne in His Times*, 383. Mellow also claims here that "to a certain extent, one can gauge Hawthorne's appraisal [of *Moby-Dick*] by the terms of Melville's response." He also notes that "there is some inkling of Hawthorne's high estimation" of the whale book in his letter to Duyckinck, after the ambivalent review in the *Literary World* (page 382).
177. *Letters of Herman Melville*, 143.
178. Ibid., 142.
179. Ibid.
180. Ibid., 128.
181. Ibid., 142.
182. Ibid.
183. Ibid.
184. Ibid., 143.
185. Nathaniel Hawthorne, *Our Old Home and English Note-Books, Vol. II*, 375.
186. Nathaniel Hawthorne, *The American Note-Books*, 215.
187. Hershel Parker, *Herman Melville: A Biography, Volume 2 (1851— 1891)* (Baltimore: Johns Hopkins University Press, 2002), 29.
188. Ibid., 25.
189. Review, Evert Duyckinck, "Melville's Moby-Dick; Or, The Whale. / Second Notice," *The Literary World*, November 22, 1851. 404. In this second part of a two-part review/essay on Melville's new book, Duyckinck is also accurate in his estimation that "there are evidently two if not three books in Moby Dick rolled into one." But he represents what he terms a combination of "romantic fictions" and "absolute fact" as a problem, and notes that the problem is compounded when "the romance is made a vehicle of opinion and satire through a more or less opaque allegorical veil." In this way, he connects *Moby-Dick* to *Mardi*, the book in which

Melville first started experimenting with a new form. But elsewhere he also heralds the writing regarding the sperm whale itself: "The information is minute, brilliantly illustrated, as it should be—the whale himself so generously illuminating the midnight page on which his memoirs are written" (all on page 403). The first installment of Duyckinck's review begins with a lengthy recap of the tragedy of *The Essex*, and this is perhaps where the reviewer's expectations cloud his view of the actual book. Having known what Melville was writing about, Duyckinck likely expected something more in that vein, albeit fictional. He did not expect the more supernatural elements or the myriad of ideas and sources that were poured into the eventual outcome. Certainly, he did not know what to do with the book's preoccupation with, in his terms, "the problem of the universe."

190. Ibid., 403.
191. Ibid.
192. Nathaniel Hawthorne, *Selected Letters of Nathaniel Hawthorne* (Columbus: Ohio State University Press, 2002), 156.
193. *Letters of Herman Melville*, 141.
194. Ibid., 142.
195. Ibid., 143.

Chapter Five

1. *The Centenary Edition of the Works of Nathaniel Hawthorne*, ed. William Charvat et al., 23 vols. (Columbus: Ohio State University Press, 1962–94), Volume 22, 163.
2. Ibid.
3. Ibid.
4. Mentioned in Andrew Delbanco, *Melville: His World and Work* (New York: Knopf, 2005), 179. The *Pierre* review was from the *New York Day Book,* 7 September 1852. The slanderous piece goes on to remark that "Melville was really supposed to be deranged, and that his friends were taking measures to place him under treatment. We hope one of the earliest precautions will be to keep him stringently secluded from pen and ink." One would be hard pressed to find another canonized author that has been subject to such willfully mean-spirited attacks in major periodicals. A fuller discussion can be found in *Pierre, Or The Ambiguities: Volume Seven, Scholarly Edition*, Northwestern University Press, 1992.
5. Ibid.
6. Brian Higgins and Hershel Parker, eds., *Herman Melville: The Contemporary Reviews* (Cambridge: Cambridge University Press, 2009), 527.
7. Herman Melville, *The Letters of Her-*

man Melville, eds. Merrell R. Davis and William H. Gilman (New Haven: Yale University Press, 1960), 228. Many of Melville's letters to his brother-in-law John Chipman Hoadley, even beyond this mournful and grieving missive, assume the same tenor as his correspondence to Hawthorne. In Hoadley, he seems to have found an acutely sensitive individual and great mind to bounce his own correspondence off of. (Hoadley's own writing to Herman confirms his sensitivity and perceptiveness where the author was concerned.) Melville's correspondence with Hoadley obviously covers a much larger span of time than the Hawthorne letters, however. Hoadley had been a widower, who met the Melvilles while living in Pittsfield. He married Herman's younger sister Catherine (born 1825) in 1853. He was a widely renowned successful engineer and inventor and also the owner of an extensive library. For a short time, he also served in the Massachusetts legislature. He was near the same age as Herman (1818), and it is clear from the correspondence between the two that they shared a friendship bond and bond of affection and affinity that went quite beyond a mere brother-in-law relationshiHoadley, born in Turin, New York, in 1818, died in 1886.

8. Robert Penn Warren, ed. and introd., *Selected Poems of Herman Melville* (New York: Barnes & Noble, 1998), 334.
9. *Letters of Herman Melville*, 121.
10. *Letters of Herman Melville*, 275. The self-deprecating description of *Clarel* appears in an 1884 letter to Englishman Charles James Billson (a.k.a. James Billson), a young Oxford graduate practicing law in Leicester. Having become an admirer of Melville's works, Billson struck up a correspondence with the aging author (then in his mid-sixties) and described to Melville a cult following of his works that was cropping up in England—what he termed a "rapidly increasing knot" of readers—and lamented the scarce availability of his published works. "[A]s soon as one is discovered (for that is really what it is with us)," noted Billson of Melville's writings, it is eagerly read & passed round." Apparently, there was not only a scarcity of published works available, but also a scarcity of information about the nearly forgotten author of *Moby-Dick*, for Billson felt compelled to communicate with the author himself to find out what other works he had written. The Englishman had read *Typee, Omoo, Mardi, Redburn, Moby-Dick, Pierre, Israel Potter, The Piazza Tales,* and *The Confidence Man* thus far. Melville responded, "You ask me to give you the names of any *other* books of mine, with the names of the publishers," and listed for Billson *White-*

Jacket, Battle Pieces, and *Clarel.* In naming the latter, he included the self-deprecating comments noted here.

11. Herman Melville, *Clarel: A Poem and Pilgrimage in the Holy Land,* eds. Harrison Hayford and Hershel Parker (Evanston, IL: Northwestern University Press, Aug 20, 2008), xv.

12. Delbanco, 292.

13. Quoted in Robert Penn Warren, introduction to *Selected Poems of Herman Melville* (New York: Barnes & Noble, 1998), 46.

14. Ibid.

15. Ibid., 44.

16. James R. Mellow, *Nathaniel Hawthorne in His Times* (Baltimore: Johns Hopkins University Press, 1998), 520.

17. Thomas Wentworth Higginson, "Short Studies of American Authors," *The Literary World,* January 18, 1879, 25.

18. Nathaniel Hawthorne, *The Marble Faun; Or, the Romance of Monte Beni,* (Boston: Ticknor and Fields, 1860), 120–121.

19. Anthony Trollope, "The Genius of Nathaniel Hawthorne," *The North American Review,* Vol. 129, No. 274 (Sept., 1879), 207. Published by University of Northern Iowa. http://www.jstor.org/stable/25100789 Accessed: 19 November 2012.

20. Ibid., 220.

21. Ibid., 222.

22. Brenda Wineapple, *Hawthorne: A Life* (New York: Random House Trade Paperbacks, 2003), 319.

23. Hawthorne, *Marble Faun,* 514.

24. Ibid., 114.

25. Review, "*The Marble Faun: Or, the Romance of Monte Beni* by Nathaniel Hawthorne," *North American Review,* Vol. 90, No. 187 (Apr., 1860), 557.

26. Both Lizzie's and Maria's letter are cited in Hershel Parker, *Herman Melville: A Biography, Volume 2 (1851– 1891),* 576.

27. Hershel Parker, *Herman Melville: A Biography, Volume 2 (1851– 1891),* 802.

28. Julian Hawthorne, *Hawthorne and His Circle, Volume 3* (New York: Harper & Brothers, 1903), 33.

29. Ibid.

30. Andrew Delbanco, *Melville: His World and Work* (New York: Knopf, 2005), 179.

31. Fiedler, quoted in Mark Royden Winchell, *Too Good to Be True: The Life and Work of Leslie Fiedler* (Columbia: University of Missouri Press, 2002), 245. In his biography, Winchell also notes that Fiedler, the renowned American critic of both high-brow and popular culture, wrote a poem called "The Whiteness of the Whale: Bologna, 1952," which concludes, "Risen at last, I took my notes by rail / Back to Bologna, back to my liver's hell, / And lectured on the Whiteness of the Whale." Winchell also describes how, on his ship journey over to Italy, Fiedler brought Hawthorne's *The Marble Faun,* opting for that over Mark Twain's *Innocents Abroad.* Thematically, Hawthorne's book seems like an appropriate choice for am expatriated American writer living in Italy.

Bibliography

Argersinger, Jana L., and Leland S. Person, eds. *Hawthorne and Melville: Writing a Relationship.* Athens: University of Georgia Press, 2005.

Arrowhead, original house and land deeds; The Berkshire Athenaeum in Pittsfield, Massachusetts; Herman Melville Room (accessed summer 2010).

Arvin, Newton. *Herman Melville.* New York: William Sloane Associates, 1950.

Booth, Robert. *Death of an Empire: The Rise and Murderous Fall of Salem, America's Richest City.* New York: Macmillan, 2011.

Bradbury, Malcolm, and Richard Ruland. *From Puritanism to Postmodernism: A History of American Literature.* New York: Penguin, 1991.

Brown, Ray Broadus, and Martin Light, eds. *Critical Approaches to American Literature, Volume 1.* New York: Crowell, 1965.

Carlyle, Thomas. *The Best Known Works of Thomas Carlyle: Including Sartor Resartus, Heroes and Hero Worship and Characteristics.* Rockville, MD: Wildside Press, 2010.

Chase, Richard Volney. *Melville: A Critical Study.* New York: Macmillan, 1949.

Coetzee, J.M. *Boyhood: Scenes from Provincial Life.* New York: Viking, 1997.

Delbanco, Andrew. *Melville: His World and Work.* New York: Knopf, 2005.

Dolin, Eric Jay. *Leviathan: The History of Whaling in America.* New York: W.W. Norton, 2007.

Duyckinck, Evert. Review of "Melville's Moby-Dick; Or, The Whale. / Second Notice." *The Literary World,* November 22, 1851, p. 403.

Eliot, T.S., in *The Criterion,* April 1933. Quoted in Jeffrey Meyers, *Hemingway: A Biography.* Boston: Da Capo Press, 1999.

Emerson, Ralph Waldo. *Selected Journals: 1841–1877.* New York: Library of America, 2010.

Epstein, Barbara, and Robert B. Silvers. *The Company They Kept.* New York: New York Review, 2009.

Freud, Sigmund. *Civilization and Its Discontents.* New York: W.W. Norton, 1989.

Freud, Sigmund. *An Outline of Psychoanalysis.* New York: W.W. Norton, 1949.

Hawthorne, Julian. *Hawthorne and His Circle, Volume 3.* New York and London: Harper & Brothers, 1903.

Hawthorne, Julian. *Nathaniel Hawthorne and His Wife: A Biography, Volume 1.* Boston and New York: Houghton Mifflin, 1884.

Hawthorne, Julian. "The Salem of Hawthorne." *The Century Magazine,* May 1884. Volume 28, No. 1, p. 6.

Hawthorne, Nathaniel. *The American Note-Books.* Newcastle upon Tyne, UK: Cambridge Scholars Publishing, 2008.

Hawthorne, Nathaniel. "The Birth-mark," in *Mosses from an Old Manse, Volume X of Works*. Columbus: Ohio State University, 1974.

Hawthorne, Nathaniel. *The Centenary Edition of the Works of Nathaniel Hawthorne,* ed. William Charvat et al., 23 volumes. Columbus: Ohio State University Press, 1962–94.

Hawthorne, Nathaniel. *The Complete Works of Nathaniel Hawthorne, Volume XXII*. Boston and New York: Houghton Mifflin, 1883.

Hawthorne, Nathaniel. *The English Notebooks*, ed. Randall Stewart. New York: Russell & Russell, 1962.

Hawthorne, Nathaniel. *Hawthorne as Editor: Selections from His Writings in the American Magazine of Useful and Entertaining Knowledge,* ed. Arlin Turner. University: Louisiana State University Press, 1941.

Hawthorne, Nathaniel. *Hawthorne's Short Stories*. New York: Vintage Classics, 2011.

Hawthorne, Nathaniel. *The House of the Seven Gables*. New York: Library of America, 1983.

Hawthorne, Nathaniel. *The Letters*, ed. Thomas Woodson and L. Neal Smith. Columbus: Ohio State University Press, 1985.

Hawthorne, Nathaniel. *The Marble Faun; Or, the Romance of Monte Beni*. Boston: Ticknor and Fields, 1860.

Hawthorne, Nathaniel. *Our Old Home and English Note-Books, Vol. II*. Cambridge: Riverside Press, 1883.

Hawthorne, Nathaniel. *Our Old Home and English Note-Books, Vol. 1*. Boston: Houghton Mifflin, 1884.

Hawthorne, Nathaniel. *The Scarlet Letter*. In *Hawthorne: Collected Novels*. New York: Library of America, 1983.

Hawthorne, Nathaniel. *Selected Letters of Nathaniel Hawthorne*. Columbus: Ohio State University Press, 2002.

Hawthorne, Nathaniel. *Twice-Told Tales*, Volume I, "The Haunted Mind." Boston: Houghton Mifflin, 1884.

Hawthorne, Nathaniel. *Twice-Told Tales*.

Columbus: Ohio State University Press, 1974.

Hawthorne, Nathaniel. *A Wonder-Book for Girls and Boys*. Chicago: Rand, McNally, 1913.

Hawthorne, Sophia, to Elizabeth Peabody. August 8, 1850. Berg Collection of English and American Literature: New York Public Library, New York.

Hemingway, Ernest. *Death in the Afternoon*. New York: Simon & Schuster, 1999.

Higgins, Brian, and Hershel Parker, eds. *Herman Melville: The Contemporary Reviews*. Cambridge: Cambridge University Press, 2009.

Higginson, Thomas Wentworth. "Short Studies of American Authors." *The Literary World*, January 18, 1879, p. 25.

James, Henry. *Hawthorne*. Ithaca: Cornell University Press, 1879.

Jung, Carl Gustav. *The Spirit in Man, Art, and Literature: Collected Works of C.G. Jung, Volume 15*. Trans. Gerhard Adler and R.F.C. Hull. Princeton: Princeton University Press, 1966.

Keats, John. *John Keats: Selected Letters*, ed. Robert Gittings and Jon Mee. Oxford: Oxford University Press, 2002.

Leyda, Jay. *The Melville Log*. New York: Harcourt, Brace, 1951.

"*The Marble Faun: Or, the Romance of Monte Beni* by Nathaniel Hawthorne" (unattributed review). *North American Review*, Vol. 90, No. 187 (Apr. 1860), pp. 557–58.

Matthiessen, F.O. *American Renaissance: Art and Expression in the Age of Emerson and Whitman*. Oxford: Oxford University Press, 1941.

Mellow, James R. *Nathaniel Hawthorne in His Times*. Baltimore: Johns Hopkins University Press, 1998.

Melville, Gansevoort to Allan Melville. From original letter. January 1841. Herman Melville Room at Berkshire Athenaeum; Pittsfield, Massachusetts.

Melville, Herman. *Clarel: A Poem and Pilgrimage in the Holy Land*, ed. Harrison Hayford and Hershel Parker.

Evanston, IL: Northwestern University Press, 2008.

Melville, Herman. *The Confidence-Man: His Masquerade.* London: John Lehmann, 1948.

Melville, Herman. 1856 passport application, housed in the Berkshire Athenaeum (Pittsfield, Massachusetts).

Melville, Herman. "Hawthorne and His Mosses." In *The Portable Melville*, ed. Jay Leyda. New York: Viking, 1952.

Melville, Herman. *The Letters of Herman Melville*, ed. Merrell R. Davis and William H. Gilman. New Haven: Yale University Press, 1960.

Melville, Herman. *Mardi: And a Voyage Thither*, ed. Harrison Hayford, G. Thomas Tanselle and Hershel Parker. Evanston, IL: Northwestern University Press, 1970.

Melville, Herman. Markings and marginalia in his copy of Hawthorne's *Mosses from an Old Manse* (New York: Wiley and Putnam, 1846. 2 vols. in 1). Houghton Library, Harvard College Library. Virtual archive available at melvillesmarginalia.org.

Melville, Herman. *Moby-Dick*, 150th Anniversary Edition. New York: Signet Classics, 1998.

Melville, Herman. *Pierre; Or, the Ambiguities.* In *The Writings of Herman Melville*, Volume 7. Chicago: Northwestern-Newberry Edition, 1971.

Melville, Herman. *Redburn: His First Voyage.* New York: Library of America, 1983.

Melville, Herman. Review of *Etchings of a Whale Cruise* (1847). In *Piazza Tales and Other Prose Pieces, 1839–1860: Volume Nine*, Scholarly Edition. Chicago: Northwestern-Newberry Edition, 1987.

Melville, Herman. *The Selected Poems of Herman Melville*, ed. Robert Penn Warren. New York: Barnes & Noble, 1998.

Melville, Herman. *Typee: A Peep at Polynesian Life.* New York: Library of America, 1982.

Melville, Herman. *White-Jacket; Or, The World in a Man-of-War.* New York: Library of America, 1983.

Melville, Herman. *The Writings of Herman Melville: Correspondence, Volume 14.* Northwestern University Press, 1993.

Menand, Louis. *The Metaphysical Club: A Story of Ideas in America.* New York: Farrar, Straus and Giroux, 2001.

Millington, Richard H., ed. *The Cambridge Companion to Nathaniel Hawthorne.* Cambridge: Cambridge University Press, 2004.

Mumford, Lewis. *Herman Melville.* New York: The Literary Guild of America/ Harcourt, Brace, 1929.

Neal, John. *American Writers: A Series of Papers Contributed to Blackwood's Magazine*, ed. Fred Patee. Durham: Duke University Press, 1937.

Parker, Hershel. *Herman Melville: A Biography, Volume 1 (1819–1851).* Baltimore: Johns Hopkins University Press, 1996.

Parker, Hershel. *Herman Melville: A Biography, Volume 2 (1851–1891).* Baltimore: Johns Hopkins University Press, 2002.

Person, Leland S. *The Cambridge Introduction to Nathaniel Hawthorne.* Cambridge: Cambridge University Press, 2007.

Phillips, Dana. "History and the Ugly Facts of McCarthy's *Blood Meridian.*" *American Literature*, volume 68, number 2 (June 1996), pp. 433–460.

Quinn, D. Michael. *Same-Sex Dynamics among Nineteenth-Century Americans.* Champaign: University of Illinois Press, 2001.

Robertson-Lorant, Laurie. *Melville: A Biography.* New York: Clarkson N. Potter, 1996.

Rohrbough, Malcolm J. *Days of Gold: The California Gold Rush and the American Nation.* Berkeley: University of California Press, 1998.

Spanos, William. *The Errant Art of Moby-Dick: The Canon, the Cold War, and the Struggle for American Studies.* Durham, NC: Duke University Press, 1995.

Stearns, Frank Preston. *The Life and Ge-*

nius of Nathaniel Hawthorne. Philadelphia: J.B. Lippincott, 1906.

Stevens, Anthony. *Jung: A Very Short Introduction*. New York: Oxford University Press, 1994.

Trollope, Anthony. "The Genius of Nathaniel Hawthorne." *The North American Review*, Vol. 129, No. 274 (Sept., 1879), pp. 203–222. Published by University of Northern Iowa. Stable URL: http://www.jstor.org/stable/251 00789 (accessed: 19 November 2012).

Turner, Arlin. *Nathaniel Hawthorne: A Biography*. Oxford: Oxford University Press, 1980.

Updike, John. "Late Works," in *Due Considerations: Essays and Criticism*. New York: Ballantine, 2007.

Wagenknecht, Edward Charles. *Nathaniel Hawthorne: Man and Writer*. Oxford: Oxford University Press, 1961.

Westbrook, Perry D. *A Literary History of New England*. Bethlehem, PA: Lehigh University Press, 1988.

Will, George. "Literary Politics." *Newsweek*. 22 April 1991, p. 72.

Winchell, Mark Royden. *Too Good to Be True: The Life and Work of Leslie Fiedler*. Columbia: University of Missouri Press, 2002.

Wineapple, Brenda. *Hawthorne: A Life*. New York: Random House Trade Paperbacks, 2003.

Woolf, Leonard. *Downhill All the Way: An Autobiography of the Years 1919–1939*. London: Hogarth Press, 1967.

Yeats, William Butler. "The Second Coming." *The Collected Poems of W.B. Yeats*. Ware: Wordsworth Editions, 2000.

Index

207